ULSTER UNDER HOME RULE

ULSTER UNDER HOME RULE

A STUDY OF THE POLITICAL AND ECONOMIC PROBLEMS OF NORTHERN IRELAND

Edited by

THOMAS WILSON

GEOFFREY CUMBERLEGE

OXFORD UNIVERSITY PRESS

LONDON   NEW YORK   TORONTO

1955

Oxford University Press, Amen House, London, E.C.4

GLASGOW NEW YORK TORONTO MELBOURNE WELLINGTON
BOMBAY CALCUTTA MADRAS KARACHI CAPE TOWN IBADAN

Geoffrey Cumberlege, Publisher to the University

PRINTED IN GREAT BRITAIN
BY BILLING AND SONS LTD., GUILDFORD AND LONDON

PREFACE

The object of this book is to provide a reasonably comprehensive survey of the social and economic problems of Northern Ireland, an area which, if notorious as a storm centre, can also lay some claim to attention on other grounds. All the contributors are personally acquainted with the conditions they describe: of the nine, five are Ulstermen and the remainder have spent some years on the staff of the Queen's University, Belfast.

Sir David Keir, who has written the Introduction, was Vice-Chancellor at Queen's before he became Master of Balliol. Professor Cyril Falls, who has recently retired from the Chichele Chair of the History of War at Oxford, was born and educated in Ulster. Professor F. H. Newark, formerly of Exeter College, Oxford, is Professor of Jurisprudence at Queen's University. Professor K. S. Isles, who formerly held the Chair of Economics at Adelaide, is also at Queen's, and Mr. Norman Cuthbert and Mr. Peter Robson are members of his Department. Mr. J. E. Sayers, who was for some years on the Prime Minister's personal staff under Mr. Churchill, is managing editor of the *Belfast Telegraph*. Mr. J. M. Mogey is Lecturer in Sociology in the University of Oxford.

Each contributor has approached his topic from his own point of view and, as might be expected, some difference of opinion about the merits of provincial self-government has emerged.

T. W.

University College, Oxford
June 1955

CONTENTS

INTRODUCTION

In terms of law and government, though in such terms alone, the country about which this book has been written was established by Act of Parliament thirty-five years ago. Its constitution, the political forms to which that constitution gives legal force, the territorial limits within which it applies are all laid down by the Government of Ireland Act, 1920. Northern Ireland, it was then enacted, 'shall consist of the Parliamentary counties of Antrim, Armagh, Down, Fermanagh, Londonderry and Tyrone, and the Parliamentary boroughs of Belfast and Londonderry'. In the territory so defined, the Act established 'a Parliament consisting of His Majesty, the Senate of Northern Ireland, and the House of Commons of Northern Ireland'.

Outwardly, at least, the political entity thus brought into being wore a strange and novel aspect. It still continued, as it still does, to form part of the United Kingdom, the new designation of which as 'The United Kingdom of Great Britain and Northern Ireland' connotes an unbroken and unbreakable connection. Yet within that connection Northern Ireland as a political, administrative and legal unit is characteristically and clearly distinguishable from all the rest. Though severed politically from the other three Provinces of the island to which geographically it belongs, it is nevertheless not co-extensive with the fourth, the historic Province of Ulster, of which it has lost the three outermost counties of Monaghan, Cavan and Donegal. While it owed much in origin to the Plantation of Ulster in the seventeenth century, its greatest strength to-day lies in the counties of Antrim and Down, which, though colonised, were not formally planted counties, whereas Cavan and Donegal were. Its six counties do not coincide with those of the Plantation. The Border, sinuously following their boundaries, three times as long as the direct distance from Newry to Londonderry at its two extremities, makes the shape of the Province look as though it had been carved out in a haphazard, even arbitrary, fashion.

The impression thus created that Northern Ireland is an anomalous and almost artificial creation seems strengthened when its statutory foundation is more closely examined. Unlike every other British territory on which self-governing powers have been conferred, it can point to no constituent Act or other instrument enacted for that sole and specific purpose, framed at its own request, related to itself alone, and fashioned in detail to meet its own interests and needs. The Act of 1920 is not of such a kind. The sections of the Act which have to do with Northern Ireland were interspersed in a larger context which deals with the rest of the country—with the twenty-six counties constituted as the separate state of Southern Ireland, with the matters, which it was hoped would become increasingly numerous and important, that might be of common concern to both North and South. That context was destroyed. The sections applying to Northern Ireland alone remained unrepealed, surviving the overthrow of a great experiment devised for the benefit of Ireland as a whole, and the gradual extinction of all the hopes on which that experiment had been founded. Its one solid and durable part, they remained as the foundation of Northern Ireland's autonomy. But they too might have been rescinded, and Northern Ireland's previous links with the rest of the United Kingdom renewed as before. The reason why they still remain in force is not that they were devised to meet its special requirements or even to fulfil any desire it had ever expressed except that of saving itself from a merger with the south; nor is it because they represent any conscious and considered attempt at devolution; it is because, however imperfect they may have been as a piece of constitution-making, a determined and vigorous people has applied itself to the task of making them work. After thirty-five years, the institutions which the Act of 1920 established have become adapted to the needs they have had to meet. Few of these needs could have been foreseen by the framers of the Act, who had harder and more urgent problems in mind than that of working out a system of government appropriate to the six counties in which alone the Act was to become effective. It is through experience, which has sometimes been arduous and difficult, that Northern Ireland has learned to operate a constitution which, though now regarded as its fundamental charter of self-determination and self-government, provided at the outset only a minimum of working rules, extracted from a far wider scheme of which they are the sole remnant.

These long years of experience have given it increasing awareness of itself as a political entity, and that fund of knowledge in the art of governing itself and regulating its relations with the central authority at Westminster which now make it so interesting as a study of the advantages and disadvantages of devolution, and so inviting as the scene of controlled experiment in such fields as education, health and agricultural and industrial development. The years have brought so many well-learned lessons that it is no longer realistic to regard Northern Ireland as simply a survival left behind by an otherwise abortive Act of Parliament. It has an independent and powerful life of its own, with characteristics, both inherited and acquired, which cannot be explained by reference to that Act or any other. Northern Ireland did not in any real sense begin, still less has it continued, simply as the creation, however interesting and important, of a British statute.

Nevertheless, the impression that Northern Ireland is somehow an artificial unit, contrived as part of a plan that failed, owing its existence to Act of Parliament, is too useful to its critics to be laid aside. It is constantly and speciously reiterated. It cannot be accepted, not only for the pragmatic reason that how things work is more important than what they were intended for, but also because it is completely at variance with the facts, not only of history during the past thirty-five years, but of Northern Irish history throughout its whole course for many centuries past. However roughly delimited, there had always existed in the North a situation, whether political, social or economic, or all three, which tended to differentiate it from the rest of Ireland. Under the pressures which the events of twentieth-century Irish history have produced, this situation became no longer vague and indefinite but sharp and concrete. Tendencies were transformed into accomplished facts. The Act of 1920 did not so much create Northern Ireland as admit that to all intents it already existed and would endure.

The facts of geography had something to do with its making as Mr. J. M. Mogey indicates in a subsequent chapter. The North of Ireland has always dwelt a little apart and aloof from the rest of the island to which it belongs. The way southwards to Leinster lies through the Gap of the North, where, between Newry and Dundalk, the route narrows between the head of Carlingford Lough and the Mountains of Mourne to the east and the slopes of Slieve Gullion to the west. The rest of the Leinster border runs through a land cut up by innumerable hills and lakes and bogs, terminating to the west at the broad waters of Upper and Lower Lough Erne. The route to Connaught breaks through the barrier presented by these two Loughs, where on the passage between them stands the island-city of Enniskillen. The lines of communication connecting the northern Province with its neighbours but also lending themselves to purposes of defence, have as often served to isolate it from them as to facilitate mutual intercourse. Conversely, the narrow seas which to the north separate Antrim from Argyll and the Highlands, and Down from the Lowlands, have encouraged rather than impeded a traffic between Ulster and Scotland which has flowed in both directions from time out of mind. It is easier and more significant to relate the affairs of Ulster to those of Scotland than to those of the other Irish Provinces. And, it has been remarked, the outlook of its people 'is naturally eastward, and their separate attitude in regard to the rest of Ireland cannot be ascribed to mere perversity'.

The isolation of the North, its closer connection with Scotland than with Leinster and Connaught, were the dominant characteristics of early and medieval Ulster. The Norman Conquest of Ireland failed to effect there even such imperfect results as it achieved elsewhere. West of the Bann the Norman colonists made very little penetration. Such hold as they gained east of the river was destroyed by the Scottish invasion under Edward Bruce in 1315 and the overthrow of the de Burgh earldom of Ulster in 1333. In the later Middle Ages the surviving remnants of Norman conquest and settlement barely extended beyond the stronghold of Carrickfergus in Antrim, small residual footholds in Down on the eastern and western shores of Strangford Lough, and the border town of Newry on Carlingford Lough. While in the South a powerful Anglo-Irish nobility was intermittently associated, whether as allies or enemies, with the Crown and the authority it endeavoured to wield from Dublin, the North went its own way and pursued its endless family feuds as though that authority did not exist at all. A land of chiefs and clans, of O'Neills whose sway spread far beyond their native Tyrone, of O'Donnels and O'Dohertys in what is now Donegal but was then Tyrconnel, of O'Cahans in North Derry, of McQuillans in North Antrim, Magennises in South Down, O'Hanlons in Armagh and Maguires in Fermanagh, it remained the last and most formidable redoubt of a Celtic Ireland still untamed. Untamed it was, in more senses than one. If elsewhere in Ireland there subsisted, however sparsely intermingled, the evidence of Celtic, Scandinavian and Norman authority and influence, monasteries such as Clonmacnois or Monasterboice, seaport towns such as Dublin, Waterford or Limerick, fortresses such as Trim, cathedrals such as Cashel, the impenetrable North remained a primitive land of mountain, bog and forest, lacking roads, towns and villages, its ecclesiastical organisation rudimentary, its few castles forming the furthest outposts of an alien and ineffective power. The borough of Carrickfergus alone was ever represented in the medieval Irish Parliament. Here, and at Ardglass with its fortified merchants' houses, the easiest lines of communication lay outwards to sea and not inwards to a dangerous and forbidding land. (Not that the sea was without its dangers for in an earlier age the great abbey at Bangor, Co. Down, had been laid in ruins by the Danes.) In this troubled Northern scene, so remote from its Irish neighbours and in many ways so unlike them, where English influence played so little part, that of the Scots constantly entered, mainly from neighbouring Argyll. Scottish settlers, chief among whom were the MacDonalds who presently Hibernicised themselves as McDonnells, planted themselves along the northern coast, farming, fishing, trading, selling their swords to the Irish chieftains in the agelong course of Ulster wars.

Not until the last years of the Tudor monarchy could any serious attempt be made by the governments in Dublin and London to reduce this turbulent and refractory land to order and obedience. As elsewhere in Ireland, the effort took the threefold form of enforcing the authority of the Crown by military conquest, organising it administratively in a shire system, and securing it politically by attracting the native aristocracy within its orbit as dutiful subjects. The policy of forfeiture and re-grant of land on which the Crown relied was subjected to its hardest test when applied to the house of O'Neill, the most powerful in all the North, lords of Tyrone and of much beside, rivalled only by the O'Donnells, supreme over all the rest. Tyrone became an earldom, as did Tyrconnel, its holders passed for Tudor ennoblement; but there was no room in the North for the dual authority of the Ulster Earls and the Queen's Lord Deputy. The bitter warfare with which the Elizabethan age closed in Ireland, bringing the rebel chiefs to defeat and Ulster to ruin, proved the futility of trying to link the native aristocracy and their clansmen to the Crown and the necessity of resort to those bolder and more thorough measures of invasion and conquest soon followed by the flight overseas of the two great Earls in 1607, furnished an opportunity such as had arisen nowhere else in Ireland.

Almost at the moment when this opportunity came, the Anglo-Scottish Union of 1603 effected a change in the external relations of the North as complete as that which was brought about in its internal affairs. English and Scottish power, hitherto somewhat ineffectually rivalling each other across the Irish Sea, were now joined together for a combined enterprise there. This unique combination of circumstances enabled the government of King James I to deal with Ulster as no part of Ireland had ever been dealt with before. The Province had long needed special treatment, and now got it. To the men of that age, the idea of organised colonisation presented itself in aspects which were bright with promise both of profit and adventure. The idea of planting the conquered districts of Ireland with English settlers, not in itself new, for it had been undertaken in Munster and Leinster with no great success, was applied very differently to the North. There was no repetition of earlier mistakes. Plans for the colonisation of Ulster, methodically framed, examined and revised, were executed with system and efficiency which were surprising in that age and would be impressive in any. The escheated lands of the fugitive Earls and their adherents were surveyed by royal commissioners during the years from 1608 to 1610. One by one the counties of Tyrone, Armagh, Fermanagh, Donegal and Cavan came under their inspection. The opportunities they offered for settlement were exactly assessed. Then followed the making of grants to Protestant English and Scottish settlers, more or less evenly mixed, except that on the whole the English predominated in Armagh and the Scots in Donegal. Such grants as were made to the Irish who had not forfeited through rebellion were on such a scale as to subordinate them effectively, both in numbers and resources, to the richly-endowed colonists.

In these planted counties settlement was by groups, organised under some one leading and responsible individual whose tenants had sometimes come in a body from their English or Scottish homes. In the region of Derry and Coleraine a separate but similar programme assigned responsibility to the City of London, grants being made to the London Companies associated in the Irish Society. In Antrim and Down, no such planned process of governmentally-directed planting took place at all. The great Scots-Irish house of MacDonnell maintained and even improved its position, raising it first to a Viscountcy and then to the Earldom of Antrim. Elsewhere, however, the ruin of the O'Neills gave opportunity for the emigration to these two counties of settlers from Southern Scotland. And in Antrim and Down the transformation, though carried out by private enterprise and not by governmental direction, proved more complete than anywhere else. So the North received that great infusion of English and Scottish blood which has determined its character and preponderates to the present day. The ancient names of Ulster history were displaced. In their stead appeared those of the Brownlows in Armagh, the Caulfields and Hamiltons in Tyrone, the Archdales and Coles in Fermanagh, the Brookes in Donegal, the Adairs, Chichesters and Montgomerys in Antrim and Down, in whose train came the host of Achesons, Alexanders, Boyds, Browns, Inglises, McCullaghs, Sloans, Watsons, who with other bearers of English and Scottish names so abound in the Northern Ireland of to-day.

Generation by generation, the Ulster settlers transformed the Ulster wilderness into a pleasant thriving province. Its nine counties (Antrim and Down, the five counties shired in 1585 and planted, save for Monaghan, from 1608 onwards, Cavan, transferred from Connaught) were completed when the tract between Antrim and Donegal was formed into County Londonderry. The settlers in the countryside built those castles and fortified yards or 'bawns', such as Ballygally Castle in Antrim, Monea Castle in Fermanagh, and Bellaghy bawn in County Derry, which, with others of the same early date, show that colonisation was a military as well as a civilising enterprise. Twice, in fact, in 1641 and again in 1688–9, the colony narrowly averted total destruction, and the memories of how near it had been to ruin and how triumphant a deliverance had been achieved became and still remain seared into the Ulster mind, whether Protestant or Roman Catholic. But, surviving these emergencies, the main purpose of the colonists, to settle and make fruitful the land they had been granted, steadily reasserted itself. The waste lands were won back to cultivation. Village life sprang up. But, above all, the North developed an urban life that was new in its history. The Planters were mighty builders of towns. Belfast virtually began with the Chichesters, as Lurgan did with the Brownlows, and Newtownards with the Montgomerys, while Londonderry, Coleraine, Magherafelt, Draperstown and others evidence in different degrees the pioneering work of London and the City Companies. These new towns, laid out to a pre-arranged plan, sometimes radiating outwards from a central square or 'Diamond', and at Londonderry and Coleraine surrounded by walls or ramparts, looked what they were—centres for the peaceful enterprise of the Planter population, strongholds and cities of refuge for their defence.

After the troubles of the seventeenth century were safely past, it was the former of these functions of the Ulster towns that predominated. Planned from the beginning to provide not only for defence but for the spiritual and material needs of the communities they housed, their traffic, markets, water, they proved the sufficiency of the original design as in the eighteenth century they began to spread beyond their earlier limits. Over their congregated roofs rose the steeples of new cathedrals and churches, as at Lisburn, Enniskillen, and Londonderry: among them were interspersed the Presbyterian meeting-houses, developing architecturally from a plain barn to a distinctive classical style which emphasised Presbyterian separateness from the Anglican Establishment: though a century or more was to elapse until Roman Catholic emancipation made possible the addition of those Italianate Gothic spires which so often complete the typical skyline of the Ulster town. As the tranquil eighteenth century advanced, courthouses like those at Armagh or Hillsborough, schools like Southwell's at Downpatrick, commercial buildings like the warehouses of Newry and Coleraine, private dwellings such as dignify the Mall at Armagh all added to the grace and seemliness of the towns which the settlers had planted or revived. There were among them characteristic differences indicative of their origins, so that Newtownards was and is as Scottish in its aspect as Armagh is English,

while Huguenot traces remain in Waringstown and those of the Wil-
liamite Dutch in Newry. But all reflect the Plantation, and the light
impact of industry on the Province has allowed most of them to retain
the aspect of the eighteenth century and always, even in industrialised
Belfast, the central design of the seventeenth.

The new towns of Ulster were its special characteristic and the foundation of its life. With them, however, villages such as Comber in Down,
the Goldsmiths' village at Muff in County Derry, the Drapers' at
Moneymore, castles restored or reconstructed as at Killyleagh and
Glenarm, eighteenth-century mansions such as Caledon and Castle
Coole and many beside, the cottages and farmhouses that dotted the
countryside, the cultivated lands, too quickly denuded of their primeval
forest, the fields of flax and the bleachgreens that denoted the beginnings
of the linen industry which Huguenot skill was founding in the Lagan
Valley, were the outwards manifestations of a stable and thriving society
whose comfortable prosperity attracted the favourable notice of travellers
coming to Ulster from the South.

Its coherence manifested itself particularly in the structure of its rural
society. The relations of Ulster landlords and tenants, who after all were
fellow-settlers and partners in a joint enterprise, and not conquerors
and conquered, differed wholly from those found elsewhere in Ireland.
The Ulster Custom which gave the tenant the right to the value of the
improvements he effected in his holding, the right to sell them to the
best bidder if he gave up his tenancy, and the right to be compensated for
them if evicted, arose from the whole nature of the Settlement. It produced a strong, self-reliant, industrious peasantry. And it raised Ulster
farming to a level comparable with that of England itself. Eighteenth-
century Ulster, though not immune from trouble between landlord and
tenant, presented as always a characteristic contrast to the other Irish
Provinces, where mass agrarian disturbances and the organised terrorism
of the Whiteboys chronically convulsed rural life. Such agrarian troubles
as the North experienced partly contributed to the considerable emigration of Ulstermen to the American colonies during the pre-Revolu-
tionary age, though a flow of emigrants was likely enough to arise in any
case from among a people of energetic character and pioneering instincts.
But the Ulster Custom ensured that agrarian strife did not disturb the
normal course of Ulster life or sap the stability of Ulster society.

Ulster's main difficulty in the seventeenth and eighteenth centuries
had a different origin. Religious divisions determined the politics of
the Province, separating Episcopalians from Presbyterians and both
from Roman Catholics. Presbyterianism entered Ulster from Covenant-

ing Scotland, militant, organised, disciplined, bent not on recognition and toleration only but on supremacy. To men of this temper, the pretensions of the episcopal Establishment in Ireland were intolerable. The Establishment employed such means as lay in its power to defend itself. Both the civil and the political rights of its opponents could be abridged by the legislation of an Irish Parliament which it dominated, in which they could hardly hope to gain any foothold so long as it remained unreformed. Though the disabilities of Presbyterians were gradually eased, partly by legislative change and partly because of the plain facts of the situation in which the whole Protestant population found itself, sectarian animosity did not greatly abate. It contributed significantly to the flow of emigrants to America. But that was not its only significance. It came to animate reforming and radical movements in the politics of Ireland. Responding to the liberal influences which leavened eighteenth-century Scottish Presbyterianism, and were specially strong in the University of Glasgow to which resorted Ulstermen debarred by doctrinal tests from Trinity College, Dublin, the Presbyterianism of Ulster changed in character. It became more latitudinarian in theological temper and more secular in political outlook as it moved away from its Covenanting tradition. Resentment of political and civil disabilities imposed by law, of the social inferiority they seemed to impute, realisation that these could be remedied by parliamentary and administrative reform, created in Ulster a radical sentiment which still permeates its political thinking and distinguishes Ulster Unionism from the English Conservatism with which later history has allied it—a theme developed by Mr. J. E. Sayers in a later chapter.

This Ulster radicalism entered fully into the Volunteer movement which, formed during the American War of Independence, liberated the Irish Parliament from subordination to the Parliament at Westminster. It gave strength to the efforts made towards reforming the Irish Parliament during the eighteen years of its sovereignty from 1782 to 1800. It supported the endeavour to extend to the Roman Catholics that relief from civil and political disabilities it sought for itself. To that extent, and for that brief and transitory period, during which reforming movements in the British Isles tended towards an apparent identity with the revolutionary movement inspired by France, Northern radicalism seemed to align itself with the Southern extremism which aimed at subverting the political, religious and social order of the country. But as that extremism gathered the force and seized the opportunities that led to the Rebellion of 1798, the Protestant North recoiled. It was one thing to free the government and Parliament in Dublin from its

bondage to Westminster, to endeavour to reform and liberalise its
Anglican and squirearchical domination, to extend to the Roman
Catholics of Ireland at least some of the rights its Protestant population
had inherited or won; but another, altogether different, to join in a
movement intended to seize power for forces which were revolutionary,
Roman Catholic and anti-British. It is not surprising that the revolutionary society of United Irishmen should in 1791 have been founded in
Belfast and counted Ulstermen among its leaders, or that handfuls of
Protestant rebels took the field at Antrim and Ballynahinch: but in-
finitely less so that such slender bonds as had ever united the main body
of Northern radicals with the Southern revolutionaries snapped at once.

Once destroyed, they were never renewed. Between the two there lay not
only a difference of race and religion but also the memories of a bitter
and tragic history, of which the unforgettable episodes were the rebellion
of 1641 and the Revolution of 1688. Such memories, which stirred in the
feuds of the Protestant Peep o' Day Boys and the Roman Catholic
Defenders, slumbered lightly in Ulster. They were easily wakened to
life. They expressed themselves in the foundation of the Orange Order
at Loughgall in 1795. The Union with Great Britain which in 1800 formed
the inevitable sequel to the suppression of the Rebellion was in its way
as effective a deliverance as the campaigns of the Cromwellians in the
mid-seventeenth century, the relief of Londonderry, and the triumph of
William of Orange at the Boyne.

The Union did more than assure the political future of the Plantation.
It brought the economic fortunes of the North into enduring association
with those of an England and Scotland in process of being transformed
by the Industrial Revolution, in which Ulster, alone again among the
Provinces of Ireland, had any substantial share. The staple industry of
Ulster had hitherto been a mere outgrowth of an agriculture in which
the production of flax was a major element. Retting, scutching, spinning,
weaving and bleaching of linens were still in 1800 domestic operations
and closely connected with farming, though their marketing was the
business of the towns. During the next half-century the industry was
completely transformed. By 1850 it had become reorganised on a factory
basis, and linen-mills had been established in almost every part of the
Province which could be conveniently reached from Belfast, through
which they imported their supplies of coal and exported their finished
products.

The impact of industrialisation diminished with distance, so that while
the inland towns developed slowly the growth of Belfast was comparable
with that of the great industrial cities across the water, of which it was

the sole Irish counterpart. At the beginning of the century, it counted less than 20,000 inhabitants, and was still comparable with Derry or Newry. At the mid-point of the century, it had far outstripped them and reached the 100,000 figure. At the close, that figure had been trebled. It now attains the half-million. To the linen industry which had been its sole major industry up to 1850, it added shipbuilding, textile engineering, rope-making and tobacco, became an ocean as well as a cross-Channel port, and the focal point towards which the road and rail system of the Province was directed. It had established economic and financial preponderance in the North, become the home of its university and professional life, and prepared the way for the time when Northern interests would spontaneously detach themselves from Dublin and the South, turn to Belfast for leadership, and transform it ultimately into the capital of an autonomous Province.

These interests, diverse as the different strands interwoven into Northern life, became increasingly coherent and unified as the century progressed. Industrialisation, though as elsewhere in the United Kingdom it created dislocation and hardship, far from destroying the rural foundations of Ulster, contributed effectively to their preservation through the Famine Years from 1845 which destroyed them in the other three Provinces, where industrialisation had made no impact at all. Its rural population, prospering as the linen industry and trade developed and towns throve on it, maintained itself in scarcely diminished number, and in a balance with the urban population which has never been significantly changed. The Ulster farmers were strong enough to maintain during the first half of the nineteenth century a stubborn defence of the Ulster Custom against their landlords, to get it put on a statutory basis in the Land Acts of 1870 and 1881, and at the turn of the century to consolidate their position through the Land Purchase Acts of 1903 and 1909 which, through a scheme of terminable annuities, converted them into peasant proprietors, an Imperial Act of 1925 ending agricultural landlordism altogether. So, in an equality with industry which is unique in these islands, agriculture became one of the twin supports of the economic and social structure of the Province.

While the gradual solution of the agrarian question increased the stability of the Province by eliminating the friction between landlord and tenant, the friction between Anglican and Presbyterian was likewise being gradually healed. To some extent, these two kinds of friction were inter-related, landlords and clergy defending their respective or common vested interests, the Presbyterian ministers and the tenant farmers united in the cause of land reform and hostile to the Establish-

B

ment. The victory of the land reformers ended one struggle which had divided Anglicans from their fellow-Protestants. The Disestablishment of the Irish Church in 1869 ended the other. By the beginning of the present century, there remained no major issue on which the ranks of Ulster Protestants could be easily broken.

The more stable and coherent this society became, the more it tended to draw away from the opinions and purposes which dominated the rest of the island. It might participate in the general resistance to the payment of tithes in the 1830s, an uneasy alliance with southern tenant-farmers in the League of North and South in the '50s, join in the agitation which led to the Land Acts, profit greatly from their success, and yet repudiate the nationalism with which such grievances were elsewhere connected and of which indeed they supplied much of the driving force. From the morrow of Roman Catholic Emancipation, Ulster was aware of what that measure must politically imply. It was opposed to Repeal of the Act of Union at that date, and subsequently when any similar proposal was mooted. As its own internal frictions were removed, it manifested at each such crisis, in 1886, in 1893, and in 1912 a spontaneous solidarity, a capacity for self-organisation, and a hard unshakeable resolution which proved that here was a State in the making. If the Union could be saved for Ireland as a whole, it would be content; but, if not, it would at least save the Union for itself.

The limits of that State were already definable, and were in men's minds in the controversies over Home Rule. They included, with Antrim and Down, the counties where the Plantation had been most effective—Londonderry, Armagh, and the evenly-balanced Tyrone and Fermanagh. Departing from a strictly county basis, they might have stretched to cover East Donegal and North Monaghan, and omitted parts of South Armagh and South Down. These marginal areas in fact remained in doubt until in 1925 the Government of the Irish Free State accepted the boundaries of Northern Ireland set out in the Act of 1920. Whatever minor imperfections these may show, they correspond with reasonable accuracy to the region within which Irish Protestantism effectively established itself by plantation or purchase in the seventeenth century. They exclude almost every area where it did not.

But they include more. The boundaries of Northern Ireland contain, with a Protestant population which in 1951 numbered almost 900,000, a Roman Catholic population of over 471,000, so distributed that while it is in a decided minority in Belfast and the North-east, it is only slightly so in the rest of the Province, and forms a decided majority in certain enclaves such as the Glens of Antrim, mid-Derry and mid-Tyrone, and certain border districts such as South Armagh and South Down. It represents mainly the survival of remnants of the pre-Plantation population of Ulster, whether Irish, or Highland Scottish as in Antrim, in regions where the Plantation was either imperfectly carried out or never attempted at all. As a fraction of the total population of Northern Ireland, this element increases very slowly in its proportion to the majority. But, as the population of Northern Ireland, here again unlike the rest of Ireland, rises instead of falling, the minority becomes larger, And as it contributes to every level of the life of the Province, professional, commercial and agricultural, its attitude and needs must be reckoned into the sum of the responsibilities of the Government. The state set up in 1920, while it arose from a recognition of the unity of the coherent and politically self-conscious majority, was a mixed state; its government was faced with a dual obligation, towards each section of the community. Founded on the interests of one, it has to seek those of both. On its success in this task, its policy and reputation must largely be judged.

Its task was no easy one. On the one hand, the Unionist majority, for reasons which are self-evident, had to undertake the unaccustomed business of self-government with hardly any main purpose in mind beyond self-preservation at a moment when terror, bloodshed and attempted revolution threatened it within as well as without. On the other, the minority could not readily bring themselves, even when order had been restored and normal processes of government had begun, to accept the situation of being citizens in a state which their own tradition led them to repudiate. Neither side could be expected very readily to conceive of a Northern Ireland in which both were freely and equally associated, which ministered to the needs of both, and the existence of which would not be called in question. While the main responsibility for evolving such ideas obviously rested on the party in power, the minority too had its share of responsibility, however much it sought to escape it. The central interest of the subsequent history of Northern Ireland is to be found in the effort made by its government to work out lines of policy which, taking the maintenance of the union with Great Britain and the effective exercise of its own authority as axioms, aimed at the advantage of the Province and its people as a whole. This was a new experience, for which the Northern majority had had little training, but from which they have learned much, both through success and failure.

Besides learning to work an untried constitutional relationship with Westminster, they have learned to apply the powers of their own government to problems which have assumed new forms since 1920. After the basic problems of maintaining law and order, those of economic development, agriculture, education, housing, health and hospital services, town and country planning, and others vital to the general welfare have come under its control to a degree varying firstly with the extent to which authority has been transferred or reserved under the constitution, and secondly with the extent to which Northern Ireland has found it advisable or necessary, in using transferred powers, to conform to lines laid down in Great Britain. Sometimes the arrangements in force there are contained in United Kingdom statutes: sometimes in Northern Ireland statutes similar in effect to those made at Westminster for England or Scotland or both: but the Northern Ireland statute-book also includes many Acts of entirely local origin and purpose. They embody the assessment of the needs of the Province made by its own government and legislature. Education, detached from its previous connection with the Irish educational system, has evolved on lines similar to those of Great Britain but not identical with them. There are variations from the British model in the pattern of health and hospital services. Above all, the economic affairs of the Province, disturbed on the one hand by the erection of a Southern Ireland tariff barrier along the Border, and on the other by the fluctuations of a world market on which its great export industries are dependent, have required governmental intervention on a large scale to redress their balance. Much of this book is devoted to the conditions in which economic policy has been made, and the measure of its success.

Under the new constitution there has grown up something of a new political life, though the predominance, or recurrence, of a single question, the fundamental one whether Northern Ireland has any right to exist at all, prevents it from assuming the typical form of British party government based on the certainty that whichever party is in office the law and custom of the Constitution will be respected and the foundations of the State will rest secure. Even so, however, political life in Northern Ireland can rise higher than these levels of discussion and no political party remains just where it was in 1920, exclusively preoccupied with that now remote event. Ulster Unionism has again revealed its composite nature in criticisms of the Government by its own backbenchers, in the occasional successes of independent Unionists, and even by the appearance in the 1930s of a splinter group, the Progressive Unionist Party. A Labour Party has come into being, achieved Parliamentary representation, undergone temporary schism with the defection of a Commonwealth Labour Party and the intrusion of the Eire Labour Party. The old Nationalist party has been replaced by new groupings of

Nationalists, some ready to take their seats at Stormont, others refusing to do so; responding uncertainly to political pressures from across the Border, sometimes as in the Northern Ireland 1948 General Election resenting Southern interference, occasionally abstaining from voting or even voting Unionist. The political life of Northern Ireland may be capricious and uncertain, finds it hard to adjust itself to changed times and get its new bearings, but it has in many respects left 1920 far behind.

This is particularly true, and naturally so, of the party which, under the leadership successively of Lord Craigavon, Mr John Miller Andrews, and Lord Brookeborough has been continuously in power throughout. In vindicating its use of authority, it has had to endeavour, as never previously, to commend union with the rest of the Kingdom, member-ship of the Commonwealth, and local self-government, in terms of their positive advantage to the whole community of Northern Ireland. Supplementing the merely negative, if necessary, aim of resisting incor-poration with the South, it has been obliged to develop policies which transcend the special interests of any one class. It can claim that the material prosperity of the Province contrasted with the rest of Ireland, the parity of its social services with those of Great Britain, the improve-ment of its education, housing and health can be justly regarded in this light. It can claim too, and not unjustly, that freedom of speech and opinion, the exercise of legitimate political activities, the absence of a literary censorship, the state of the arts, of learning and science, of the social conscience, offer their own proofs that Northern Ireland can offer more than material prosperity to its citizens. Competent and even-handed administration, initiative and vigour in experiment with new ideas, increased contact with the other States of the Commonwealth, can become the means of providing a better life and a richer field of opportunity, as Northern Ireland grows to maturity.

It is in the domain of ideas that its final justification must lie. This should not be difficult for a people whose annals are adorned through three-and-a-half centuries of history by so many famous names and among whom energy of mind is as evident as of character. It has been a land not only of great soldiers, in a long list of whom the names of Brooke, Dill and Alexander are among the latest and most famous, but of leaders in the advancement of every branch of human endeavour. From Sir Hans Sloane, of Killyleagh, whose collections formed the nucleus of the British Museum, to Lord Kelvin, Sir Almroth Wright and Sir Joseph Larmor, Ulstermen have contributed to British science and medicine: James Bryce to historical and legal learning: Lord Russell of Killowen to the eminence of the English Bench: Sir Samuel Dill to classical studies. Among its imperial pro-consuls Ulster can count the name of the first Marquis of Dufferin and Ava, Governor-General of Canada, Viceroy of India, and in a different but analogous sphere that of Sir Robert Hart, creator of the Chinese Customs Service: its artists and men of letters have included Sir John Lavery, George William Russell, and a succession of writers in prose and verse such as Carleton, Allingham, 'George Birmingham' and Robert Lynd. There is power in the Northern people, both of the Plantation and the older race. In the self-governing Province and the world to which it ensures them entrance, there is scope for that power to be used even more effectively than in the past.

D. LINDSAY KEIR

Balliol College, Oxford
June 1955

CHAPTER 1

ULSTER'S SIX COUNTIES

By J. M. MOGEY

1. THE ancient name of Ulster, itself a teutonic version of the still more ancient Celtic word "Uladh", is commonly applied to the six counties of Ireland that still remain within the United Kingdom: Antrim, Down, Armagh, Tyrone, Fermanagh and Londonderry. This use of the term is sometimes held to be improper on the ground that three counties of the old Province now form part of Eire—Donegal, Monaghan and Cavan— and the term "Northern Ireland", though also ambiguous, seems to enjoy some official favour. On the other hand, it may be fairly urged that the nine-county province was essentially a product of the English conquest, and the boundaries of the ancient Gaelic province were, to say the least of it, fluctuating and ill-determined. At all events popular usage tends to defy the pedants, and in everyday speech "Ulster" has become the title of the area. It is true that Irish republicans sometimes prefer to talk about the "Six Counties" with the intention presumably of implying that these six would be like the other counties of Ireland were it not that they had been arbitrarily lopped off by an alien power. If this, indeed, is the implication it needs to be qualified. However much one may regret the division of the island, one must accept the fact that its northern part, like the Catalan fringe of the Iberian peninsula, differs in some crucial respects from the rest of the country and has long maintained a certain consciousness of regional autonomy. The purpose of this opening chapter is to give some description of the land of Ulster and of the people who live there.

2. A glance at the map reveals that Ulster's coastline is only a few miles away from south-west Scotland. Although the crossing of these treacherous narrows must have presented more difficulty to primitive craft than the short distance would suggest, the two areas have been of immense importance to each other since prehistoric times. England was far less important to Ulster until her leadership in the British Isles made her the main political influence and even then the social and cultural links with Scotland were stronger. Southern Ireland, by contrast, was more closely associated with England and Wales and had more direct, if tenuous, links with Continental Europe.

Within Ireland, geography also fostered some degree of isolation in the north, although it is important not to exaggerate this factor or to imply that it affords a major explanation of partition. Four hill masses mark out the province. The Sperrin mountains, whose old rock formations stand up as bare hill ranges, occupy much of Tyrone and Londonderry and are interspersed with long, deep valleys. The Antrim hills in the north-east are high peat-covered moorlands, forming rough hill grazings and divided into several smaller regions by the river valleys.[1] In the third hill mass may be included the Mournes, which rise steeply from the sea to granite crags of over 2,000 feet, and, across Carlingford Lough, Slieve Gullion with its associated ring of volcanic hills; this range roughly follows the south-eastern frontier with Eire. To the south-west of the Province, beyond Lough Erne, is the fourth mountainous region. Here the frontier with Eire runs along the summit of a great block of limestone, separating the bog and lake-strewn area of the Erne river from its larger counterpart, the central plain of Ireland. These hills rise in a series of steps, each marked by long escarpments to the long flat-topped mountain called Cuilcagh. A free translation of the name is "the big, rough fellow" and the country is wild and remote; being limestone, it is reminiscent in some of its formations of the Pennines in England, and like the Pennines it has an elaborate network of underground streams and caverns.

If the mountains form the background to the inhabited landscape, its central feature is Lough Neagh, filling a hollow in the Antrim basalt. Draining the lake northwards, runs the River Bann in a broad valley of considerable fertility. South of the lake begins a country of little rolling hills, which cover almost half the province in Down, Armagh and Fermanagh. These are *drumlins*, evidence of the Pleistocene ice cap which also smoothed the hills and in places caused the growth of peat bogs by interrupting the natural drainage. From Belfast Lough to the edge of Lough Neagh the valley of the Lagan is a fertile farming area and the main route by which road and rail traffic reaches the remainder of the province. Only one part of the province is not reached by easy gradients from these central plains around Lough Neagh: this area, the valley of the Foyle, forms part of County Londonderry. School-children used to

[1] These hills are the result of a geographically recent outpouring of basalt. The uptilted edges of this sheet of basalt form a bold escarpment overlooking Belfast Lough and the Lagan valley, and cliff formations continue northwards along the coast of County Antrim. Underneath the basalt is a layer of chalk of the same age and formation as the Downs of Southern England. "With its high moorlands, deep valleys, precipitous headlands and sandy beaches . . . (with) the strong contrasts of black basalt, white chalk and sparkling sea . . . (the Antrim coast has) a type of scenery which is unique in Western Europe." (*The Ulster Countryside*: Interim Report of N.I. Planning Advisory Board, 1946, 12.)

be told that Ireland, with its ring of coastal hills, is like a saucer, and someone has added, a little inaccurately perhaps, that Ulster is like a small saucer inside a big one.

Ulster has an intimate landscape: the intricate geological background of many different rock types, of ice-transported soils and of accumulated soils like peat and alluvium, all compressed into an area of 5,000 square miles, prevents the development of large-scale physical features. The climate too is almost as variable as the topography. The dominant influence is the Atlantic ocean, which makes for a temperate, equable, humid, rather cloudy and very changeable climate with rainfall evenly spread throughout the year. Belfast has on the average 231 days a year with at least a shower of rain, compared with 163 days in London. The amount of rainfall varies from one part of the Province to another: in the west and in the mountains there is usually over 50 inches a year, but in the Lough Neagh lowlands and eastern coast lands about 35 inches. With cool, cloudy summers due to the high latitude and the proximity of the Atlantic Ocean, even the lower figure is more than sufficient for agriculture. Amongst the major problems of the countryside, land drainage ranks very high, and it is because of the good natural drainage they afford that the patches of ice-transported sand are so much prized by the farmers. Spring is normally the driest season with March or April the driest month; whilst the wettest month is either October or December, there is a secondary wet period in August, which interferes considerably with cereal harvesting. The frost-free period normally runs from the end of April to the beginning of October, but the heating up process in spring is slow and halting and, while dryness may encourage sowing, late frosts are a real hazard. At 700 feet the growing season extends only from June to September, and even the hardy oats may refuse to ripen at higher altitudes. In general the landscape is green and fertile; gentle slopes, tall hedges, small lakes or bogs, and clear rivers characterise the farming area, and the hills are never out of sight. This pleasant landscape of small fields with its rivers controlled by locks and sluice gates is a far cry from the swamps, forests and primeval bogs which the first literate English invaders described in their despatches to the London of King John and which were still in large measure a feature of the countryside as late as the seventeenth century when the Plantation took place.

3. The Norman invasion in the twelfth century hastened the break-up of one of the oldest social systems in Europe. The Irish in their isolation seem to have been little affected by the Roman invasion of Britain; both the aristocracy and the petty kings appear to have maintained their rule uninterrupted for many centuries. As might be expected the records

are scanty and those that survive are so full of fancies and myths that they are not to be relied upon, but it seems to be a clear fact that no Irish high-king ever united the island effectively. It was a regional civilisation, backward and barbarous, perhaps like that of England before King Alfred. Within the island Ulster, for its part, was always a distinct if loosely-defined region and with such mythological heroes as Cuchulain and the Red Branch Knights. In this shadowy period the archaeologist has provided the only firm foundation and the record of excavations makes it clear that there were numerous cultures. The Pictish tribes against whom the Romans fortified their northern boundary in Britain may have been close kin with the men of Ulster. The earliest records of human settlement suggest that the two sides of the North Channel were inhabited by the same peoples, and later invaders, bringing Neolithic stock-rearing and agriculture with them also settled on both sides of the sea, the megalithic burial tombs that they erected being known as the Clyde-Carlingford type. The Neolithic population in Ulster was already some centuries old and local styles were developing by 2,000 B.C., long before any written records began.

In modern Ireland, where the nationalist movement has been associated with a revival of interest in the ancient Celtic culture, the origin of the Gaels is naturally a question of some interest. The popular belief that they were the original inhabitants of Ireland is contradicted by modern research and is, indeed, inconsistent with some of the old Celtic legends themselves where the Gaels are represented as an aristocratic ascendancy that conquered the earlier peoples. It is of interest to note that Ulster features in the legends as a centre of opposition to the newcomers just as, in subsequent centuries, it was the main Celtic stronghold that resisted the English invaders. There is still a good deal of uncertainty about the date of the arrival of the first Celtic speakers in Ireland, but the invasion appears to have begun several centuries before Christ, and to have been completed in about the sixth century A.D. The Celtic law and language were then well established throughout the country, although there was no effective central government. The distinction between conquerors and conquered appears to have survived in some measure for many centuries—indeed till the eve of a fresh conquest from across the Irish sea.

We know little about the coming of a knowledge of iron to Ireland, but its introduction appears to have been both long-retarded and gradual. Although the first Celtic speakers may have come in the Bronze Age, later Celts are believed to have introduced the use of iron of which there are some traces in the fourth century B.C. The fact remains that for nearly two thousand years, from 700 B.C. to A.D. 1200, the archaeological remains suggest little change. Circular earthen enclosures were both habitation and cattle corral; some big farmers or petty chiefs lived in these houses or on similar circular artificial islands built in rivers or lakes. These water-defended crannogs were used in the Bronze Age, and even as late as the time of Elizabeth I one or two of them were still inhabited.

Cereal crops were known and cultivated in Celtic Ireland, but the staple foods seem to have been milk and meat, evidence of a pastoral society and a non-exchange economy. The Irish built no towns or ports along the coast, and had few roads worthy of the name. Without these each region could remain autonomous, free from political servitude to any central power, but at the cost of a wasteful use of land and a low standard of living. This form of life may be called Irish or Celtic, for it was common to the whole of Ireland. While England was experiencing successive conquests by Romans, Danes, Saxons and Normans, Ireland remained largely isolated, but for the Danish assaults, till the twelfth century.

With the waning of the Roman power in Britain, the Irish themselves —or the Scots as they were termed—became invaders. Northern England was raided and a large part of Wales was conquered, but these were passing incidents as compared with two other events of this disturbed period. The first was the crossing of the North Channel early in the sixth century by a tribe of Scots from County Antrim who were to give their name to the whole of the country they had invaded. The comparative ease with which such small-scale migrations took place shows how close the links have always been between the North of Ireland and the country now called Scotland. The Celtic spoken in the Scottish Highlands to-day is practically the same as that spoken in Donegal and similar to that known to have been the speech of Antrim and Londonderry. The second event was the capture of St. Patrick, who was first brought to Ulster as a herd. The coming of Christianity to Ireland, although it did little or nothing to unify the country, marked the beginning of a great period of Irish culture.   The church gradually developed on monastic rather than episcopal lines, and of the many monasteries established two of the greatest were in Ulster, one at Bangor and the other at Moville. It was from Ulster that St. Columba and St. Columbanus set out, the first to bring back Christianity to a ravaged and pagan Britain, the latter to the Continent itself. Thus during the Dark Ages Ireland was one of the few surviving centres of Christian culture in Western Europe, and her own confused and disorganised political life did not prevent her from making a major contribution to the renaissance of learning. This "golden age" was rudely shattered in the ninth century when the Viking invasions began. Ulster suffered severely, as did the rest of Ireland, but there was an important difference. It was the Northmen who first established towns in Ireland, Dublin itself being one of their creations, and these towns survived the Norse defeat at Clontarf in 1014 and contributed to the growth of Irish commerce and the development of civilised life. In Ulster, however, no towns were established and the devastated province had no compensation for its heavy losses, which included the destruction of the great monastery at Bangor. Moreover the triumph of Brian Boru broke the ancient tradition that the High King should be an O'Neill from Ulster, and there followed a confused period of tribal warfare.

It was the English who first united Ireland and even they did not succeed in doing so for a very long time.[1] Although the Anglo-Normans built some coastal fortresses, Ulster retained its independence and was indeed for centuries the main Celtic fastness and place of refuge for defeated leaders from the rest of the country. It was not till the sixteenth century, when the Tudors embarked upon a thorough-going policy of conquest and centralisation, that the province was finally subjected, after a bitter struggle in the course of which the countryside was devastated, its population reduced and impoverished and its native leaders discredited. The Celtic chiefs soon afterwards secretly left Ireland and sailed to Europe, and much of Ulster was then declared forfeit to the English Crown. An unsuccessful attempt to plant two southern counties had been made by Mary Tudor, whose Catholicism did not make her gentle in her treatment of Ireland, and Elizabeth had also embarked on an experiment in Munster; but the new plan of James I was more ambitious and vastly more important in its results. The six counties planted were Armagh, Cavan, Donegal, Fermanagh, Tyrone and Coleraine.[2] The two eastern counties, Antrim and Down, were not included, but had already attracted large numbers of settlers, expecially from Scotland, and continued to do so after the official Plantation began. The procedure of plantation was to distribute the land in lots of varying size to "undertakers" who were committed to sub-let smaller portions only to farmers who professed the Protestant religion: another group, the "servitors", also received land in smaller lots and they were allowed to sub-let to the Irish. Thus, in Ulster alone of the provinces of Ireland, conquest was to

---

[1] For an admirable brief account of these matters, see *A Short History of Ireland*, by J. C. Beckett.

[2] Most of the county was allotted to the Livery Companies of the City of London, which is the origin of the name "Londonderry".

mean not only a change in the ruling élite, but also—over at least part of the area officially planted[1]—a gradual change in the rank and file of the population.

Over the Province as a whole the new colonists were small in number, and many of the previous inhabitants remained as tenants and farmers despite edicts to the contrary from London. After twenty years it was estimated that, outside Antrim and Down, only 13,000 adult male British settlers had arrived. They were working in a devastated land, improving its drainage, building houses, erecting mills and experimenting in iron smelting with the use of the plentiful local charcoal. It was a hard, pioneering type of life, with the added peril of attacks by the original inhabitants. The latter attempted a counter-revolution in 1641, just as the Civil War broke out in England. Troops from Scotland enabled the colonists to hold their own, but not before many of the new settlements and most of the embryonic towns had been sacked and burnt. The colony in Ulster was not to know any security until 1690, when William of Orange defeated the armies of James II at the Boyne river. After 1690 there was a renewed inflow of Scots settlers; one record says that by 1715 "50,000 families had settled in Ulster since the Revolution". Not that the Scots were the only settlers: English families came from Warwickshire, from the Welsh border country and from the south-west of England to settle on estates owned by English landlords in the Lagan valley, in Co. Armagh and around Dungannon in Tyrone. These immigrants, whether English or Scottish, knew more about agriculture than the native Irish, and their efforts slowly turned Ulster into a fair and fertile land of farms, fields, roads and towns.

The Scots, who soon outnumbered the other colonists, brought Presbyterianism to Ireland. Thus—if one may generalise a little wildly—it may be said that whereas law and the market came from England, the family and the church came from Scotland. Presbyterian ministers were soon at work among the colonists, and we may suppose that their uncompromising doctrine of the elect became a personal anchor of stability and assurance in a world of social, economic and political turmoil for these farmers in their "cottages and boothes . . . of sods and saplings of ashes and birch trees, with rushes for thatch and bushes for wattles". Naturally these Presbyterians of the North of Ireland stood firmly on the side of the civil authorities in the later wars between James II and William

---

[1] It will be observed that two of the counties included in the Plantation are now in Eire (Cavan and Donegal) and very substantial parts of Londonderry, Fermanagh and Tyrone have a majority of Catholics to-day. In these areas the Plantation may be said to have failed to achieve the object for which it was designed.

III, but were not thereafter immune from civil disabilities. On the face of it, it might be supposed that favour would have been shown to such firm Protestants, but the claims of episcopacy confused public policy by cutting across the obvious desirability of treating the "garrison" well. Although an official grant to the Presbyterian church (regium donum) was renewed,[1] its members were not deemed worthy in future of holding civic office, and a number of them were dismissed even in Derry. An attempt was even made to deny the validity of all marriages except those performed by the established church, and great hostility was not unnaturally aroused. Throughout the eighteenth century, when civil disabilities and the abuses of landlordism were at their worst, the Dissenters in Ulster constituted a third force that was hostile to the episcopal ascendancy as well as to the Catholics; indeed for a time the two persecuted groups tended to draw together and presented England with the alarming prospect of the United Irishmen. It was in this century of oppression that Ulstermen migrated to America in such numbers that something like a sixth of the population of the colonies is believed to have been of Ulster descent at the time of the War of Independence. These immigrants played an important part in that struggle, and like the Catholic Irish who crossed the Atlantic in the next century, many of them bore the English no good will.

In the nineteenth century, the division between Anglican and Dissenter became gradually much less sharp. The Penal laws had been abolished, and the Church of Ireland was ultimately disestablished in 1869. Economic developments also favoured both greater unity between the Protestants and the preservation of the British connection: the old mercantilist restrictions in Irish trade had been swept away, and the rising industry of the North became more and more closely linked with the British economy. In the later part of the century successive land acts met what was now the principal demand of the powerful liberal group among the Ulster Protestants. As the twentieth century opened it could be said that the distinction between Anglican and Dissenter had long ago lost most of its political significance, and the landed Anglican Ascendancy was itself on the point of losing its traditional economic power. Moreover, in face of rising Irish nationalism, both groups tended to draw together for what they believed to be their self-protection.

The Catholics, both in Ulster and in the rest of Ireland, also benefited from these developments but were not for that reason reconciled to English rule. Much has been written about the Irish nationalist movement and its sentiments are sufficiently well understood and appreciated

---

[1] It had first been given by Charles II.

to make any attempt at explanation or description redundant here. But it may be in place to observe that the South was also closely linked with the British economy where it found a market for its agricultural produce and a source of supply of manufactures; nationalist sentiment, however, has proved too strong to be undermined either by the removal of old grievances or by any modern benefits of the English connection. The slow and reluctant acts of reform in Ireland failed to win over the Catholics but succeeded in winning over the Ulster Dissenters. Herein lies a basic explanation of much that has happened since.

4. The churches remain to-day a potent force in the lives of the Ulster people. Although here, as elsewhere, the "new paganism" has rapidly advanced, especially among the Protestants, church attendance, even in the towns, is more regular and more normal than in England. It has often been claimed, and there is some validity in the claim, that the major religious bodies represent the various social groups that have settled in Northern Ireland. Thus the Roman Catholic population is held to represent the "native Irish", the Presbyterians to be the descendants of the Scottish settlers who flooded into Antrim, Down and Londonderry during the seventeenth and early eighteenth centuries; and the Church of Ireland is held in like manner to represent the English element in the settlement, being concentrated for the most part in the Lagan valley, and in selected areas of Armagh, Tyrone and Fermanagh. Admittedly, any local historian could produce exceptions to this generalisation, both as regards individual families and particular districts within Northern Ireland. Thus, although immigrations from Scotland to the glens of Antrim were well documented from as early as the fifteenth century, these were Highland Scots, and they remain within the Roman Catholic Church; to take another example, many of the English element were dissenters and joined with other nonconformist groups in the province. Notwithstanding these exceptions there is some truth in the historical generalisation and, at the present time, it remains broadly true to say that political affiliations and religious faiths tend to coincide, the Protestants being in the main supporters and the Catholics opponents of the British connection.

An old organisation, the Loyal Orange Order, still brings together members of the different Protestant churches on issues which have direct bearing upon the survival of the State in its present form in Northern Ireland. The Order publishes no membership figures, but it is probable that two-thirds or more of the adult male Protestants belong to it. Its public "walks" have the fervour of popular festivals, in particular those held on July 12 to commemorate the victory of William III over the armies of James II at the Battle of the Boyne.[1] Preceded by colourful silk banners of orange, blue and green and by the great cane-beaten drums and bands of many kinds, the members, wearing sashes and signs of their rank within the hierarchy of the Order, walk through some town chosen as a local rendezvous to hear speeches delivered by representatives of the Order, the Protestant churches and the Unionist political party. This emotional mechanism, making use of many separate devices, has been an important factor in maintaining the unbroken record of the Unionist party at the polls since 1920. In the countryside and small villages each local unit of the Orange Order fulfils, politics apart, a real social need, linking together the diverse classes of the population—wage-earners, independent farmers, factory owners and local aristocracy—into a close-knit association. Social gatherings such as these, restricted to men, have replaced older informal gatherings which have a long history in Ulster and in similar communities of small farmers elsewhere in Europe.[2] Recently subsidiary associations for women and juveniles have been formed and may be said to reflect the assimilation of this century-old, male-dominated organisation into the value system associated with equal and democratic citizenship in a modern State. The corresponding Catholic organisation, the Ancient Order of Hibernians, has a much smaller membership, which is not surprising because the Catholic Church itself can speak with a unified voice for all age, sex and social groups in its section of the population

The figures below show the relative importance of the different sects in 1951:—

Religion	Persons	Per Cent
Presbyterian	410,259	30
Church of Ireland	337,395	25
Methodist	66,544	5
Other (including not stated)..	85,182	6
TOTAL PROTESTANT (including not stated)	899,380	66
ROMAN CATHOLIC	471,329	34

Source: Census of Population, 1951, Preliminary Report
(Belfast H.M.S.O.) 1951.

[1] William was at that time allied with the Papacy, a fact which both sides in Ulster must view with resentment.

[2] Arensberg, C. M., and Kimball, S. T., *Family and Community in Ireland*, pp. 158–201; Mogey, J. M. *Rural Life in Northern Ireland*, pp. 117–9.

All the Protestant groups taken together showed a gain of 47,000 adherents over the figures for the previous census in 1937, and the Roman Catholics a gain of 43,000. We may regard these two figures as approximately equal and note that although this implies a larger proportionate increase in Catholics the difference is small; the relative proportions of Catholics and Protestants in the total population has not changed greatly since 1920.

The division that separates these two groups is a sharp one, although it must not be supposed that hatred and ill-feeling, or even ill-manners, are a general characteristic of the day-to-day relations between people in the two groups. The nature of this division can perhaps be illustrated by considering a small town, similar in its social structure to that of the area as a whole. In this town with a population of 4,500 and a market area about five times that number, there existed in 1946 some 260 separate shops, a large figure for such an area which can be in part accounted for by the fact that many of the shops drew their customers predominantly either from the Protestant or the Catholic section of the community. (Historical accident and a Presbyterian sense of values explains the fact that all but one of the public houses were owned by Catholics; the customers were by no means all of the same persuasion.) The two sections of society here support four secondary schools, one for the boys and one for the girls of each section; a fifth school, for technical education, is interdenominational. Voluntary societies also exist in duplicate: thus the town has two music festivals, two drama festivals, two sports meetings and similarly duplicated arrangements for cultural societies. It is true that a few organisations attempt to bridge the gap, and some have a certain success. The division is not an absolute one, not to be compared with the emotional barriers associated with colour caste in the United States; yet in the field of social relationships, as in the sphere of politics, it is very real. The unyielding attitude of the Orange Order is notorious, and, on the other side, certain basic principles of the Catholic Church hinder a rapprochement. Thus the division would be less sharp if Protestant and Catholic children went to the same schools, but here as elsewhere the Catholic hierarchy will not sanction secular education. Nor is there much hope of fusion by inter-marriage, for even a lukewarm Protestant—and there are now many in this category—may be reluctant to get married in a Catholic church when he finds he must first sign a declaration to the effect that any children of the marriage will be brought up as Catholics.

5. If the religious and political difference between Catholics and Protestants are so much sharper in Ulster than in Great Britain, those

C

between economic classes are probably less so. The explanation lies in part in the importance of agriculture: nearly half of the population lives in rural areas as compared with 5 per cent in England and Wales, and it is important to recall that these family farms are run almost entirely by owner-occupiers. The farmers may still have to repay the State by means of small annuities for buying out the landlords half a century or more ago, but for all practical purposes they own the land and certainly have the traditional mentality of small independent farmers. Even before the Land Acts, the farmers in Ulster enjoyed rather more security of tenure than elsewhere in Ireland, but here, as elsewhere, the landlord was often an absentee who exercised far less personal influence on social and economic life than in England. In order to understand the curious combination of conservatism and radicalism in Ulster's political life—more curious, perhaps, from an English than from an American point of view—it is necessary to remember how large a proportion of the people are owner-occupiers or their dependents, and allowance should also be made for the close family ties with the country among a large part of the urban population. In industry itself there are some very large firms—notably the world's largest shipyard—but in general family concerns are relatively more important than in England. Whether in agriculture or in industry, the likelihood of being self-employed seems greater, and the personal contact between boss and worker seems closer, than in many places across the Irish Sea. Moreover, if landlords were less important historically so was the established church, a point of no small social importance. The bulk of the people were Catholics and Dissenters, and their clergy usually came from their own ranks, not from a different class as was so often the case in the Church of England. There is plenty of snobbery in Ulster, of course, but the society in general gives the impression of being more fluid—more like America or Scotland or Lancashire —than the South of England.

Whether this impression is true or false, it must be strongly emphasised that the main class division, that between Catholics and Protestants, reflects different views on religion and the British connection rather than economic differences. To try to identify one group with workers and the other with capitalists would be most unwise and would, indeed, imply that the significance of the Plantation of Ulster had not been appreciated: the Loyalists there are not a mere upper-class ascendancy but comprise all classes of society. Indeed the Orange Order itself is recruited almost entirely from small farmers and workers, with the Protestant bourgeoisie standing aside and expressing that slightly disdainful amusement with which middle classes everywhere react to public spectacles. The average income is no doubt somewhat higher among the Protestants than the Catholics, mainly perhaps because some of the worst land is farmed by Catholics, but it may be doubted whether the Catholics are in general more left-wing than the Protestants. The class division in Ulster does not follow Marxian lines, if these are crudely drawn, and in so far as economic forces have contributed, their effect has been subtle and indirect.

CHAPTER 2

THE LAW AND THE CONSTITUTION

By F. H. NEWARK

Introduction

THE Constitution of Northern Ireland represents an experiment in the government in this kingdom and, apart from its own intrinsic interest, has an importance in that it is regarded by some as a prototype of constitutional devolution which might be applied to other parts of the United Kingdom. In our constitutional history we trace from early times the establishment of a strong central government which has reached its culmination in the democratic parliament of King, Lords and Commons at Westminster. The final establishment of parliamentary supremacy at the revolution of 1688 was succeeded by a development of local, county and municipal government which proceeded at a great pace in the nineteenth and twentieth centuries. Now in Northern Ireland we find added a third type of representative government, the provincial legislature which divides with the Westminster parliament the main legislative responsibilities though occupying a somewhat subordinate position.

Even after thirty years from the establishment of the Northern Ireland parliament and government it is not possible to assess the full implications of this new development. To some it may seem a step towards the perfect democratisation of government by providing the subject with one more popularly elected body in which he can make his voice felt. Some may regard it as a happy way of combating the over-centralisation of power in Westminster and Whitehall. There are critics who believe that it has in fact rendered possible the creation of a fascist State within the framework of a democratic State. And there are others who are convinced that the implications are in fact slight and the changes effected of no real importance.

The purpose of this chapter is first to describe the circumstances which led to this particular experiment in devolution being carried through in Northern Ireland in 1920. We shall see that the experiment was not the fruit of long deliberation but was thrust upon us as a result of violent political events, and has subsequently been carried through in an area where the temper of political passions is unlike anything known in England or Scotland. We shall then examine in outline the structure and function of the parliament and government in Northern Ireland, its relations with the central parliament and government, and the legal system which operates in Northern Ireland.

It must never be forgotten that devolution in Northern Ireland is an experiment and not necessarily a pattern. Had there been less political pressure in the events of 1914 and 1920 devolution might have taken a different form. And though the advocates of home rule in Scotland and Wales have displayed a keen interest in the working of the Northern Ireland Constitution, it must not be supposed that if a measure of home rule were ever given to these two countries it would necessarily take the same form as in Northern Ireland. The purpose of experiments is to increase knowledge, and there have not been wanting lessons to be learned from this particular experiment.

Constitutional History—1171–1914

The origin of the English influence on the government of Ireland is well known but often misrepresented. The statement that Henry II invaded Ireland in 1171 and subjected it to the English Crown by force of arms is a misleading simplification of the events which did in fact occur, and those who suppose that an independent Irish nation was brought under alien political domination as the result of a military campaign have not even begun to approximate to the truth.

The Ireland of the twelfth century was still in a tribal state with only the vaguest forms of national government. The traditional belief that there was an Irish nation of five provinces ruled by five kings with a high king above all "did not in historic times square with the facts".[1] Instead the evidence presents us with a picture of endless civil wars between tribal chiefs, wars which were petty in their conception and cruel beyond belief in their waging. Meanwhile the one national institution in Ireland, the Irish Church, wrung its hands at the sight of so much barbarism and evil in the land.

In 1166 Dermot MacMurrough, the King of Leinster and a great founder of churches and ravisher of nuns, was worsted in one of these tribal strifes, and he thereupon sailed to England in search of foreign aid. An application to Henry II for active assistance was refused, but Henry did give a licence to Dermot to recruit English subjects in a campaign to recover his lost territory. It was in these circumstances that Dermot returned to Ireland in 1167 with a force of Anglo-Norman barons and their followers, to be joined later by the most famous Anglo-

[1] Orpen, *Ireland under the Normans*, i. 25.

Norman baron of all, Richard Earl of Pembroke, the renowned "Strongbow".[1]

Norman military skill speedily recovered for Dermot his lost territory, and Strongbow's reward was the hand of Dermot's daughter, Eva, in marriage with the promise of a right of succession on Dermot's death. Thus when Dermot died in 1171 Strongbow found himself in the anomalous position of being at once a subject of Henry II and the king of a province of Ireland. In recognition of his feudal allegiance Strongbow made it clear that he held his Leinster territory as the subject of the English king, and it was to receive this submission in person that King Henry crossed to Ireland in 1171. It was during this visit that the Irish chiefs outside Leinster did homage to the English king, but this did no more than establish a vague suzerainty over the "mere Irish" territories. When Henry returned to England in 1172 the constitutional position was that in the eastern part of the island—Leinster and Meath—there was a settlement of Anglo-Normans; in the rest of the country were territories held by Irish chiefs; and the Anglo-Norman colonists and the Irish chiefs recognised the King of England as a feudal superior. Ireland had not fallen to Henry II by conquest in the same way that England fell to William the Conqueror, and the style of Henry II shows this. He was King of England, but merely Lord of Ireland.

In the succeeding three centuries there was little substantial change in the constitutional position. The greater part of Ireland was divided into forty or more lordships held nominally of the English king but in substance independent. Some of these lordships were held by the mere Irish and were governed by Celtic custom; others were held by the descendants of the Anglo-Norman settlers, and these in the course of time had in a large measure absorbed the habits and outlook of the Irish. Only in the eastern part of Ireland—the Pale—was English control in any sense real, but even here the control was not direct. The same influences which had brought into being a Parliament in England had led to the establishment of a like institution in Ireland, and it was this Irish Parliament which was the supreme and effective authority within the Pale. But the king who stood at the head of the Irish Parliament was an absentee king represented by a deputy who might be a statesman but more often was one of the Anglo-Norman nobles who happened to dominate the political scene at that particular time. In effect the heyday of Home Rule in Ireland was in the fourteenth and fifteenth centuries.

It was with the Tudors that the weight of English governance first

[1] Strictly speaking, Strongbow and his companions were Norman-Welsh rather than Anglo-Norman.

came to be felt in Ireland, and the medium was Sir Edward Poynings and his famous Poynings' Law. In 1487 the Irish House of Lords had committed the political error of backing the pretender Lambert Simnel, and in 1491 they repeated the error with Perkin Warbeck. Henry VII decided that the time had come to exact due obedience, and Poynings was sent from England as Lord Deputy to enforce a policy of effective supremacy of the English government. At a meeting of the Irish Parliament held at Drogheda in 1494 was passed the statute known as Poynings' Law[1] which subjected the Irish Parliament to control from England. Under the terms of this statute the Irish Parliament could not meet without the permission of the King and the English Privy Council, and then could only approve legislation which had been previously approved by the King and Privy Council. But it should be noticed that the subjection of the Irish Parliament was to the King and his Council: there was no suggestion that Ireland was in any sense subject to the English Parliament.

The subjection of Ireland to the English Parliament came at the beginning of the eighteenth century. It arose out of a dispute in the forensic sphere concerning appeals from the Irish courts. In the closing years of the seventeenth century both the English House of Lords and the Irish House of Lords claimed to be the ultimate court of appeal from the Irish courts. An intermittent conflict between the two Houses came to a climax in *Annesley v. Sherlock* in 1719 where neither of the litigants was satisfied with the decision of the Irish court and one appealed to the Irish House of Lords while the other appealed to the English House. The Irish House pressed its claims to the length of committing some of the Irish judges for contempt, but at that point the British Parliament intervened and passed the Act of 6 George I, c. 5, which not only deprived the Irish House of Lords of its appellate powers but went further and declared that the British Parliament had the right to legislate so as to bind the people of Ireland.

This Act did not mean the disappearance of the Irish Parliament. Indeed, the middle years of the eighteenth century were a period of considerable legislative activity in Dublin; but the Irish Parliament worked under a growing sense of what was regarded as an unwarrantable subordination of its sovereignty to the Parliament at Westminster. By 1781 the Irish Parliament was in a mood to assert its independence, and taking advantage of Britain's difficulties in the American war it managed to

---

[1] *Irish Statutes*, 1494, c. 9 (printed as c. 4). The name "Poynings' Law" is also at times applied to another statute of the same session which provided that certain public general statutes recently passed in England should extend to Ireland.

secure from Westminster the repeal of the Act of 6 George I, c. 5. And having shaken off the bonds of an alien parliament it now modified the control exercised by an alien executive by passing an Act to modify Poynings' Law. The effect of this modification was to ensure that the royal assent should be given to Irish bills in the exact form in which they passed the Irish Parliament "without addition, diminution or alteration".

This emancipated Irish Parliament lasted for two decades, and the constitutional position during this period was most unsatisfactory. In theory there were two independent parliaments in the two countries, each sovereign in its own realm. In theory the King could prevent collision between the two bodies by the exercise of discretion in giving the royal assent to bills. But in fact the King's power to veto bills had fallen into disuse since the beginning of the eighteenth century and a revival of that power would have been contrary to accepted constitutional convention. There remained the executive as the only tie between two equal parliaments, and an executive maintained in office by the votes of the Westminster Parliament could only ensure retaining office in Dublin by resorting to bribery. Fortunately the executive found in the Irish Parliament a legislature "corrupt beyond example",[1] and the sham of an independent Irish Parliament was kept up until 1800. In that year the Parliaments of Great Britain and Ireland by identical Acts of Union confirmed Articles of Union which established that after January 1, 1801 the kingdoms of Great Britain and Ireland should "for ever be united into one kingdom", and this United Kingdom was to be represented "in one and the same Parliament, to be styled the Parliament of the United Kingdom of Great Britain and Ireland".

Though agitation for the repeal of the Union may be said to have begun the day the Act of Union was passed, in fact for the first forty years of the nineteenth century the "Irish problem" was less a constitutional problem and more a problem, or series of problems, relating to specific grievances. Catholic emancipation, Irish Church revenues, electoral reform and the land question provided plenty of scope for those who were minded to attack the government. After 1840 there emerged the Young Ireland movement and the Fenian Society, but the first serious agitation for Home Rule may be said to begin with Isaac Butt's establishment of the Home Rule Association in 1870. At such a pace did the agitation for Home Rule make headway that by 1886 the Prime Minister was actually introducing a government measure for Home Rule in the House of Commons.

Gladstone's 1886 Bill proposed an Irish Legislature with two Houses

---

[1] See Ingram, *Irish History*, i, 334.

which were to sit and vote together unless a separate vote was demanded. This Irish Legislature had a general legislative power with a number of subjects reserved for the Imperial Parliament. Representatives from Irish constituencies were not ordinarily to attend at Westminster, though they could be summoned when certain matters affecting Ireland were under discussion. This "casual and partial interference in Imperial affairs"[1] by the Irish members would almost certainly have proved unworkable, but it was never tested, for the Home Rule Bill was rejected on its second reading in the Commons, and with it there passed out of the Liberal Party Joseph Chamberlain and his fellow Liberal-Unionists.

In 1893 Gladstone introduced his second Home Rule Bill. The general principles were the same as in 1886 except that the eighty Irish members were to be retained at Westminster, at first without power to vote on any matter purely British, but by amendment made in the Commons they were retained for all purposes. This bill passed the Commons[2] but was decisively rejected in the House of Lords.

At this point it is necessary to consider the quarters from which came opposition to Home Rule. Among Englishmen opposition from the Conservatives is easily explainable, since that party is traditionally an Imperialist party, and moreover it contained in its ranks a number of landowners with Irish estates who naturally had no reason to suppose that a Dublin parliament would be sympathetic to their interests. In Ireland the opposition came from the Protestant minority. Since the repeal of the penal laws against Roman Catholics, the bishops and priests of that church had come more and more to identify themselves with Irish nationalism, and by the middle of the nineteenth century the division between Catholic and Protestant corresponded, by and large, with the division between Nationalist and Unionist. Through most of Ireland the Unionists were a scattered minority, but in the north-east corner of Ireland there was a compact majority on which the Constitution of Northern Ireland came to be built.

Ulster was the last part of Ireland to be affected by British influence. Up to the end of the sixteenth century it was largely outside the control of either the English king or the Irish parliament. But in the seventeenth century Ulster was the scene of extensive "plantations" involving wholesale confiscations of the land of the native Irish and a resettlement with English and Scots colonists, and this produced entirely different conditions from those which obtained in the rest of Ireland. Firstly, the

---

[1] *The Times*, May 11, 1886.
[2] The majorities of 43 and 34 on the second and third readings were rendered possible by the presence of 81 Home Rulers returned for Irish constituencies.

extent of the confiscations and the fact that steps were taken to prevent the new grantees taking the native Irish as tenants ensured an English-Scots majority. Secondly, the Scots brought with them Presbyterianism, the least likely form of Protestantism to become reconciled to living under a predominantly Roman Catholic parliament in the South. And thirdly, there had developed in Ulster one of the kingdom's greatest industrial cities—Belfast—a city whose trade and industry had begun with and essentially depended on the maintenance of the Union.

Consequently it is not surprising that from the time when a movement towards Home Rule got under way it became apparent that this concentrated opposition could not be disregarded. Unfortunately this fact did not become apparent to Mr Gladstone who, it would seem, never appreciated the nature and strength of Ulster's opposition.[1] On the other hand, even before he left the Liberal party Joseph Chamberlain realised that the special conditions of Ulster demanded special treatment which would have to take the form either of an exclusion of Ulster from any Home Rule measure, or the provision of a separate parliament at Belfast quite distinct from that at Dublin. It cannot be said that if Ulster opinion had been conciliated Home Rule for the South could have been achieved in 1886 or 1893, but it is clear that without such conciliation the two Home Rule bills of Gladstone were doomed from the moment they were drafted.

When the Liberals returned to power in 1906 they showed at first no desire to return to the promotion of a Home Rule measure. Ireland was reasonably quiet, and the Government, with a full programme of social reform before it, did not wish to raise a constitutional controversy on an issue which had not been a lucky fighting ground for the party on previous occasions. It was the elections of 1910 that altered the picture: the Liberals lost heavily and remained in office only with the support of the Irish Nationalists. The outcome was a bargain between Liberals and Nationalists: the Nationalists would support the Liberals in their scheme to limit the power of the House of Lords if the Liberals would take advantage of this limitation to force through Home Rule. The Nationalists had discharged their obligation under this bargain when the Parliament Bill became law in August 1911, and the Liberals began to implement their obligation when the Government of Ireland Bill was introduced in the following April.

The new bill was on the general lines of previous Home Rule bills: an Irish legislature with limited powers was to be established and executive

---

[1] See Hammond, *Gladstone and the Irish Nation*, pp. 515–18 for an examination of Gladstone's attitude to the problem of Ulster.

power over purely Irish matters was to be transferred to an Irish government; Irish members would continue to sit at Westminster without any
restriction on the right to speak or vote. As a piece of draftsmanship and
as a genuine attempt to reconcile the claims of Irish Nationalism with
continued association in the United Kingdom it was a manifest improvement on its predecessors. The one flaw was that it purported to be a
Home Rule bill for all Ireland and there was nothing in it likely to con-
ciliate the opposition from Ulster.

It was evident from the day on which the bill was introduced that
though Liberal and Nationalist votes would see it through the Commons
it was bound to be rejected in the Lords and could only pass into law
under the terms of the Parliament Act, 1911. The Lords could hold up
the bill for a little over two years, and it would not get on the statute
book until the middle or latter part of 1914. The Northern Unionists
thus had two years' notice of their impending subordination to a Dublin
parliament, and in these circumstances they acted in the manner in
which every sagacious political observer expected they would. The Ulster
Covenant "to use all means" to prevent a Home Rule parliament being
established was signed in September 1912; a year later a Provisional
Government under Sir Edward Carson was set up, and then the drilling
of unarmed volunteers began in earnest. In the spring of 1914 the Liberal
Government decided to intimidate Ulster by military action, but the
plan was foiled by the refusal of British troops to advance against people
whose offence they felt to be simply that of loyalty to the British connection. Shortly afterwards weapons were smuggled into the north, the
Ulster volunteers became an armed force and the stage was set for civil
war. Covenant, Provisional Government and armed volunteers were, of
course, quite illegal, and as such have no place in the course of constitutional events. Their political importance, on the other hand, was tre-
mendous: for the first time in English history over half a million subjects
had publicly and solemnly announced that they intended to oppose an
Act of Parliament by force.

The force of these events was not lost on the politicians, who searched
desperately for some accommodation between the opposing views. But
none was forthcoming, for the causes of Irish Nationalism and Ulster
Unionism were direct antitheses. The Government then for the first time
decided to treat Ulster as a special case: the counties of Ulster were to be
given the option of voting themselves out of the new Act for a period of
six years, after which they would be incorporated automatically in a
united Ireland under the proposed Dublin parliament. A bill to this
effect was introduced by Lord Crewe in June 1914. Time was short, for

the Government of Ireland Act had nearly run its course under the Parliament Act and Lord Crewe's bill—even if the compromise it contained had been acceptable to Ulster—could only get on to the statute book in time to avert a crisis if it passed Parliament virtually as an agreed measure. In fact the House of Lords amended Lord Crewe's bill by rejecting temporary exclusion by counties in favour of permanent exclusion for the whole Province, but it was clear that this amendment would, in its turn, be rejected by the Commons. Thus it appeared that the Home Rule Bill would become law with the Ulster question unresolved, and the country seemed on the verge of civil war.

It was then that King George intervened by calling a conference of the Irish leaders, but no agreement was reached and the Conference broke up in failure. But by now war clouds of a different kind were blowing up on the horizon, and before any further steps could be taken August 1914 had arrived. The Government of Ireland Act reached the statute book in September 1914, but there was now no question of bringing it into immediate effect. On the same day as the Government of Ireland Bill received the royal assent, another bill also received the royal assent and this provided that the Government of Ireland Act, 1914 should not come into operation until the end of the war. Both Carson and Redmond promised support against Germany[1]; and the Government believed that the greater emergency had brought temporary peace to Ireland. Those hopes were to be dashed in 1916.

The Creation of Northern Ireland

Though the Government of Ireland Act, 1914, thus lay shelved for the duration of the war, political speculation about the future of Ireland was not stilled, and in all subsequent discussion it was clearly perceived that the Ulster problem would have to be solved at the same time as the Irish problem. In other words, it was clear that the 1914 Act could not be brought into force as it stood, and the new promised amending bill had not yet appeared.

The unsuccessful Dublin rebellion of 1916, organised by Sinn Fein extremists, who were now gaining ground from Redmond's more moderate nationalists, led the Government to resume its attempts to solve the Irish problem. In 1916 "Headings of a Settlement as to the Government of Ireland"[2] were presented to Parliament: these anticipated immediate application of the 1914 Act with the six counties of Antrim,

[1] Members of the Ulster Volunteer Force joined the army to form the Ulster Division.
[2] Cmd. 8310.

Armagh, Down, Fermanagh, Londonderry and Tyrone excluded, these to be governed by Order in Council, and the whole situation to be reviewed after the war. The "Headings" pleased nobody and no settlement was effected. Again, at the Irish Convention in 1918, a proposal to exclude the whole Province of Ulster was made, but no rapprochement between Unionist and Nationalist was possible on these lines. And so the war drew to an end with the prospect of the 1914 Act being brought into operation and civil war in the North being superimposed on the general state of anarchy into which the whole country was gradually slipping.

In these circumstances the Government decided to abandon the idea of bringing in the 1914 Act with some sort of temporising provision to safeguard the interests of the North; instead they produced a new bill which went on to the statute book as the Government of Ireland Act, 1920, and which still remains as the foundation document of the Constitution of Northern Ireland.

The vital principle of the new bill was that it contained a definite and permanent exclusion of six counties in the North and conferred on this area a separate parliament. Indeed, it is perhaps inappropriate to speak of the "exclusion" of the North: the North was no more excluded from the South than the South was excluded from the North. The Westminster Parliament at last recognised the diversity of interest between North and South and conferred on each the benefit of Home Rule in the form envisaged in the 1914 Act.

In so far as the South was concerned the gift was unacceptable, partly because Irish nationalism had advanced far beyond the limited degree of Home Rule which might have been acceptable in 1914, and partly because Irish nationalism insisted on the essential unity of all the island of Ireland. In so far as the North was concerned the gift was received with mixed feelings, for though it gave security from the fear of domination by a Dublin parliament, it was accompanied by the creation of a Belfast parliament which had never been asked for. In short, the Unionists in Ulster were put in charge of a Home Rule parliament of their own. And there was one additional disappointment for the Northern Unionists: Northern Ireland was not to be the Province of Ulster but only the six counties where there was the greatest concentration of Unionists. However, the Northern Unionists decided to work the Act loyally on the footing that this was to be the final settlement: there were to be no more concessions to Nationalist aspirations at the expense of the territory or powers of Northern Ireland.

The broad scheme of the 1920 Act was to establish in each of the two provinces of Northern Ireland and Southern Ireland a parliament with limited powers, and separate governments responsible to each parliament. There was to be one representative of the King for the whole of Ireland—the Lord Lieutenant—and in order to bring about harmonious relations between the two governments and parliaments there was to be a Council of Ireland consisting of twenty representatives from each parliament. The Act optimistically looked forward to the two parliaments by mutual agreement yielding up their powers to one parliament for the whole country. It will be seen that "partition" was never a policy of the British government.

As far as Southern Ireland was concerned the Act proved entirely unworkable, as everyone could have foreseen. The Southern Parliament was called into being, and amid the ambushes and arsons an election was held for members to serve in the Southern House of Commons. The successful Sinn Fein candidates were pledged to sit in their own self-constituted Dail;[1] so it was not surprising that when the faithful Commons of Southern Ireland met on June 28, 1921 only four members took their seats. At the next meeting a fortnight later only two members appeared. The farce was now ended and the attempt to put the Act into operation in the South was abandoned.

Meanwhile the British Prime Minister, Lloyd George, was proposing negotiations with the Sinn Fein leaders in the South, and these eventually led to a truce and a visit of a Sinn Fein delegation to London. It was these London talks that ended in Articles of Agreement for a Treaty between Great Britain and Ireland signed on December 6, 1921—the document always simply referred to in Ireland as "the Treaty".

It is an odd document, and to constitutional lawyers a rather irregular document. This is due to the fact that the Sinn Fein delegates insisted on regarding themselves as delegates of a Republic of Ireland, whereas the British Government could only deal with them as a group of intransigent subjects. Treaties are entered into between sovereign States and the "Republic of Ireland" was not a sovereign State; hence the evasive title "Articles of Agreement for a Treaty". Furthermore, the Sinn Feiners, who signed as the "Irish Delegation", insisted on treating for the whole of Ireland, though none of the signatories can have imagined for a moment that the status of Northern Ireland was to be interfered with. What the Treaty did in effect was to make the whole of Ireland a self-governing Dominion under the style of "the Irish Free State" (Article 1), provided that the powers of the Irish Free State Government should not

---

[1] At the general election in 1918 the Sinn Fein candidates had used the electoral machinery for choosing candidates for a republican assembly—Dail Eireann. They now used the same method for reconstituting that body.

extend to Northern Ireland until the expiration of one month after ratification (Article 11), and gave Northern Ireland the option of contracting out of the Irish Free State during that month (Article 12).

Needless to say as soon as the Treaty was ratified the Parliament of Northern Ireland quickly elected to contract out of the newly-born Irish Free State. This had been foreseen in the Treaty, which had provided that in such an event a Boundary Commission of three persons, one each to be appointed by the British, Northern Ireland and Free State Governments, should determine the boundaries between Northern Ireland and the Free State. The Northern Ireland Government had protested against this Boundary Commission on the ground that there had been pledges by the British Government before the Treaty that the territorial integrity of Northern Ireland would not be infringed. Accordingly the Northern Ireland Government declined to appoint a representative, and when the Judicial Committee of the Privy Council was asked whether the King or the Governor of Northern Ireland could legally appoint a representative for Northern Ireland in the absence of a recommendation from the Northern Ireland ministers it was ruled that there was no such power. So a new "Treaty" was entered into between the British Government and the Irish Free State Government in August 1924 by which it was agreed that if Northern Ireland remained obdurate the power to appoint a Northern Ireland representative should pass to the British Government. Eventually the British Government appointed J. R. Fisher, an Ulster lawyer, as the Northern Ireland representative, and with Mr Justice Feetham of South Africa as British representative and Professor Eoin McNeill as Free State representative the Boundary Commission was at last constituted late in 1924.

The Boundary Commission laboured for a year, perambulating the border area and studying the wishes of the inhabitants and the economic and geographic conditions. It was about to report in November 1925 when Professor McNeill suddenly resigned. No report was ever published, but the broad outlines of what the report would have contained and the reasons for Professor McNeill's resignation are well known. The Irish Free State had gone into the Boundary Commission in the belief that the result would have been to award large portions of the Six Counties to the Irish Free State.[1] It seems that the Boundary Commission was prepared to award parts of the Six Counties to the Free State, but it was also prepared to award parts of the Twenty-Six Counties to Northern

---

[1] Michael Collins's idea of boundary revision was the cession to the Free State of the counties of Fermanagh and Tyrone and parts of the counties of Down, Londonderry and Armagh.

Ireland. And it was a premature disclosure of this scheme which alarmed the Free State Government and induced Professor McNeill to resign.

At this point Mr Baldwin appeared on the scene as a peace-maker, and convened a conference between representatives of Northern Ireland and the Irish Free State. On December 3, 1925, nearly four years to the day from the Treaty, an agreement was signed by which it was agreed "in a spirit of neighbourly comradeship" that the Boundary Commission's powers should be revoked and that the extent of Northern Ireland should be such as was fixed by the Government of Ireland Act, 1920— that is, the six counties.[1]

This question of the delimitation of Northern Ireland has been considered in some detail because of the contention so often advanced that Ireland was arbitrarily partitioned by Britain. In fact, to-day the terms "Nationalist" and "Unionist" have almost gone out in favour of the terms "Anti-Partitionist" and "Partitionist". Partition does not, as will have been seen, depend to-day on the Government of Ireland Act, 1920. If we accept the Southern view that the document of December 1921 was a Treaty signed by a delegation entitled to speak in the name of "Ireland" there was a recognition by "Ireland" in articles 11, 12 and 14 of the Treaty that a part of the country was entitled to retain its *status quo* under the 1920 Act. Again in 1924, in the Agreement which supplemented the Treaty and by which the Boundary Commission was finally constituted, the Irish Free State by its Prime Minister recognised and ratified the right of Northern Ireland to remain outside the Irish Free State. Finally we have the Agreement of 1925 where again the Irish Free State signatories recognised the separation of the six counties from the rest of Ireland and did so "in a spirit of neighbourly comradeship."

The establishment of the Irish Free State naturally rendered much of the 1920 Act obsolete. The Westminster Parliament passed an Irish Free State (Consequential Provisions) Act, 1922, which did a certain amount of tidying up of the statute book, and in 1927 all that part of the 1920 Act which related to Southern Ireland was repealed.[2] The rest

---

[1] The official title of the State which is under consideration is "Northern Ireland". It is often referred to however as "Ulster" or "the Six Counties". "The Six Counties" is politically tendentious, for it is the favourite term in use among Nationalists who suppose that "Northern Ireland" implies that Ireland is divisible. Perhaps the Nationalists do not know that the term "Six Counties" was invented by George V. "Ulster" is historically and geographically inaccurate to describe the territory, but it is a short and convenient word, and the inhabitants of Northern Ireland are best described as "Ulstermen".

[2] The reader who turns up the Government of Ireland Act, 1920, in the volume of statutes, will see the original text which related to both Northern and Southern Ireland. The best reference to the text of the Act as it now stands is in Queckett, *Constitution of Northern Ireland*, vol. ii.

remains to form the Constitution of Northern Ireland, and it is this Constitution that we may now examine.

The Parliament of Northern Ireland

(1) The centre of gravity of the Northern Ireland Constitution is the Parliament which is given power to pass legislation for the "peace, order and good government of Northern Ireland" subject to certain limitations. "Peace, order and good government" is the traditional phrase which the Westminster Parliament uses when it establishes a legislature in a dominion or colony. It is a phrase intended to carry the amplest powers except where otherwise specified. So the Northern Ireland Parliament is truly a sovereign body except in so far as its powers are expressly limited. In short, we must not approach a consideration of the Parliament's powers by looking into the 1920 Act to see what it can do; we look into the Act to see what it cannot do.

The first and broadest limitation on the powers of the Northern Ireland Parliament is that it can only legislate in respect of matters exclusively relating to Northern Ireland. This sharply distinguishes it from the Westminster Parliament and from the Parliaments of the various dominions in the Commonwealth. These other Parliaments have the power to pass legislation with extra-territorial effect binding persons and things outside the territory over which the Parliament exercises immediate control. Thus the Westminster Parliament can legislate so as to regulate or prohibit acts done by its subjects, or even by foreigners, in another country.[1] But the Northern Ireland Parliament can legislate only in respect of acts and things within the territory of Northern Ireland. The effect of this limitation is twofold: firstly it means that a direct attempt on the part of the Northern Ireland Parliament to legislate on matters outside Northern Ireland would be *ultra vires* and invalid; and secondly, where general words appear in a Northern Ireland statute which grammatically could refer both to matters within and without Northern Ireland it is to be assumed that the Northern Ireland Parliament has acted *intra vires* and words are accordingly construed as relating only to Northern Ireland.

The 1920 Act, after imposing this general limitation on the powers of the Northern Ireland Parliament, then proceeds to set out a list of "*excepted*" matters on which that Parliament has no power to make laws.[2] Many of these are matters which in any event do not exclusively relate

---

[1] Thus under a United Kingdom statute bigamy can be punished in our courts though the bigamous marriage may have taken place abroad.

[2] Section 4 of the 1920 Act.

D

to Northern Ireland; all are matters on which it is essential that there shall be uniformity throughout the United Kingdom. These excepted matters are: the Crown, peace and war and matters arising from a state of war, the armed forces, treaties with foreign States, dignities and titles, treason, naturalisation, domicile, trade with any place outside Northern Ireland, cables and wireless, air navigation, lighthouses, coinage and negotiable instruments, weights and measures, trade marks, copyright and patents.

Next there are certain matters which are *"reserved"*, and on these the Northern Ireland Parliament has no power to legislate. The reserved matters are few in number and they are topics which the Westminster Parliament decided in 1920 to reserve to itself for a time with the intention that when Northern Ireland and Southern Ireland united these powers could be transferred to an All-Ireland Parliament. Reserved matters include the postal service, savings banks, designs for stamps, the registration of deeds, land purchase, the Supreme Court in Northern Ireland and certain highly important reserved taxes.[1] In recent years the registration of deeds and land purchase have been dereserved and the power to deal with these matters handed over to the Northern Ireland Parliament.

Next there are two prohibitions imposed on the powers of the Northern Ireland Parliament—a prohibition against legislation discriminating on grounds of religion, and a prohibition against taking property without compensation.[2] The prohibition against religious discrimination forbids the endowment of religion, restrictions against the free exercise of religion, the giving of any preference or the imposing of any disability on grounds of religion, and also protects the property of religious bodies. These provisions have been an invariable feature of all Home Rule bills. The prohibition against taking property without compensation was not in the original draft of the 1920 Act, but was inserted in the bill's passage through Parliament and rather incautiously put at the end of the section dealing with religious discrimination. This fact has led some to contend that the prohibition only deals with the taking of *religious* property without compensation, but this view has been rejected by the Northern Ireland Court of Appeal. Such a prohibition is, in fact, quite a common feature in written Constitutions, and was certainly inserted in this instance in order to prevent confiscatory legislation. In practice its importance is slight, for there is no reason to suppose that the Northern Ireland

---

[1] For the powers of the Northern Ireland Parliament with regard to taxation see *post* pp. 38–9.
[2] Section 5 of the 1920 Act.

Parliament would in any event fail to follow the well-settled tradition at Westminster (where there is, of course, no such limitation) that the State does not take the subject's property without paying compensation.

We can therefore summarise the position set out above by saying that all matters which could concern Northern Ireland fall into one of the three classes: *excepted* matters, *reserved* matters, and *transferred* matters. With regard to *excepted* and *reserved* matters the only Parliament which can deal with them is the Westminster Parliament, and the administration of these matters in Northern Ireland is in the hands of Imperial civil servants.[1] With regard to *transferred* matters the Northern Ireland Parliament is fully competent to legislate provided that it does not purport to give its legislation extra-territorial effect and does not infringe the prohibitions against religious discrimination and the taking of property without compensation.

Naturally when legislative functions are distributed between two Parliaments as in the present case, there is bound to be a certain haziness on the boundary line, however well the statute dividing the functions is drafted. It might therefore be supposed that from time to time collisions between Westminster and Stormont would arise as to which was the appropriate Parliament to legislate on some particular topic. In fact such collisions are unlikely. There is the closest co-ordination between civil servants at Stormont and their opposite numbers at Whitehall, and the Parliamentary Draftsman at Stormont is an expert at ensuring that the bills which he draws are within the competence of the Northern Ireland Parliament. Furthermore, when a bill has passed the Northern Ireland Parliament and is presented for royal assent it has to be accompanied by a certificate from the Attorney-General for Northern Ireland to the effect that the bill does not infringe the provisions of the Government of Ireland Act, 1920.

Also it should be observed that when the courts come to interpret a Northern Ireland statute they, according to a well-known rule, apply a benign canon of construction known as the "pith and substance" doctrine. This means that if the pith and substance of the disputed legislation is within the powers of the Northern Ireland Parliament the courts will not hold it to be *ultra vires* because incidentally and in some slight degree it may purport to go beyond the competence of the Parliament.

---

[1] This remark has to be taken with the qualification that sometimes the Northern Ireland civil service acts as agents for the Imperial civil service in administering excepted and reserved matters. It will be appreciated that the emergence in recent years of a number of new and important ministries, e.g. Ministry of Food, Ministry of Supply, etc. has greatly increased the activities of Imperial civil servants in Northern Ireland.

Thus, a Northern Ireland statute which imposed control on hygienic grounds over the sale of milk in Northern Ireland was held valid notwithstanding that in a few cases it could apply to milk producers selling milk in Northern Ireland whose farms were actually across the border in the Irish Free State.[1]

Nor, on the other hand, is there any "poaching" by the Westminster Parliament on the preserves of Stormont. Legally the Westminster Parliament could legislate for Northern Ireland on any transferred matter, for the Government of Ireland Act expressly preserves the authority of the Westminster Parliament "over all persons, matters, and things" in Northern Ireland.[2] But this saving of supreme authority is an "iron ration" of legislative power which remains on the statute book to be used in an emergency. In the normal course of things by well-established constitutional convention the Westminster Parliament will not legislate where the matter is within Stormont's competence. Indeed, the Westminster Parliament has on many occasions permitted Stormont to legislate on matters which under the original division of functions were assigned to Westminster. Since 1920 it has been found in various instances that the limitations imposed on Stormont were working with unnecessary strictness, and on each occasion the Westminster Parliament has relaxed the limitation.[3] One example will suffice. Criminal offences are in general a matter on which the Stormont Parliament can legislate, but because the Post Office is a reserved service it meant that though Stormont could legislate against stealing in general it could not legislate against the stealing of postal packets. When this anomaly came to light the Westminster Parliament conferred on the Stormont Parliament the power to legislate with respect to criminal offences in connection with reserved services.

Again, the Stormont Parliament has no power to legislate with regard to matters arising out of a state of war. The war of 1939–45 demonstrated that modern war leaves untouched practically no aspect of social life, and such subjects as the effect of war on the superannuation of civil servants, emergency housing, control of employment, control of war charities, etc., were originally all beyond the competence of the Stormont Parliament. What in fact happened was that in most cases whenever the Westminster Parliament legislated on such matters for Great Britain it included in the Act a section enabling the Stormont Parliament to legislate for similar purposes.

---

[1] *Gallagher* v. *Lynn* (1937).   [2] Section 75 of the 1920 Act.
[3] See the Northern Ireland (Miscellaneous Provisions) Acts of 1928, 1932, 1945, and the Northern Ireland Act, 1947.

We thus see that the division of legislative functions between the two Parliaments has worked harmoniously, and that while Stormont is scrupulously careful in not going beyond the limits laid down, Westminster for its part is ready in all reasonable cases to enlarge the original limits of Stormont's jurisdiction. In the event of this harmony ever breaking down there is, of course, no doubt where the whip hand is to be found: it rests with Westminster. Stormont legislation which oversteps the prescribed limits is *ultra vires* and of no effect. And if Westminster chooses to legislate on a transferred matter, that Westminster legislation is law in Northern Ireland.

The conception of an *ultra vires* statute which was introduced by the Government of Ireland Act is novel in our constitutional law. It is a trite remark among lawyers that "an Act of Parliament can do anything except make a man a woman", and this is true of Acts of the Westminster Parliament. No court can declare that an Act of the Westminster Parliament is invalid because it is unreasonable or contrary to natural law or for any reason of that kind. It is otherwise in many other countries where there are written Constitutions which set limits beyond which the legislature cannot go. Thus in the United States of America it is no infrequent thing for the Supreme Court to declare that an Act of Congress is unconstitutional and therefore void because it is at variance with the provisions of the American Constitution. Northern Ireland legislation can likewise be declared to be void, and there have been one or two minor instances.

No special procedure is necessary to invalidate an *ultra vires* Act. Any court, even the humblest magistrate, before which the question of validity is raised can declare that the Act is *ultra vires* if it so believes. There is, however, a special provision in the 1920 Act by which legislation can be tested before any concrete question arises. A Northern Ireland Act, or even a Bill which has not yet become an Act, can be referred by the Governor of Northern Ireland to the Judicial Committee of the Privy Council, and it is possible in this way to get a speedy and definite decision which is binding on all courts.

As far as can be ascertained six Acts, or rather sections in Acts, have been challenged.[1] In five cases the challenge came in the course of ordinary litigation; in the sixth case the matter was referred to the Privy Council under the procedure mentioned above. In four of the cases the courts sustained the validity of the legislation, but in two cases—both cases arising out of the Transport Acts which transferred transport

---

[1] In each case the point involved was highly technical and devoid of political importance.

undertakings to public ownership—it was held that the impugned legislation was *ultra vires* as constituting a taking of property without compensation.

(2) The Parliament of Northern Ireland is of the two chamber type
which is known at Westminster and has been exported thence to the
various parts of the Empire. But though the model is Westminster we
shall see that those who designed the Government of Ireland Act were
at pains to avoid some of the anomalies and archaisms which existed
in the older legislature.

The Parliament consists of King, Senate and House of Commons.
The House of Commons is composed of fifty-two members, forty-eight
of them representing territorial constituencies and the remaining four
being returned for the Queen's University of Belfast. The 1920 Act
provided that the system of election was to be that of proportional representation, but the Northern Ireland Parliament was given power to
change the electoral system after the lapse of three years. Advantage was
taken of this in 1929 when a return was made to the old system of direct
vote in single-member constituencies, except in the four-member constituency of the University where proportional representation still exists.
The change was strongly criticised as a political manœuvre to increase
the number of government supporters. The actual result in operation
was to increase the number of both government supporters and supporters of the main opposition—the Nationalists. It was the smaller
"splinter" parties, always a feature of any system of proportional representation, which received the full impact of the change. The real
justification of the change was that proportional representation requires
multiple-member constituencies, and the sparse population in rural
areas of Northern Ireland meant that such constituencies were fantas-
tically large. When, as provided in the 1920 Act, the whole of two counties
—Fermanagh and Tyrone—was one constituency, territorial representation became a farce.

The House of Commons of Northern Ireland continues for five years
unless sooner dissolved. In fact, in accordance with the Westminster
practice, no House of Commons has ever expired by effluxion of time:
an election is always held as the result of a dissolution which the Governor grants on the advice of the Prime Minister of Northern Ireland.

The Senate consists of twenty-six members—two ex officio members,
the Lord Mayor of Belfast and the Mayor of Londonderry, and twenty-
four members elected by the House of Commons by proportional representation. The Senate is not dissolved when Parliament is dissolved:
Senators hold office for eight years, but the body is revivified periodic-

ally by an arrangement by which half the members retire every four years.

The relationship of House of Commons and Senate is similar to that of House of Commons and House of Lords at Westminster. Financial legislation must be initiated in the House of Commons, and the Senate has no power of amendment to such legislation. The procedure on legislation is similar to that at Westminster; that is to say, there are the customary three readings and committee stage. In the event of a disagreement between the two Houses the Governor can convoke a joint sitting of the two Houses, and if the bill passes at this joint sitting it is deemed to have passed both Houses.[1] In fact there has never been such a joint sitting, for there has never been serious disagreement. The Senate's amendments have invariably been such as could be accepted by the Commons. Indeed, since the Senate is elected by the members of the House of Commons it is naturally to be expected that the second house will represent the political opinions of the first. The only circumstances in which the two houses could be politically at loggerheads would be where, after a landslide at a general election, the newly formed government majority found itself burdened with a Senate composed of members elected by its predecessor. Up to the present there has been no sign of such a landslide.

The fact that the Senate so faithfully represents the political opinions of the Commons raises the question of its value in the Constitution. The House of Lords had a historical growth of several centuries, and the dignity of its antiquity atones to some extent for its anomalies. Several second chambers have been formed in imitation but none has been wholly successful. A second chamber elected by popular vote is an unnecessary duplication of democratic control. A nominated second chamber opens up the way to complete control of the legislature by the executive. What is really wanted is a second chamber consisting of single-minded men of wide interests and complete integrity who can be trusted to have a clearer insight into our social and economic needs than those whom the people have chosen; but such perfection is hard to achieve.

It will be observed that the Parliament of Northern Ireland is on a very small scale compared with that of Westminster. A House of Commons of fifty-two members looks diminutive beside the parent body of over six hundred members; and though the House of Lords never musters all its seven-hundred-odd peers, an average debate attracts forty or fifty, whereas the Senate of Northern Ireland is only twenty-six all told. One consequence of the small size of the Commons at Stormont is that

[1] Section 17 of the 1920 Act.

the ratio of government back benchers to the Treasury bench is much lower than at Westminster.

It must be admitted that the normal working of the parliamentary system as seen at Westminster cannot be reproduced at Stormont. The Westminster system is based on the healthy alternation of parties in power, the opposition of to-day being the government of to-morrow, and vice versa. This system is usually styled "healthy" because it is realised that a spell out of office acts as a necessary corrective to ministers who are in danger of magnifying their own importance; and on the other hand it has been discovered that a spell in office can work wonders in the case of the irresponsible critic. But at Stormont the Unionist party has never gone out of office since 1921, and there is no likelihood of this happening in the foreseeable future. The reason for this is that the main opposition party, the Nationalist, stands for the abolition of Northern Ireland as a part of the United Kingdom, and this is more than a plank in its platform—it is virtually its whole platform. The result is that every election is fought on the constitutional issue, and the Constitution can only survive if the government survives. The day that the government goes out of office the Constitution will go out of existence. In fact for some years after the establishment of the Northern Parliament the Nationalist members refused to take their seats, but from 1928 the policy of abstention has been abandoned, though the party still disclaims to be the "official" opposition.

The remaining part of the legislature is the King, whose functions are exercised by the Governor. The Government of Ireland Act, 1920, had envisaged two Parliaments in Ireland with one representative of the King—the Lord Lieutenant—and the text of the Act speaks of "Lord Lieutenant" throughout. But on the setting up of the Irish Free State in 1922 the Irish Free State (Consequential Provisions) Act was passed at Westminster, and this substituted a Governor of Northern Ireland for the Lord Lieutenant. The Governor is appointed by the King and holds office for a term of six years which may be renewed.[1]

With regard to the Governor's powers in connection with legislation we have to distinguish between the strictly legal position and what in fact happens by constitutional convention. The theoretical position is that, unless the King gives the Governor special instructions to assent to, or withold assent from, or to reserve[2] a bill, the Governor can please

[1] The first Governor—the Duke of Abercorn— had his term renewed twice. The second—the Earl Granville— had one renewal.

[2] To reserve a bill is to retain it for consideration by the King (i.e. by Whitehall). Where a bill is reserved the royal assent can be given later at any time up to one year after the bill passed Parliament.

himself whether he gives or refuses assent. In fact the Governor acts like a constitutional monarch, and if a bill passes the Commons and Senate he must give his assent. Nor, in fact, can the King, either of his own accord or on the advice of his Whitehall ministers, give instructions to the Governor to refuse assent or to reserve.

When the Government of Ireland Act was passed no one imagined that the Governor was going to exercise a personal discretion whether he would assent to legislation or not, but apparently it was assumed that he might be required to reserve a bill on the orders of Whitehall given through the King. The experiment was tried once in 1922 when a Local Government Bill was reserved. This procedure evoked sharp comment in Northern Ireland, where the view was taken that on transferred matters the Northern Ireland Parliament had in fact the last word. "We must be masters in our own house!" was the expression used in the Northern Ireland Parliament, and doubtless the sentiment was conveyed to Whitehall in more diplomatic language. At any rate this bill was speedily assented to and, as far as is known, there has been no similar reservation since.

(3) The inhabitants of Northern Ireland are represented, not only in the Parliament of Northern Ireland, but also in the Imperial Parliament at Westminster. Some sort of Irish representation at Westminster had been a feature of all the Home Rule bills, for it was clearly necessary in order to preserve the democratic principle that as long as some affairs were withheld from the subordinate parliament representatives must be present at the superior parliament where these matters were dealt with. The Government of Ireland Act, 1920, provided for thirteen members for Northern Ireland to sit at Westminster, but the number has now been reduced to twelve with the abolition of the University constituency at Belfast. These twelve members are, of course, part and parcel of the Westminster Parliament and have nothing to do with the local parliament as such: that is to say they are returned in elections for the Westminster Parliament and their tenure is unaffected by a dissolution of the Stormont Parliament. There have been instances of an individual being elected to both parliaments.

For the same reason that ensures a Unionist majority in the Stormont Parliament, the majority of the twelve Ulster members at Westminster are always Unionists. No matter what controversies of domestic or foreign policy agitate the electorate in Great Britain at the time of a general election, one may be sure that the contest in Northern Ireland will be fought on the constitutional issue.

This dual representation naturally results in some dissipation of political talent in Northern Ireland. Not many will attempt the exhausting task of trying to do duty in both Parliaments, and faced with the choice of Stormont or Westminster there are great temptations to forsake Northern Ireland for the more august assembly. This is understandable, for the more attractive topics of politics, such as foreign affairs come up for consideration at Westminster. No politician worth his salt would prefer to discuss drainage in Derry at Stormont instead of deliberating on the fate of nations at Westminster. It is true that Sir James Craig, later Lord Craigavon, abandoned a promising career to Westminster to come into Northern Ireland politics, but it was generally accepted that he was making a great sacrifice.

The disparity in importance between Westminster and Stormont has been aggravated by a ruling, or rather a series of rulings, of Speakers of the Northern Ireland Parliament which have prevented discussion at Stormont on excepted and reserved matters. While it is clear under the Government of Ireland Act that Stormont cannot legislate on such matters there is nothing in that Act which in terms prohibits discussion. Indeed, it seems to have been assumed during the passage of the various Home Rule bills at Westminster that the Irish legislature would discuss and pass resolutions on matters not within its legislative competence.[1] After all, as the name of the institution shows, a parliament is a place for talking, and legislation is, historically, a secondary function. However, from an early date the Speaker in the Northern Ireland Commons[2] has prohibited discussion on excepted and reserved matters. The justification for this is that since no minister in the Northern Ireland Parliament is responsible for these matters, question and criticism are out of order. The only ways in which any sort of discussion on excepted or reserved matters could take place would be where a Northern Ireland minister had actually undertaken some action in respect of an excepted or reserved matter, or where the exceedingly cumbersome procedure of an Address to the Crown were resorted to.

The Executive

Legislation is, of course, only part of government. The executive today wields ever-increasing powers, as the prerogative powers of the King have been added to by Parliament's delegation of powers to the executive. Another fact which enhances the importance of the executive is that the

---

[1] "The addresses of the Legislative Body, if founded on reason, would on excluded matters have no power, but they might have a great deal of influence." Gladstone in 1885, cited in Hammond, *Gladstone and the Irish Nation*.

[2] The same rule has been laid down by the Speaker of the Senate.

executive is at work day by day, whereas Parliament, in Northern Ireland at any rate, confines its activities to a few weeks in the year all told.

According to our constitutional law the executive power in the Constitution resides in the King and is exercised on his behalf by ministers.[1] Before 1920 the executive power in relation to Irish affairs was exercised through the Lord Lieutenant and the Chief Secretary for Ireland in Dublin Castle. The Act of 1920 does not tamper with the political theory that executive power is vested in the King: section 8 declares that "the executive power in Northern Ireland shall continue vested in His Majesty the King". The section then goes on to distinguish: executive power in relation to "transferred services", i.e. those services with respect to which the Northern Ireland Parliament has power to legislate, is contrasted with executive power in relation to excepted and reserved matters. The latter is exercised by the King through his Whitehall ministers and the Imperial civil service. The former may be delegated to the Governor. In fact the King delegated all executive power in relation to transferred services to the Governor[2] as soon as the Act came into operation. The Act provides that the powers so delegated to the Governor shall be exercised through such departments as he or the Northern Ireland Parliament may establish. Immediately after this delegation of executive power to the Governor in 1921 he established seven departments: Prime Minister's Department, Ministry of Finance, Ministry of Home Affairs, Ministry of Labour, Ministry of Education, Ministry of Commerce and Ministry of Agriculture. These have now been added to by the creation in 1944 of a Ministry of Health and Local Government.[3] At the same time as the Governor established these departments he assigned functions to each, i.e. distributed executive powers in connection with transferred services over the various departments.

The heads of these departments are designated by the Act as the Ministers of Northern Ireland. Every person made a Minister must be a member of the Privy Council of Northern Ireland, and he must be a member of one or other of the Houses of the Northern Ireland Parliament or become such a member within six months. The Ministers collectively

---

[1] Ministers are, as the name implies, merely servants of the King, and until modern times they remembered that fact in the language which they used. To-day it is not uncommon to hear ministers speaking of "*my* ministry" and "*my* officials", or even "*my* army". One Prime Minister of the United Kingdom went so far as to speak of "*my* ministers".

[2] I have used the term "Governor", though it will be remembered that during the short period between the establishment of Northern Ireland and the passing of the Irish Free State (Consequential Provisions) Act, 1922, the chief officer was "Lord Lieutenant", and it was in fact the Lord Lieutenant who took the steps described.

[3] During the war period there was also a Ministry of Public Security.

form what the Act styles "an executive committee of the Privy Council of Northern Ireland (to be called the Executive Committee of Northern Ireland)"—in fact it is the body which is known as the Northern Ireland Cabinet.[1] The functions of this Cabinet are stated in the Act to be "to aid and advise the Governor in the exercise of his executive power" in relation to Northern Ireland services. That is to say, the Northern Ireland Cabinet behaves in exactly the same way as does the British Cabinet: it acts as the body which co-ordinates the activities of the various ministries and formulates a general government policy.

Provided that the Ministers are members of the Northern Ireland Parliament, there is no stipulation that they must be members of a particular House. The dominance of the Commons means that in practice Ministers tend to seek seats in that House, but the situation is much better than at Westminster owing to a very useful provision in the Act that a Minister may appear and speak in either House. He can vote only in the House of which he is a member, but this provision does mean that a Minister who has piloted a bill through one House does not have to hand it over to some one who is less familiar with the subject matter when it goes to the other House.

Taxation and Expenditure

The general course of financial legislation and the constitutional principles underlying it are similar to those in Great Britain. The Government of Ireland Act, 1920, secures the pre-eminence of the Commons in financial matters, a pre-eminence which was won by the Commons at Westminster after centuries of struggle culminating in the Parliament Act, 1911. The Government of Ireland Act also provides that no appropriation of public revenue shall take place except in pursuance of a recommendation from the Governor: this is to secure that the promotion of financial policy rests entirely with the Government and so prevents private members sponsoring schemes for the particular benefit of their own constituents.

The scheme of the 1920 Act was to split the taxing power between the two parliaments as follows: the Northern Ireland Parliament was given

---

[1] It is presumably a relic of the seventeenth-century Parliamentary suspicion of government by a Cabinet that the Legislature could not, even in 1920, bring itself to use the hated word. Even to-day in Britain the Cabinet is, broadly speaking, a device not recognised by law. It will be noted that in Northern Ireland the Act establishes as law two rules which obtain at Westminster only by convention: (a) Ministers must be Privy Councillors since the Cabinet is in theory merely a meeting of a Privy Council committee; (b) Ministers must be in Parliament in order to maintain the principle of parliamentary control of the executive.

power to impose taxes other than (a) customs duties, (b) excise duties, (c) excess profits duty, (d) corporation profits tax, (e) any other tax on profits, (f) income tax and surtax, (g) any tax substantially the same as the foregoing, (h) a general tax on capital not being a tax substantially the same as an existing tax. These taxes mentioned as being beyond the competence of the Northern Ireland Parliament are the "reserved taxes"; they are imposed by the Westminster Parliament and collected by Westminster officials. A perusal of the list will show that there is not much scope left to the Northern Ireland Minister of Finance unless he wishes to experiment in new and unheard-of (and therefore unpopular) forms of taxation. In fact the taxes imposed by the Northern Ireland Parliament—the "transferred taxes"— are estate duties, motor licence duties, entertainments tax, stamp duties, and a few minor excise duties.

The division of the taxing power does not mean that the reserved taxes are collected by Imperial officials and never seen again in Northern Ireland. Though they are first paid into the Westminster Exchequer, a substantial portion is handed over to the Northern Ireland Exchequer, after certain deductions have been made, as "the Northern Ireland share of reserved taxes". This is essential since the Northern Ireland government is responsible for a much larger proportion of the expenditure on public services than the proportion of the revenue which is raised under its control. The deductions which are made from the reserved taxes before the residue is handed over are: (i) the cost of reserved services, e.g. the cost of the postal services in Northern Ireland, the cost of the running of the Supreme Court of Judicature in Northern Ireland, etc.; (ii) Northern Ireland's Imperial contribution.

The principle of the Imperial contribution is that as the inhabitants of Northern Ireland derive substantial benefits from certain services which are excepted matters under the Government of Ireland Act, 1920, it is only fair that they should make an appropriate contribution to the cost. For example, the inhabitants of Northern Ireland enjoy the benefit of the dignity of the Crown being maintained, enjoy the protection of the armed forces, benefit from the existence of diplomatic and consular services, not to mention advantages arising from the fact that the National Debt is properly serviced.

When the Government of Ireland Act, 1920, was passed the amount of the Imperial contribution was fixed at £18,000,000 a year from all Ireland of which Northern Ireland was to pay 44 per cent. This figure was provisional for the first two years, and thereafter the figure was to be such as the Joint Exchequer Board should determine as "just having regard to the relative taxable capacities" of Northern Ireland on the one hand and the whole United Kingdom on the other hand. This Joint Exchequer Board consists of three persons, one representing the British Treasury, one representing the Northern Ireland Ministry of Finance, and an independent chairman.

The expectations of the framers of the Act of 1920 that Northern Ireland could provide a contribution of 44 per cent of £18,000,000 (approximately £8,000,000) was soon belied. The financial details of revenue on which the 1920 Act figures were founded were those for 1920–21, a year of inflated post-war taxation, and these proved to be unreal in the years that followed. In point of fact the United Kingdom revenues as a whole fell by about 43 per cent between 1920–21 and 1924–25. Whilst, therefore, a contribution of £2,821,000 for that part of the year 1921–22 after Northern Ireland assumed its separate responsibilities maintained the 1920 Act standard, in the following years account had to be taken of the fact that a period of falling revenues and increasing local expenditure had begun. In order to assist the Joint Exchequer Board in deciding what was meant by having regard to relative taxable capacities a committee—the Colwyn Committee—sat between 1923 and 1925, and in its report[1] resolved that due regard would be had to relative taxable capacity if the Imperial Contribution were based on the extent to which the total revenue raised exceeded the actual and necessary expenditure required to give Northern Ireland an equivalent standard of services compared with Great Britain.[2]

Elsewhere in this book will be found a critical examination of the financial relationship between the two Exchequers from the point of view of economists,[3] and we are here only concerned with this relationship in its broad constitutional aspect. It has come under a certain amount of criticism, both on political and on academic grounds, though often the attacks are based on misunderstandings or misrepresentations.

One line of attack is directed to the fact that the elected representatives of Northern Ireland people in their own Parliament have so little control over their financial affairs. It is said that the essence of self-government is self-taxation, and it is highly anomalous that the Stormont Parliament which administers about 90 per cent of governmental expenditure in Northern Ireland should only control the raising of 11 per cent of the revenue. This is in one sense a legitimate criticism, though it is difficult to see how any other arrangement could fit into the scheme of devolution

[1] Cmd. 2073.
[2] This "Colwyn formula" has been modified in detail by subsequent agreements between the Treasury and the Northern Ireland Ministry of Finance.
[3] See chapters 6 and 8.

which has been established. Probably the only person who finds the deprivation of the full taxing power to be a real hardship is the Northern Ireland Minister of Finance, whose sphere of activity is so severely limited, and even in this limited sphere he is too often compelled by force of circumstance to follow the policies framed at Westminster.

Perhaps the most frequently voiced criticism relates to the Imperial contribution. This criticism comes, oddly enough, from the two opposing camps of Nationalists and Unionists. The Nationalist representation of the Imperial contribution is that of a sort of a dane-geld levied in favour of an alien power on the inhabitants of Northern Ireland. The complaint from the less well-informed members of the Unionist party is to the effect that charity begins at home and that the Northern Ireland Government has no right to give away money which could be usefully applied in Ulster. Perhaps both criticisms derive a little sustenance from the unfortunate word "contribution", which does tend to suggest that the hat has been passed round for a contribution to keep the Empire going. In fact, as explained above, the Imperial contribution is merely the appropriate share of those Imperial expenses which Northern Ireland in proportion to its taxable capacity ought to bear as a component part of the United Kingdom. Nor is the Imperial contribution peculiar to Northern Ireland: the proportionate part of the taxes levied on the inhabitants of Lancashire which is needed to meet expenses of an imperial nature could very well be shown in the national accounts as "Lancashire's Imperial Contribution" if it were worth anyone's while to do so. The full implications of the criticism directed against the Imperial contribution are that Northern Ireland should get the benefits of Imperial services without paying for them—a doctrine which is morally improper and politically dangerous.

Another criticism is directed against payments from the British Exchequer to the Northern Ireland Exchequer, such as payments under the reinsurance agreements and the like. This criticism is usually contained in a further Nationalist argument to the effect that Northern Ireland is a dead loss to the United Kingdom because these outward contributions exceed the Imperial contribution.[1] It is submitted that the basis of this criticism is invalid because it supposes that Northern Ireland and Great Britain are two separate entities instead of, as they are, component parts of one state. To take the case of unemployment reinsurance—it was never suggested in the days before the war when South Wales was a depressed area that the cost of unemployment should fall exclusively on

---

[1] This criticism may have been supported by evidence in the days before the war when the Imperial contribution was low, but it has long since lacked validity.

the shoulders of taxpayers in South Wales, and equally, when the incidence of a particular charge is felt more heavily in Northern Ireland, there is no case that this should be borne by the inhabitants of Northern Ireland in its entirety. In family life it is not unusual for the husband to help the wife when the "housekeeping exchequer" has had an unduly heavy week, and a similar family arrangement exists between what are not two States at arm's length, but partners in one realm.

Parliamentary control of finance does not end with the voting of supply and the enactment of Finance Acts and Appropriation Acts. One of the first statutes ever passed by the Northern Ireland Parliament was an Exchequer and Audit Act which reproduced the same stringent control of public finance as obtains in Britain. Under this act all revenues raised under the authority of the Northern Ireland Parliament are paid into the Northern Ireland Exchequer's bank account and so constitute the Consolidated Fund of Northern Ireland. Money can only be paid out of this fund under the authority of an Act of Parliament and under the supervision of the Comptroller and Auditor-General. This official occupies a position of complete political independence: he holds office during good behaviour and can only be removed by an address from both Houses of Parliament. It is his duty not only to see that every penny extracted from the taxpayer reaches the Consolidated Fund, but he is also responsible for seeing that it comes out of the Fund only for purposes approved by Parliament. At the end of the financial year the Ministries must submit their accounts to the Comptroller and Auditor-General, who examines them and certifies them with any observations he may think fit to make. Finally the audited accounts are laid before the Commons and examined by the Select Committee on Public Accounts. There is thus every safeguard that moneys raised by taxation are applied to the public service, and that the moneys applied to the public service are properly spent.

The Legal System

The legal system of Northern Ireland is broadly similar to that of England. The original laws of Ireland consisted of Celtic customary law which, probably by reason of the geographical separation of Ireland, had been completely untouched either by the civilising influences of Roman law or by the less civilised but very virile Germanic law which the English had brought to Britain. When Henry II arrived in Ireland in 1171 he is said to have held a Council at Lismore "where the laws of England were by all freely received and confirmed with due solemnity".[1]

1 Matthew of Paris, *Life of Henry II*, 1172.

If this event did take place, it certainly did not amount to a complete extension of English law to Ireland. All that would be intended was that the relations between the settlers and the English king, and perhaps also between settlers and those Irish chiefs who had done homage to Henry II, would be regulated by English law. There was no suggestion that the native Irish should use English law or have access to the King of England's courts; they would remain under Celtic law.

In all probability it was the original intention that the settlers should continue to litigate in courts in England, but it soon became apparent that it was inconvenient to cross the sea in search of justice, and as early as 1204 we find English legal proceedings taking place in Ireland. From that time the development of a distinct system of courts went forward, and by 1400 there had come into existence in Ireland a system of courts identical with that in England: King's Bench, Common Pleas, Chancery, Assizes and so on were all reproduced on a slightly smaller scale. And the law enforced in these courts was English law, uniformity between the two countries being secured partly by frequent mandates from the King commanding his judges in Ireland to conform to English practice, and partly by the appointment of English lawyers to the Irish bench.

But in 1400 the Irish courts were still offering justice only to the Anglo-Irish. Not only were the "mere Irish" immune from having English law thrust upon them, but they were positively refused its benefits. It was recognised that it was a good defence to an action brought in the courts to plead that the plaintiff was an *Hibernicus* and therefore unable to sue. There were a few exceptions: from the middle of the thirteenth century the practice had arisen of selling to individual Irishmen or to families the right to use English law, and eventually—within the Pale at any rate—English law became general, but it was not until the seventeenth century that English law became of universal application. Then decisions of the courts held that the native Celtic customs must be suppressed as being barbarous and contrary to the common law, and from that time the only law recognised in Ireland has been the law that the settlers had brought from England.

For the past two hundred and fifty years the identity of English law and Irish law (i.e. the law enforced in the courts in Ireland) has been assisted by the fact that with one short interval of eighteen years the House of Lords at Westminster has been the ultimate court of appeal from the courts of each system.

The present system of the administration of the law in Northern Ireland can be considered under these heads: (i) the Supreme Court; (ii) the county court system; (iii) the magisterial courts.

E

(i) *The Supreme Court.* The Government of Ireland Act, 1920, established a Supreme Court of Judicature of Northern Ireland. This continues in Northern Ireland the functions formerly exercised by the Supreme Court of Ireland which sat in pre-1921 days at the Four Courts in Dublin. The Northern Ireland Supreme Court is divided into a Court of Appeal in Northern Ireland and a High Court of Justice in Northern Ireland. Both courts sit in Belfast in the Royal Courts of Justice. There are five judges: a Lord Chief Justice, two Lords Justices of Appeal, and two High Court Judges. The High Court comprises two divisions: a King's Bench Division and a Chancery Division. There is no Probate, Divorce and Admiralty Division as there is in England, and probate, matrimonial and admiralty work is dealt with in the King's Bench Division. The Lord Chief Justice and the two High Court judges normally do the work of the High Court, and the Lord Chief Justice and two Lords Justices normally constitute the Court of Appeal; but it is not infrequent to find a Lord Justice sitting in the High Court to assist with the work, and likewise the High Court judges are often invited to sit in the Court of Appeal. The practice and procedure of the High Court and Court of Appeal are virtually identical with that obtaining in the two similar courts in England. Appeal lies from the Court of Appeal to the House of Lords.[1]

The judges of the Supreme Court go round the six counties of Northern Ireland on assize in exactly the same way as in England.

(ii) *The County Courts.* The County Court system in Northern Ireland differs in a number of respects from the system in England and Wales. The County Courts of England and Wales are a comparatively modern statutory invention dating from 1846, but the Irish County Court has a pedigree of respectable antiquity. From very early times the assize judges in Ireland had been accustomed, in addition to their ordinary assize duties, to hear plaints dealing with petty matters where the sum involved was not more than £30. Such plaints were made by what were known as "English bills" or "civil bills".[2] This practice had begun to die out at the end of the seventeenth century, but it was revivified by an Act of 1703. By the end of the eighteenth century this informal mode of litigation had become so popular that it began to interfere with the ordinary

---

[1] This right of appeal is not absolute. There are certain cases where the Court of Appeal in Northern Ireland is a final court of appeal. However, an appeal will always lie to the House of Lords where the validity of Northern Ireland legislation is under consideration.

[2] "Bills" because the case was begun by an informal document called a bill, instead of the more formal writ; "English" because the document was in English at a time when most legal documents were in Latin.

assize work, and in 1796 Assistant Barristers were appointed for each county whose duty it was to hear these civil bills, with an appeal lying to the next going judge of assize. In 1877 these Assistant Barristers were replaced by the present County Court judges.

To-day there are County Court judges for each of the six counties of Northern Ireland, except Fermanagh and Armagh, which share one judge. The two cities of Belfast and Londonderry each constitutes a County Court area by itself with a Recorder to act as judge, but in practice the Recorder of Belfast is also County Court judge for Antrim, and the Recorder of Londonderry is County Court judge for the County of Londonderry.

The present jurisdiction of the County Court is a general jurisdiction where the amount claimed is not more than £100, and a somewhat wider jurisdiction in certain equity and probate cases.

Another substantial difference between Northern Ireland and England and Wales is that in Northern Ireland the County Court and Quarter Sessions are virtually identical. The justices-of-the-peace system has never worked as satisfactorily in Ireland as in England and Wales, and in 1851 the Assistant Barristers who presided in Civil Bill courts were given the additional duty of sitting in Quarter Sessions as Chairman of the Bench with authority to act independently if no other justices appeared to sit. When County Court Judges replaced Assistant Barristers in 1877 they continued to act as Chairmen of Quarter Sessions, and the last stage was reached in Northern Ireland in 1935 when the County Court Judges were made sole judges at Quarter Sessions.

(iii) *Magisterial Courts.* It has already been observed that the justices-of-the-peace system did not work satisfactorily in Ireland. One reason was that in the eighteenth and nineteenth centuries that class of landed proprietor from which appointments to the commission of the peace were usually made was an absentee class. Consequently in 1836 the Constabulary (Ireland) Act, after noting that the absence of magistrates was facilitating serious disorder in the country, gave the Lord Lieutenant authority to appoint salaried magistrates who should be resident in their districts. Up to 1935 benches of summary jurisdiction consisted of lay justices sitting with these resident magistrates, but for a number of years there had been grave dissatisfaction with the conduct of lay justices, especially in licensing and betting cases, and the Summary Jurisdiction and Criminal Justice Act (Northern Ireland), 1935, deprived the lay justices of virtually all their judicial functions, and courts of summary jurisdiction are now composed of a single resident magistrate—a paid magistrate similar to the Metropolitan Police Court Magistrates of

London, or the Stipendiary Magistrates which exist in some of the bigger English cities.

The course of litigation in Northern Ireland is the same as in England. There are the same two branches of the legal profession—barristers and solicitors—and their status and duties are the same as their English counterparts. To all outward appearance the Northern Ireland and English legal systems are but parts of one whole. For instance, the motorist who is involved in an accident, the wife with the unfaithful husband, the business man in trouble over a contract—all these will find their cases dealt with in the same manner and the same principles of law applied no matter whether the case be tried in Belfast or in London. An English lawyer coming to Northern Ireland will find himself completely at home in the courts and familiar with the law enforced in those courts, except possibly in the one subject of conveyancing. Land law in Ireland is complicated by the Land Purchase legislation of the last and present centuries and by the existence of a different, and very efficient, system of registration. Furthermore, the simplifications of English real property law which were carried through in England in 1925 have not been attempted yet in Northern Ireland. But for the general identity of the law in the two countries no more convincing evidence could be forthcoming than the fact that there are no printed books on Northern Ireland law: all lawyers in Northern Ireland use the standard English text-books.

Likewise in the sphere of constitutional law the same principles apply in the two countries. There are the same principles of the interrelation of the legislature, executive and judiciary, and the courts enforce the same principles of liberty within the framework of the common law. This last statement will run counter to many preconceptions of political conditions in Northern Ireland, preconceptions which have resulted from the fierce controversy which has centred on the Civil Authority (Special Powers) Act, and it is therefore necessary to deal with this Act in some detail.

The Special Powers Act

In order to appreciate the Special Powers Act (as it is usually called) it is necessary to consider the political circumstances in which it first came to the statute book. The Government of Ireland Act had come into operation on May 3, 1921, and the various ministries were established in the course of the following month. Then began a process of devolution of power to these ministries. The Act had provided that the Royal Irish Constabulary should remain a reserved service until a date not later than three years after the coming into force of the Act, which showed that the constabulary service might reasonably be expected to be one of the last services devolved.[1] The situation, therefore, during the opening months of the life of the new Northern Ireland Government was that it had no control over the armed services (being an excepted service) and no control over the Royal Irish Constabulary (being still a reserved service). Meanwhile the utmost disorder prevailed: it was the period of "the troubles" when murders and arsons committed by political malcontents were of daily occurrence, and it appeared that the newly constituted province might dissolve at any time into complete anarchy.

The British Government had armed its own forces in Ireland with emergency powers by means of the Restoration of Order in Ireland Act, 1920, under which emergency regulations could be made by the British Government, and regulations of a very drastic character were in fact made and executed, and formed a model for many of the regulations made under the Special Powers Act. But the Restoration of Order in Ireland Act offered little practical help to the Northern Ireland Government in its plight, partly because of administrative difficulties which made liaison between the Northern Ireland Government, the Lord Lieutenant and the military authorities very difficult to achieve, and more particularly because the British Government was at that time inclined to stay its hand in pursuance of a policy of truce with the Sinn Fein rebels in the South.

In these circumstances the Northern Ireland Government decided to equip itself with powers similar to those possessed by the British Government in the Restoration of Order Act. This fact explains the title of the Act—*Civil* Authority (Special Powers) Act: the new Act was to supply the civil authority with the same powers that the Restoration of Order in Ireland Act supplied to the military authority. The new Act was foreshadowed in the King's speech when the Northern Ireland Parliament was opened on March 14, 1922, and the necessary bill was speedily brought forward. It was, as the mover observed, "an exceptional time and requires exceptional measures", and the Parliament approved it almost without demur.[2] Only one member recognised that even in an age of delegated legislation the bill was extraordinary for the extent of the powers which Parliament was prepared to delegate: the bill was, he

[1] In 1922 the British Government decided to disband the Royal Irish Constabulary, and it was never in fact transferred.

[2] It will be remembered that Nationalist members did not take their seats at this time.

said, too long—all that was needed was one section: "The Home Secretary shall have power to do what he likes, or else let somebody else do what he likes for him".

What the Act does in fact is to confer on the civil authority, i.e. the Minister for Home Affairs,[1] power "to take all such steps and issue all such orders as may be necessary for preserving the peace" according to regulations made under the Act. Some regulations were appended to the Act and the civil authority was given power to make further regulations which have to be laid before Parliament. Offences against the regulations are tried by a court consisting of two resident magistrates, or on indictment, and the maximum penalty is two years' imprisonment and a fine of £100. There is also a provision that if any person does an act calculated to be prejudicial to the peace or the maintenance of public order not specifically provided for in the regulations he shall be deemed to be guilty of an offence against the regulations, but in fact no action is taken except on a specific charge.

A clear distinction must be drawn between the Act and the regulations and orders made under the Act. Though the Act remains on the statute book, regulations and orders are by no means permanent. Thus in 1949 the Minister of Home Affairs considered the settled state of the country justified the revocation of forty-one regulations, and though five new ones were made in 1950 owing to an outbreak of violence, in 1951 a further thirteen regulations were revoked, and in fact most of those regulations which have provoked controversy in the past are no longer in existence.

The matters dealt with in the regulations covered a wide field. Some, such as the regulation imposing curfew (i.e. requiring persons in a particular area to be indoors during specified hours) and the regulations against firearms and explosives, were directed against open disorder. Others, such as the regulations against unlawful drilling, illegal uniforms and keeping explosives, were directed against a planned rising. Others, dealing with unlawful meetings and membership of illegal organisations such as the I.R.A., were directed against the promotion of sedition. There were also regulations dealing with detention orders and exclusion orders which are treated in more detail below.

Probably the most effective way of commenting on this Act is to discuss the criticisms that have been brought against it. Criticism of the Act is a commonplace of political controversy in Northern Ireland, and in 1936 the controversy was somewhat heightened by a report on the working of

---

[1] The Minister has power to delegate his powers to his Under-Secretary or to a police officer.

the Act issued by the National Council for Civil Liberties.[1] The critics may be divided into two classes: those who criticise the political conceptions which lie behind the Act, and those who are more anxious to expose the hardships and absurdities in its operation.

The more abstract criticism is based on the contention that the Act abrogates the "rule of law" in conferring virtually unlimited powers on the executive to create criminal offences and "suspends Habeas Corpus" by permitting persons to be detained in prison otherwise than after trial and conviction. The view to be opposed to this is that the "rule of law" requires a reasonably settled community in which to operate—that desperate situations require desperate remedies, and that legal and constitutional niceties must give way to the ultimate security of the constitution. The Northern Ireland Government has never delighted in the existence of the Special Powers Act; indeed, it is noticeable that it is inclined to be touchy on the subject. But, on the other hand, no one can doubt that the circumstances which the Act was framed to meet were truly alarming. A generation has now grown to maturity that cannot remember what "the troubles" were like, but a reference back to the newspapers of the early twenties will show a horrible picture of murders and damage to property which confronted the Government of that day with the final challenge that can be put to a government—govern or get out. This period was not, of course, the first occasion on which Irishmen had resorted to the bomb and pistol to reinforce their political arguments, and the Special Powers Act should rightly be considered, not as a unique piece of legislation, but as taking its place in that long line of repressive statutes which the unsettled state of Ireland has called forth.

Also it must be remembered that to the theorist the Special Powers Act must now appear somewhat less alarming than it did in 1922. In 1936 the National Council of Civil Liberties expressed itself shocked at the "complete delegation of law-making power to the Executive", but the Special Powers Act is but a shadow in this respect of the Supplies and Services Act which the Westminster parliament itself was subsequently to enact. Since 1936 we have made closer acquaintance with emergency legislation, and have also seen the special powers which the republican South of Ireland assumed to protect itself against political conspiracy by the I.R.A. The fact is that in these islands we have deteriorated politically since the end of the last century when the "rule of

---

[1] Quite apart from its contents this was a remarkable production. In a blue paper cover with all the format of a Government Blue Book it was calculated to deceive the unwary into believing that in some way it emanated from Whitehall. In fact it was sponsored by a body well leavened with individuals whom we now recognise as Communists and fellow-travellers.

law" was at its zenith. Unstable conditions and revolutionary tendencies do not permit us the luxury of unlimited freedom of the individual; just as he who wishes for peace must prepare for war, so he who wants freedom must be prepared to use restraint.

The criticisms against the Act in its operation involve a catalogue of hardships said to be suffered by those who have come under its operation. There were undoubted cases of hardship, as might well be expected. The completely innocent are sometimes wrongly suspected, and may in consequence suffer arrest and detention; in a country where political passions run high there are times when individuals charged with the execution of orders under the Act exceed their powers or act in a rough and oppressive fashion; there are times when the authorities appear to use the powers with that particular brand of stupidity which is endemic in government departments throughout the world. But against these facts must be set the fact that the Act was, as we have said, a desperate measure taken to deal with a desperate situation.

The Detention Regulation (Reg. 23) provided that a person suspected of having acted or being about to act in a manner prejudicial to the preservation of peace or maintenance of order could be arrested and detained until discharged by direction of the Attorney-General. Detention without conviction but no mere suspicion is properly regarded as the hall-mark of the despotic State, and many pages in our constitutional history books are devoted to the struggles of the seventeenth and eighteenth centuries by which freedom from arbitrary arrest and general warrants was established. But there is this difference, that the struggles of the seventeenth and eighteenth centuries were waged against a high conception of the extent of the royal prerogative, whereas the powers under the Special Powers Act were conferred by the vote of a popularly elected legislature.

The Exclusion Regulation (Reg. 23a) enabled the civil authority to exclude a person from certain areas of Northern Ireland and to confine him to a specified area where he must stay under penalty of committing an offence. This regulation has been extensively used to enable the authorities to prevent republican sympathisers from the South from entering Northern Ireland and carrying on operations in cities and towns, but it has also been used against persons domiciled in Northern Ireland. The Council of Civil Liberties Report concluded that these exclusion orders were illegal as being *ultra vires* the Parliament of Northern Ireland, but certainly none of the persons on whom such orders have been served ever thought it worth while to test the point in litigation.

A final criticism of the Act has been that whereas it was originally intended to be an annual Act for temporary purposes and was renewed from year to year from 1922 to 1928, in 1928 it was renewed for five years, and in 1933 was made permanent. There is nothing particularly sinister in this. In Stuart and Hanoverian times, when it was by no means certain that Parliament would otherwise be summoned to meet each year, there was a good reason why Parliament should make certain Acts annual Acts so that the Government could not continue to govern by means of them without the continued concurrence of Parliament. But now that Parliament is in virtually constant session this reason no longer holds good. The Special Powers Act can be repealed whenever the Parliament of Northern Ireland so desires. All that has happened is that the annual recriminations between the two parties in the House have been avoided.

Reference here may be made to two Acts which deal specifically with certain aspects of political strife and which are now taken out of the ambit of the Special Powers Act. The Public Order Act (Northern Ireland), 1951, imposes control on disorderly meetings and processions, and the Flags and Emblems Act (Northern Ireland), 1954, secures the right to fly the Union Jack on premises and enables the police to seize provocative emblems.

Is Devolution a Success?

After thirty years' working of the Constitution of Northern Ireland it is possible to make at least an interim assessment of its success. In one sense it must be admitted at once that it has failed. The predominant intention of those who carried the Act of 1920 was to devise a scheme which would satisfy nationalist aspiration in Ireland and yet retain the whole of Ireland within the United Kingdom. This aim was defeated within a year of the Act coming into operation, and thirty years after the passing of the Act sees the greater part of Ireland not only out of the United Kingdom but out of the Commonwealth as well.

But there was another, if secondary, reason behind the passing of the Act, as there had been behind all the earlier Home Rule bills. This was to effect some measure of devolution. The advantages of devolution are said to be, (1) that the labours of the central legislature are lightened; and (2) the local region is given the chance of pursuing policies appropriate to the peculiarities of local conditions. There is no doubt that this first advantage has been attained: whereas the Irish problem consumed an inordinate amount of time at Westminster in the fifty years before 1920, at the present day Northern Ireland affairs occupy at the most a few hours in each year. Whether the second advantage has been achieved is more doubtful.

Since 1920 the Government of Northern Ireland has avowedly pursued a policy of "step by step". This aims at securing to the inhabitants of Northern Ireland similar legislative benefits to those conferred by Westminster on the inhabitants of Great Britain. There is not necessarily an automatic adoption of British legislation, and even where the principle of a British Act is adopted there may be adaptations to suit peculiarities of Northern Ireland administration. But by and large the legislative reforms which have marked the past thirty years at Westminster will be found to have had their counterparts enacted in Belfast shortly afterwards.

It is doubtful whether "step by step" is a policy which could have been avoided. When devolution was first conceived in the Gladstonian era, it might have been possible to have a United Kingdom in which the distinct regions had differing systems of law relating to such matters as health, housing, labour, agriculture and the like. But to-day the urge is towards uniformity, and uniformity has been rendered all the more essential by reason of the "contraction" in the Kingdom which improved transport, radio, newspapers, and increased facilities for education have brought about. In 1850 a labourer in Antrim and a labourer in Sussex might have lived in different worlds. To-day they are conscious of being fellows in the same community. They read the same papers, listen to the same Broadcasting Corporation, enter for the same "pools" and belong to the same unions. So it is not surprising that when legislative benefits are being given away they expect similar treatment. The intercourse between Great Britain and Northern Ireland is so complete that almost of necessity Northern Ireland must have Rent Restriction Acts like England, Road Traffic Acts like England, a Hire Purchase Act like England, Industrial Injuries Acts like England, and so on.[1]

---

[1] The following table illustrates the manner in which some of the more important English Acts of the past twenty-five years have been immediately or shortly followed by parallel Northern Ireland legislation:

English Act	Northern Ireland Act
Legitimacy Act, 1926	Legitimacy Act (N.I.), 1928
Adoption of Children Act, 1926	Adoption of Children Act (N.I.), 1929
Trade Disputes Act, 1927	Trade Disputes Act (N.I.), 1927
Road Traffic Act, 1930	Motor Vehicles and Road Traffic Act (N.I.), 1930
Children and Young Persons Act, 1933	Children and Young Persons Act (N.I.), 1950
Law Reform Act, 1934	Law Reform (Miscellaneous Provisions) Act (N.I.), 1937
Road Traffic Act, 1934	Motor Vehicles and Road Traffic Act (N.I.), 1934
Hire Purchase Act, 1938	Hire Purchase Act (N.I.), 1940

This has raised the question whether the advantages of devolution are real. Has Northern Ireland benefited as a result of having a separate Parliament and a separate Government? It has been said that it is no argument in support of devolution to point to the efficiency of Northern Ireland administration. There is no reason to suppose, for example, that the officials of the Ministry of Agriculture in Northern Ireland would be less efficient if they were administering Westminster statutes instead of Northern Ireland statutes. And when attention is drawn to the improvements in administration effected since 1921, it is pointed out that Dublin Castle administration was notoriously ineffective.

It is difficult to say whether the ordinary citizen notices much difference in living under a scheme of limited devolution, instead of being subject only to the Imperial parliament. The less intelligent part of the Ulster electorate almost certainly does not comprehend the nature of the division of powers between Westminster, Stormont and the local authority: indeed, a quite common attitude is to suppose that Stormont exists merely as a constitutional barrier to the ending of "partition", though this is probably the result of the alignment of political parties in Northern Ireland which subordinates economic and social questions to the constitutional question. Even those who are more educated politically often fail to distinguish between what is and what is not within the competence of Stormont. On the whole, in matters other than foreign affairs, the man in the Belfast street inclines to lay all blame on Stormont and its officials: either they are at fault themselves, or if not at fault themselves they should try to put more pressure on their Westminster counterparts to right matters.

As far as the citizen's pocket is concerned it is safe to say that he notices little if any difference between living in Northern Ireland and living in Yorkshire. The major taxes—income tax, purchase tax, customs and excise—are the same, and the "step by step" policy is pursued in the case of the transferred taxes as in other departments of legislation.

But these criticisms must not obscure the positive achievements of Stormont. The industry, commerce and, in particular, the agriculture of

Holidays with Pay Act, 1938	Holidays with Pay Act (N.I.), 1938
Evidence Act, 1938	Evidence Act (N.I.), 1939
Prevention of Frauds (Investment) Act, 1939	Prevention of Frauds (Investment) Act (N.I.), 1940
Truck Act, 1940	Truck Act (N.I.), 1940
Law Reform (Frustrated Contracts) Act, 1943	Frustrated Contracts Act (N.I.), 1947
Family Allowances Act, 1945	Family Allowances Act (N.I.), 1945
Law Reform (Miscellaneous Provisions) Act, 1949	Law Reform (Miscellaneous Provisions) Act (N.I.), 1951

Northern Ireland has received attention such as they never knew in the old days. Furthermore, Ulster's domestic matters are dealt with more expeditiously than when Irish, along with Scottish, affairs took a very subordinate place in the Westminster programme. If the public of Northern Ireland is sometimes apathetic about its local parliament and government, the administrators at Stormont exhibit all that enthusiasm which might be expected of those who are intimately concerned in the worthwhile task of bringing Northern Ireland services up to the level of the best in the United Kingdom.

What, then, is likely to be the future development of the Constitution of Northern Ireland? Apart from a maintenance of the *status quo* there would appear to be three theoretically possible courses ahead. One is that course which leads to an absorption of the six Northern counties into an All Ireland Republic, but it would be completely ignoring the facts of politics to suppose that this lies in any foreseeable future. The second course is in the direction of dominion status, and there are a few influential figures in Northern Ireland politics who are known to favour this course. The advantage of dominion status lies in financial autonomy; its disadvantage lies in the fact that Northern Ireland would have to step down from being an integral part of a world power to become the least significant dominion in the Commonwealth. A third course would be "back to Westminster"—a repeal of the Government of Ireland Act and a reversion to the original principles of the Union.

One cannot ignore the fact that the situation has been considerably affected by the events since the war. The advent of a Socialist government at Westminster added an entirely fresh problem to complicate the inter-relations between Great Britain and Northern Ireland. Once the constitutional question is excised from discussion between Ulstermen it is usually found that their political make-up consists of a hard core of conservatism with a certain overlay of old-fashioned radicalism on such matters as religious liberty, independence of thought, and the like. Certainly the average Ulsterman is no socialist, and yet he now finds that the step-by-step policy has of necessity lured him into socialistic experiments of which he disapproves in principle and which he finds expensive in practice. Consequently it is not surprising that the question of union is now sometimes discussed from a new angle. Can a scheme be devised by which complete financial and economic independence for Northern Ireland is combined with continuance as a part of the United Kingdom? The politician who discovers such a scheme in which union is paradoxically combined with independence will certainly merit the title of Statesman!

CHAPTER 3

THE POLITICAL PARTIES AND THE SOCIAL BACKGROUND

By JOHN E. SAYERS

ULSTER Unionism does not fall into any of the political categories with which the observer in Great Britain is familiar. Particular local stresses have given it a characteristic form embracing a whole community of people who might otherwise be ranged from the Right to the Left. The term Unionism does not connote alone the unity of the kingdom: it represents also the coalescence in a single party of Conservatives and breakaway Liberals who first took up the Ulster cause when Home Rule was proposed for Ireland as a whole. In course of time a continuing pre-occupation with Partition, as well as the responsibility of Government, has tended to overlay the strongly radical element contributed to the alliance by the Liberals, but the spirit of the party is none the less foreign to the oligarchic conceptions of the extreme Right Wing of Toryism. Yet this term in its more hoary and unyielding sense is often applied to the party by its opponents at home and some of its critics elsewhere. These are doubtless encouraged to think on such lines by the now tradi-tional closeness of the association between the party organisation and the Conservative and Unionist Party in Great Britain, and the inclusion in its ranks of many important employers of labour. Colour is also given even to a belief in the existence of a semi-dictatorship by the fact that Unionism has been in power since 1921 without any material reduction in the strength of its hold. But the varied impressions of this kind that are current fail to allow for the fact that the party is one composed of all levels of society to a degree not often encountered in Parliamentary democracies. Nor has the fusion of classes been brought about solely by a common loyalty to country and religion, powerful as this influence can be; the nature of the party derives from the character of the people themselves. Such solidarity, together with the absence of marked class distinctions, has given the vital strength to the stand for self-deter-mination.

This is no more than the lesson of history. The Scots who settled in the North of Ireland and became its dominant strain were in some ways strongly individualistic, but they were a disciplined race accustomed to governing themselves through the Presbyterian synods. By reason of the religious and economic disabilities to which they were subjected as Dissenters[1] they tended to become more politically conscious than the English stock joined with them in the Plantation. For them the issue in the eighteenth century, after William III had made Ireland secure, was a simple one of personal liberty. Ultimately their objective was won, but not before thousands of the most virile of the Scots-Irish had emigrated to America, where they and their descendants were to be the leaders in the War of Independence and founders of the United States. As events fell out these emigrants embraced republicanism, but it is not too much to say that Ulstermen today, as monarchists, have inherited the same ideal of freedom. The common misapprehension about Northern Ireland is that once Partition was established its people lost these distinctive and historic characteristics; in fact, they are still to be found in greater or lesser degree and this despite the defensive attitude into which the planter population has been forced. In the long and often bitter Home Rule struggle the Nationalist urge to be free from the British has usually received most attention outside Ireland. Unionist Ulster, in consequence, has not been fully credited with the will to preserve the civil and religious liberty that under Protestantism has become the basis of the British Constitution.

Historically, the argument is not weakened by the support given by Presbyterians to the rebellion of 1798, which aimed at the creation of an Irish republic on the model of France. These were revolutionary times, and a section of society discriminated against by the Tories of the day and fired by new doctrines from America and the Continent were ready, even in company with oppressed Roman Catholics with whom they had long been in conflict, to rise against authority. The rebellion was short-lived and was soon followed by the Act of Union, which so restored the unity and common aims of the Scots and English settlers that its preservation has been their guiding principle ever since. The excesses of the rising also aggravated their religious and racial differences with the Irish, and the new Act, together with the threat from Napoleon, combined to turn the mass of Protestants back to the British allegiance. At the same time the Union established and guaranteed the equality of rights longed for by the Presbyterians, and the freedom of trade with Great Britain and abroad which survives to-day as a primary economic requirement

[1] In the eighteenth century the Dissenters, like the Roman Catholics, could not vote; their clergy could not perform legal marriages; they were frequently rack-rented by the Anglo-Irish landowners. British economic policy also prevented direct trade between Ireland and countries overseas: all goods had to pass through British ports, frustrating the capacity of the Ulster-Scots for industry and commerce.

and the key to the success of Ulster industry. Henceforward the Protestants of the North were assured of the full protection of the British Constitution: the Union was their restoration to their own kith-and-kin. So that, significant as the part played by the Dissenters in the rebellion of 1798 may have been, the more important fact is that so soon afterwards the great body of Protestants were united in their loyalty to Britain.

Under the Union, with Ireland an integral part of the kingdom, politics in the North began to follow a natural course of development. The alignment of Conservatives and Liberals that emerged in the Victorian era was hardly different from that seen in England. The landed and professional classes, mostly Episcopalian, were Tory, and the farmers and merchants generally Liberal. The latter included many Ulstermen of humble origin whose manufactures rapidly brought Belfast into the front rank of industrial cities and earned the wealth which played its part in the prolonged resistance to Home Rule. The farmers, too, were bent on the agrarian reforms which eventually enabled them to buy out the lands they held as tenants of the gentry. By the time the cry of Home Rule was raised in earnest these measures were completed or far advanced and reform, begun under the Liberals, was completed by a Conservative government before the Third Home Rule Bill had appeared as part of the policy of "killing Home Rule with kindness". Thus, with the old penal laws long since gone, the episcopal church itself disestablished and the farmers on their way to becoming owner-occupiers, there was no grievance or ideological obstacle to deter Liberals and Conservatives from presenting a common front and forming the Unionist Party that exists to-day. The fusion was brought about most of all by the fear of domination by a Roman Catholic-controlled Parliament in Dublin, but almost equally strong was the apprehension that Customs barriers would be raised between the agriculture and industries of the north and their principal market in Great Britain. In the early days of the Irish controversy it does not appear that fidelity to British institutions, especially the Crown, was directly in question, but subsequent events in the Irish Free State, later to become the Irish Republic, have shown that the Unionist misgivings were not without foundation, and that Ulster's attachment is sentimental as well as practical.

It is true that among the Home Rulers there was a Protestant element which in the North of Ireland was again chiefly confined to Presbyterians. These were persons of independent mind whose traditional liberalism was such that they were prepared to support Gladstone's policy. Some were also influenced by the contemporary revival in Gaelic culture, but mostly they were moved by a normal will for constitutional reform; in this way they perhaps marked themselves as the more obvious spiritual descendants of the first Scottish planters and of those who went to the American colonies. By now, however, it has been recognised that their aspirations were at heart similar to those of the majority of Liberal-Unionists, the more so as Northern Ireland was to receive the devolutionary powers which first attracted men interested more in liberty and self-expression than in any other end. Some of them may not in the past have been profound in their loyalty to things English; yet, at least until Socialism in power began to instil doubts in their minds, they decided that twentieth-century democracy on the British model was the best protection for their way of life. Not least in this was freedom of thought; the Ulsterman, though well grounded in religion and apt to be something of a theologian, is by nature anti-clerical and scorns nothing in the Roman Catholic faith so much as the authoritarianism that would not allow him to think for himself. Such an intervention as that made by the hierarchy against the "Mother and Child" Health Service in the Irish Republic he regards as a perfect justification for the Partition of Ireland; literary censorship no less.[1]

This apart, the radical strain has mainly found its expression in the upholding of Northern Ireland as a unit of the United Kingdom where politics have so developed that, save for the more extreme acts of Socialism, the older Liberals have had less and less with which to quarrel. To some extent the evolution of political theory has been retarded by the constant demand for a unified front against the Anti-Partitionists, but independence of mind, if not a perfect liberality, can still be seen in the recurring appearances of unofficial Unionist candidates at elections. Against the partial submerging of radicalism and the absence of any large-scale swing to the Left as in Great Britain must be set the unity by which the Ulster Protestants secured local self-determination and the right to share fully in the advances in social welfare made by the British nation. Without this identity of interest, and failing the discovery of an alternative form of common denominator between classes and parties, the Union could hardly have been maintained.

At this point it is necessary to remember that self-government was accepted only as a compromise solution to the Irish problem. Unionists who had long been opposed to Home Rule found themselves undertaking, to quote one of the unconvinced Presbyterian Liberals, "a form of Home

---

[1] In 1951 the objections of the Roman Catholic hierarchy "on the grounds of faith and morals" to proposals for a "Mother and Child" Health Service without a means test led to the resignation of the Minister of Health, Dr Noel Browne. The objections were accepted by the other members of the inter-party Government as a decisive reason for the abandonment of the measure.

Rule that the Devil himself could not have imagined". There was, however, a positive as well as a negative reason for such a change of heart. The Government of Ireland Act which gave the six counties of Northern Ireland the right to opt out of the Irish Free State could not have been passed on other terms. Carson and Craig also foresaw that once a Parliament was established in Belfast it was unlikely ever to be abolished without its own consent. In constitutional practice it is an axiom that once the Imperial Parliament devolves powers upon a subordinate, such powers cannot be arbitrarily or unilaterally revoked. To-day that axiom has been clearly defined in the Ireland Act of 1949, which lays down that the Constitution of Northern Ireland cannot be altered except by the will of its own Parliament.

Thus, before any questions of domestic policy and their political interpretation can arise, the main purpose of the Unionist Party must be understood. Its overriding aim is to preserve in the provincial House of Commons a majority in favour of the Union, and it has become instinctive among the people to safeguard the unity, not to say the single-mindedness, that makes this possible. All other matters are secondary so long as there is any attack upon the right of self-determination. The Union, in turn, represents loyalty to the Throne and the British Commonwealth, and to the Protestant conception of civil and religious liberty, and it stands only a little less urgently for the economic advantages of free trade within the United Kingdom, and the raising of the standard of life to the highest national level. These objects, at once idealistic and pragmatic, are not to be derogated, but it is perhaps open to question whether for all their importance they have not been allowed to hold back the natural development of political thought in domestic affairs. The argument is, of course, that without a firm degree of unity Northern Ireland could not survive, and that such compromises as become necessary are made within the Unionist fold. On the other hand, general elections too often demonstrate that even those in favour of the links with Britain are not acknowledged as "loyal" if they do not support the official party which will allow little or no respectability to other loyalists, whether Independent, Liberal or Labour. This attitude finds a response throughout the party ranks, more especially at the level at which all issues are seen as between Protestant and Roman Catholic. As a result, the Government has rarely been seriously challenged on its administrative policy and the purpose of successive general elections is not so much to seek endorsement of its actions as to prove to the outside world that there is no weakening of Unionist conviction.

It must be admitted, however, that in a small area in which the people

F

have never been wholly self-confident, little room exists for a variety of parties. Lord Craigavon recognised this when he abolished Proportional Representation.[1] and all the conventional arguments against this system were reinforced by the situation with which he had to deal. Yet from the point of view of Parliamentary government the consequences have left something to be desired. Since the Anti-Partition parties have never properly fulfilled the functions of Opposition, only very small groups of Independents or Labour have been available to act as critics of the Administration. In a House consisting of only fifty-two members, thirty-eight of whom at the time of writing are Unionists (thirteen in official positions), a fair balance is lacking and debates suffer accordingly. From time to time back-benchers freely attack the Government, but this leads only to the settlement of differences at private meetings of the party. The small number of seats in the Commons, as laid down by the Government of Ireland Act, also gives the Prime Minister a narrow field of choice in the selection of Ministers. The calibre of Parliamentary representatives is a familiar problem in a democracy, but in Northern Ireland a tendency to return men for the strength of their partisanship rather than their ability as public servants has caused a dearth of responsible political leadership that does not augur well for the future. The weaknesses of the House of Commons are duplicated in the Senate, which the lower Chamber elects on a method of Proportional Representation. Here the members are chosen more for party services than for intellectual or administrative attainments, and as a consequence the Upper House has little influence on law making and contributes in only a minor way to the discussion of affairs.

No charge is more frequently levelled against Unionist control than that of gerrymandering. The Nationalist case is that Roman Catholics, numbering one-third of the population, should have at least this proportion of the seats in Parliament. But no arrangement of single-seat constituencies could produce this result, since the minority inevitably suffers from the handicap of being widely dispersed. On the other hand, the party in power has enjoyed certain positive advantages. Plural voting in the case of business premises is substantially in its favour, and the small electorate in Queen's University, Belfast, returns up to three Unionists for its four seats, an unjustifiably high percentage of the total membership of the House of Commons. No move has been made by the Government to follow the British example in abolishing the business and university franchises and their party value may, perhaps, be measured accordingly. The allegations of manipulation, however, are discounted

---

[1] *Cf.* Chapter 2, p. 32.

by the experience of the other elections held in Northern Ireland for the Imperial Parliament, in which there is single voting and the electoral divisions are determined by Boundary Commissions. In 1955 ten out of twelve seats were gained by Unionists and the conduct of the General Election was unexceptionable. On the population figures representation on local councils is more open to question, but in elections of this kind Northern Ireland adheres to a franchise based on rateable valuations, another case of its declining to follow Great Britain, where universal suffrage has been adopted. The efficacy of this reform in Great Britain has yet to be established, and the exercise of such a discretion in Northern Ireland, though undoubtedly strengthening Unionist supremacy, may possibly give a better type of local administration.

Because the Liberal Party was the first to father the Home Rule desired by the Irish Nationalists, it has been natural that Unionists in Ulster should look to the Conservatives as their allies and defenders, and that with the passage of time they should have come to gear their thought to the pace of Conservative policy. This was particularly pronounced in the early years of self-government when the Tories were usually in power at Westminster. In Northern Ireland the first tasks were the restoration of internal security and reconstruction; it was not to be expected that the Government would seek immediately to experiment in other fields with its new and untried powers. Neither was the time one for liberal measures, so violent became the Republican attack on law and order. At this point the Civil Authorities (Special Powers) Act was brought in to combat a reign of terror, but having done so successfully it was maintained on the Statute Book as a weapon against similar outbreaks. Since the last war most of the extraordinary powers given to the Government and police have been relinquished; yet a people who are at heart opposed to measures of this kind have come to regard them as a normal means of defence. Such is an example, for all the sparing use that is now made of the Act, of the way in which the more liberal instincts of the Unionist Party have been somewhat weakened by the difficult conditions prevailing in the country. Some Members of Parliament who show no anxiety for such legislation to be repealed can still be relied upon to speak with indignation against any invasion of common law and private rights that is Socialist in origin.

The post-war annulment of many of the more extreme powers, including that of internment without trial, and the passing of the Public Order Act, 1951, based on the Imperial measure of the same title, is however evidence of the Government's desire not to stretch the law beyond the normal limits, as well as of the realisation that to the outside world nothing weakens the case for Partition more than the suggestion that it is maintained by some form of dictatorship. It is notable that while violence and sedition have been proceeded against so vigorously, freedom of speech and of the press has remained virtually intact.

In the Irish Republic the threats of the same subversive movement—the I.R.A.—have caused equally stringent counter-measures to be taken.

So far it has been indicated that the cardinal and overriding point of Government policy is the continuance of Northern Ireland's place as an integral part of the United Kingdom. Side by side with this is the policy of raising the standard of public services, and with it the standard of living, to a state of parity with Great Britain. But while the one object has been constant the other has taken time to develop. When the Unionist Party first took office under Lord Craigavon it did not go further than to adopt the principle of "step-by-step" in the cash social services of the day, pensions and unemployment benefit. As it happened, it inherited an unbalanced economy and much that was relatively backward in community services. From its first days unemployment ran at a level much higher than in Great Britain, and the cost of benefit and relief caused to be negotiated in 1926 the first of a series of Re-insurance Agreements assimilating the burden with the Treasury. Finance was, indeed, a problem which reached its most serious proportions in the depression of the early thirties, when Northern Ireland was barely able to balance its Budget. The state of trade and industry had a corollary in the retarded state of economic development, and as a result the area found itself at the end of the period between the wars with a greater "leeway" behind Great Britain than existed even before the grant of self-government.

It might appear that this was due to the failure of the Unionist Party to realise its responsibilities and to move with the times, and partly this is true. The Cabinet and its supporters in Parliament were preoccupied with the defence of Partition and were loath to give their opponents the opportunity to say that Northern Ireland required to be subsidised. It is worth noting that controversies about the subsidisation of a region tend to be engendered by measures of Devolution such as the Government of Ireland Act. Northern Ireland may be said to be no more subsidised than a Development Area within the United Kingdom, but the effect of introducing separate, though similar, regional schemes for social insurance and the like is to turn a spotlight on subsidies which in a centralised area like Great Britain are largely concealed. In so far as it may be necessary to measure the value of the province to the nation, its output of agricultural produce and livestock, goods for export and weapons for defence must outweigh all such considerations.

The financial relations with Great Britain are discussed elsewhere in the book, but in commenting here on the general record of the Unionist Party, it is in place to observe that the backward state of development passed on to the first Northern Ireland Government tended to be perpetuated by the Colwyn Report of 1925. This laid down that expenditure "should not be in excess of the strict necessities of the case having regard to any lower general level of prices, wages, standards of comfort and social amenity existing in Northern Ireland".[1] How far this provision was responsible for the increase in leeway, and how far the fault lay with the slowness of the Government to press on with the building up of public services, is now difficult to say. To some extent local authorities themselves were to blame, since they were reluctant, in the absence of normal pressure from the electorate, to proceed with schemes which would add to the burden on the rates. In this respect they may not have differed very much from public bodies in parts of Great Britain, but generally speaking it could be said that Northern Ireland as a predominantly agricultural area was somewhat behind contemporary ideas in regard to housing and welfare. For that matter Ulster radicalism has usually found more expression in ideas about social justice. Since the start of post-war reconstruction "step-by-step" has been superseded by the new principle of parity and the Colwyn conditions suspended. It is now laid down that in return for parity of taxation Northern Ireland is entitled to parity throughout the social services and that, in addition, an annual allowance should be made to enable the leeway to be overtaken.

It will be seen that the effect of all this, at least so far as the provincial Parliament is concerned, has been to remove from party politics much of its normal stock-in-trade, the share that the needier classes should have of the national wealth. It was and is enough for the Unionist Party to argue that Northern Ireland, by remaining part of the United Kingdom, can have, in good times or bad, exactly the same standard of State benefit as Great Britain, and its best guarantee of employment. Nor has the Labour Party been able to challenge the fact that the prevailing British scale faithfully followed is the highest to which the people of Northern Ireland can hope to attain. So that while the Unionist Party is sometimes accused of discouraging political experiments by concentrating its appeal on "loyalism", its fidelity to the Union has secured for

[1] The Simon Declaration of 1938 enunciated a different principle, i.e. that not only should Northern Ireland be entitled to enjoy the same social standards and services as Great Britain, but that if a deficit occurred on the Northern Ireland Budget which was not the result of a higher standard of expenditure or a lower standard of taxation means would be found to make good this deficit. (*Cf*. Chapter 6 below). Reference may also be made to the valuable survey of these matters in the *Ulster Year Book* for 1951.)

Ulster its share of the social betterment brought in by British Govern-ments whether of the Right or Left. The new conception of parity and the more expansive ideas of the post-war period, together with the visible surplus of revenue in the Stormont Exchequer, have—among the less wealthy at least—given a greater urgency to social reform. The interest that is now taken in re-housing, in the improvement of public utilities like water and sewerage and electricity, and in education and health, is serving to widen the range of the average Unionist's outlook. It also reflects a growing maturity based on the experience of self-government over thirty years, on pride in its achievement and on the knowledge that the Constitution is stable and secure.

This is not the place to analyse whether the present social services in the United Kingdom are inspired by the Conservatives, the wartime Coalition or the Socialists; the matter may be no more than one of de-gree. Inevitably, however, the return to power of a Socialist Government in 1945 and the strengthening of the Welfare State have had disturbing effects on the relationship between Northern Ireland and the rest of the kingdom, though it is only right to record that the Unionist Government under Sir Basil Brooke (now Lord Brookeborough) overcame the poli-tical differences that arose with more success than might have been anticipated when the results of the fateful post-war General Election became known. It did so by its early decision that the new social legis-lation, whatever its party origin, should be extended to Northern Ire-land. National Insurance did not present any exceptional difficulty, but it is probable that a majority of the Cabinet and of middle- and upper-class Unionists, not to speak of doctors, were not really in favour of the Health Service, certainly not on the scale at which it was introduced. Yet, partly because the Minister of Health of the day was a former ship-yard worker who believed sincerely in the ideals of the Health Service, but mostly because it was felt that Northern Ireland could not afford to get out of step, the Act was passed. Significantly, the English procedure was varied in a number of ways to remove what were regarded as its more Socialistic features. The Minister, for instance, conceded that there should be appeal from him to the courts in certain cases, and paid his due to the merits of private enterprise by debarring the projected health centres from dispensing prescriptions. In this way, and by leaving somewhat undefined the powers of the Ministry over the bodies appointed for its management, the Service was inaugurated on the same day as in Great Britain and has become an accepted part of everyday life.

The anti-Socialist nature of many Unionists, businessmen and farmers who own their own lands was much more effectively demonstrated in the case of the Statistics of Trade Act. This measure was dutifully presented to Parliament in the same form as at Westminster. It was obvious that if statistics were to be collected for the United Kingdom as a whole, Northern Ireland must conform, but Unionist back-benchers forced the Government to withdraw the Bill and to revise as many of the provisions as it safely could. That the objections should have been on the grounds that such statistics were the precursor of the nationalisation of production, distribution and exchange, showed that the Unionists concerned were unable to share even the Conservative view of the requirements of economic oversight by the State.

The Government's leanings have been seen in a fairer light in its housing policy. In this, generous subsidies have been available to private builders and owner occupiers (as well as to public authorities) and no quota was placed on the number of houses built by public authorities for letting. In the event, the Housing Trust, a State agency which has proved to be one of the most successful original ventures Northern Ireland has made, has with the help of local councils provided a large number of homes for tenants: but private enterprise in building, whether for personal occupation or letting, has been consistently encouraged. An independent policy was also embarked upon in the Rent Restriction Law (Amendment) Act, 1951, which has permitted increases in certain controlled rents. As at that time no such increases had been made in Great Britain, this was a step of some boldness.

A pledge given by the present Prime Minister not to acquire compulsorily any of Belfast's municipal trading services, while it was a gesture to the city's strong influence in regional affairs, is another indication of the Government's dislike of outright nationalisation. But, on the other hand, it aroused much criticism in 1935 by trying to solve the transport problem by the buying out of passenger and freight services operated by private road hauliers. Since the war nationalisation has had to be extended to the railways, though any encroachment on the right of traders to carry their own goods has been avoided. Thus, even before the war, Parliament was induced to cut across the accepted ideas of the sanctity of private property. If it was at first without success, the legislation anticipated by at least a decade the efforts in Great Britain to bring about closer co-ordination between road and rail services.

The power of compulsory acquisition has similarly been used by the Electricity Board for Northern Ireland, in this case with hardly a protest.

The conventional faith in private enterprise may equally be contrasted with the enthusiasm shown by manufacturers, particularly in the linen industry, for the Re-equipment of Industry and Capital Grants to

Industry Acts, under which the Government gives outright grants from public funds towards the cost of schemes of modernisation. To make an estimate of opinion even more confusing, some of the same manufacturers are prone to insist that public transport should be made self-supporting and independent of subsidy. If in this aspect of domestic politics a consistently firm attitude of mind is difficult to find, the antipathy to planning is perhaps the best index to the Unionist's belief in the rights of property. "Compensation and Betterment" were not adopted in Northern Ireland, and since no Government grants are available for compensation, local authorities are not encouraged to exercise more than an elementary control over building development.

Most of those engaged in the direction of trade and commerce, the larger farmers and people on whom the weight of taxation falls most severely, are undoubtedly firmly anti-Socialist, and as such were ready to blame the post-war ills of the country almost exclusively on the Socialist Government. The Welfare State is often decried despite the fact that Northern Ireland has adopted its principal features at as fast a pace as the rest of the kingdom. The arguments against the Welfare State and the Labour Party are of familiar pattern, but they have been the more coloured for the suspicion with which the generality of Unionists regard the Nationalist sympathies of many of the Labour rank and file in Great Britain. For Mr Attlee and his Government this must be considered an injustice, since in the Ireland Act of 1949 they gave Northern Ireland the cherished and final right of self-determination. Notwithstanding this gesture and the helpfulness of many Departments towards Ulster, there developed first a movement in favour of dominion status, and later one for the exercise of greater autonomy by the provincial Parliament. The first movement died a natural death: it would have ended the Union and was, moreover, a financial impracticability. The second is still alive, and the more often the Socialist Party gains control at Westminster, the more agitation of this nature is likely within the Unionist Party.

Of the more informed criticism that has been made of Northern Ireland as an experiment in devolution, the most pointed has come from a retired senior civil servant of Conservative hue who has charged successive Governments with abdicating the functions of original thought by following too slavishly the policies set forth in London.[1] It is noticeable that charges of this kind were not made until Socialism began to be practised at Westminster; but what is essentially implied is that Northern

[1] "Northern Ireland, Success or Failure," by Dr G. C. Duggan (Dublin, *The Irish Times*, 1950).

Ireland should exercise more freedom and that in order to do so it should have new powers over finance. This has since been taken up by a section of the Unionist Party which has directed its attack on the law relating to death duties, and therefore against the principle of equality in taxation with Great Britain.

In this matter the late Major J. Maynard Sinclair as Minister of Finance made no secret of his dilemma; his Budget speech in 1946 showed plainly that he had no liking for the steep rise in duty on all but the smaller estates. But to exercise his right to propose a different scale he avowed that he would have had to find, in order to preserve parity of taxation, a commensurate sum from an alternative source without causing hardship to any one section of the community. This problem, under pressure from the wealthier elements in the Unionist Party, has since borne heavily on the Government, and a number of concessions have been made. In 1951 the five-year period before death in which gifts *inter vivos* were free from liability was restored to three years, and in the following year a reduction was allowed of from 1 to 5 per cent in the scale of duties on estates ranging in value from £20,000 to £125,000. These variations purported to recognise the high proportion of private companies and family businesses in Northern Ireland and to be offset by the introduction of a Pool Betting Tax and an increase in the Stamp Duties payable by banks on their fiduciary issues, bills and promissory notes. Mr W. B. Maginess, who became Minister of Finance in 1953, further reduced the scale of Estate Duty on estates of between £10,000 and £85,000, this over and above the adoption of the reliefs given in the Imperial Budget of 1954. In doing so he abandoned Major Sinclair's requirement of alternative taxation to offset the cost of his own concessions, estimated at £200,000 in a full year—admittedly a small sum. Neither in the Budget statement nor in the subsequent debates did the Minister acknowledge any departure from the principle of parity.[1] The proposals, in themselves, have also been criticised on both political and economic grounds. The preferential nature of the taxation was held on the one hand to bring in a class distinction, and on the other to be far from sufficient to achieve a material reinforcement of the economy. Indeed, by trying to buttress the many family concerns forming a large part of Ulster business, the Government was thought by some to have pitted itself against a financial trend that has long been running its course in Great Britain. The survival of private companies, many of which continue to pass into the control of large public concerns elsewhere, is of understandable importance, but it does not meet the even

[1] *Cf.* p. 131 n. 1 below.

more urgent need for greater investment in local industry. Until more can be done to retain capital it is certain to flow steadily outwards across the Irish Sea. The crux has therefore seemed to be that the advantages in taxation must be of a much more positive order to anchor money and to attract more from investors outside, and that Northern Ireland cannot go so far without final sacrifice of parity. Under the Government of Ireland Act it possesses power to levy a lower rate of income tax, the likeliest of all means of stimulating investment in the area, but the consequences are recognised as too serious to be contemplated. It must appear that the present attempt to escape from the full weight of Imperial taxation cannot be carried much further without being detrimental to the right of the mass of the people to parity of benefit in return for parity of payment. The pursuit of an independent fiscal policy, aimed as it is at greater economic stability, would soon be followed by divisions in the united front of the Unionist Party.

Working men and small farmers in Northern Ireland are by nature self-reliant, yet no matter what their politics few of them will let themselves be deprived of advantages to the cost of which they make, in indirect taxation at least, their due contribution. The farmers, especially, have gained too much from the national system of guaranteed prices, and from the promise of treatment equal to that accorded to other distant areas on the mainland, to consent to their exclusion. In industrial areas, too, the Unionist Party could not go to the polls without pledging the highest contemporary standards of public welfare.

In this way the ordinary man is, perhaps, more loyal to the Union than those Unionists of extreme Conservative predilections whose distaste for taxation and Socialist legislation has tempted them to stretch the principle of devolution beyond its intended limits. Part of this controversy, as expected, ended with the Imperial General Election of 1951, but it may recur whenever the Left Wing returns to power. Broadly, however, the Northern Ireland Government, notwithstanding its Conservative affiliations, made a fair and wise settlement with the Socialist Administration in the post-war period. The reverse is also true, despite the inclination of many Labour M.P.s to be hostile to Northern Ireland, partly because it does not add to the number of seats in their possession. It has been suggested that the Conservative Government elected in 1951 did more for Ulster in the economic field, but while the advance in co-operation was notable it was probably hastened more by the recession in Northern Ireland in 1951–52 than by the fact of a change of régime.

At the same time the settlement made with the Socialists by the Unionist Government at Stormont was not without some embarrassment to Unionist members at Westminster who, having joined with the Conservative Opposition in resisting Socialist proposals, have seen the same proposals adopted by the Government in Belfast. Some of these members, like the more Right Wing Unionists at home, have not always been diplomatic in their references to Socialist policy in view of Northern Ireland's dependence on the goodwill of the Imperial Government of the day, and of what the Labour Government, in particular, did to safeguard its position. There has arisen here the question whether the Unionist Party should not act more independently of the Conservative Party, the more so as it has been felt on occasion that the latter, when in Opposition, failed to give its full support in Parliament when Ulster was in need of defence. In its opportunist form, the proposition is that the votes of the Unionist *bloc* should go to the highest bidder—the narrow majority after the 1951 election has been cited as an example of how they could be used—but, more morally, the reasoning is that, as Unionism is a blend of people of many political sympathies, it should hesitate to submerge its identity in the Conservative Party, as it does at annual conferences and by its members taking the Whip in the House of Commons.

The wage earners from whom the party draws so much of its massive strength may not be Socialist in outlook, but beneath their first loyalties is at least a sympathy with social reform that until the post-war period would have been probably a little in advance of Toryism. In this their belief in equality of opportunity outweighs any class envy; for socially Ulster may be compared more with the United States than with England, and in terms of American politics the Ulsterman would rank as a Northern Democrat, not a Republican. Yet while the accent in party policy is now on such once radical aspirations, it is a pity that the ordinary people themselves have not taken a greater share in forming it. The Unionist Labour Association, founded to demonstrate the identity of working men with Unionism, has not grasped the chance to influence the party councils. Of its members the late Mr William Grant, who became Minister of Health and Local Government, was the last to speak with authority for those who are trade unionists as well as Unionists. Otherwise the Association tends to allow constitutional matters to overshadow the more everyday questions of human welfare and to say no more than is said by the leaders of the party proper. Similarly the Orange Order, though it embraces thousands of working men and is a democratic movement of formidable power, confines its pronouncements to the defence of Protestantism; whereas, if so minded, it could effectively balance the upper- and middle-class elements that more often provide the voice of Unionist doctrine.

We now come to the other political parties in Northern Ireland. Most of these have as a common link a belief in a United Ireland, but between them there is no unity; nor, with the exception of the Irish Labour Party, itself a prey to divisions, are they directly associated with any of the principal parties in the Irish Republic. In the beginning the Ulster Home Rulers were Nationalists of the constitutional order: later many of them were ousted from Parliament by the more militantly republican movement known as Sinn Fein. To-day what is left of the old Nationalism is found in the Anti-Partition League, but for most of the lifetime of the Northern Ireland Parliament it has lacked cohesion and failed to be an effective force in opposition. Within its ranks have been men steadfast in their refusal to recognise what they regard as alien rule, and this has led to a reluctance to enter the House of Commons and take the oath. Others, notably under the leadership of the late Mr Joseph Devlin and the late Mr T. J. Campbell, K.C., have believed in speaking and acting on behalf of their people; yet even after thirty years there are Nationalist M.P.s who abstain from attendance. The record in the Imperial Parliament has been similar.

Beyond its aspirations to end Partition the League has no clear political faith. Northern Nationalists themselves differ essentially in character from other Irishmen, which perhaps accounts for the fact that they have so long refrained from allying themselves with either Fine Gael or Fianna Fail, the main parties in the Republic. The Anti-Partition League in the North has inherited its own tradition of Conservatism; it looks for backing to the more substantial businessmen and farmers, and to the Roman Catholic clergy. These, for all their interest in politics, as the Irish know them, do not show themselves eager for reforms of any kind. They have, indeed, been described as the "green Tories" by those opponents of partition who are more conscious of modern issues. The latter are found mostly in the industrial areas of Belfast which return to the Northern Ireland Parliament two Irish Labour (or Socialist Republican) members and one member who is Labour but independent of party. It may be considered in some quarters that faithful adherents of Roman Catholicism cannot contrive to add to the sentimental appeal of Irish unity their own agitation for the improvement of living conditions and against the upper classes. At all events since the Roman Catholic Church always has the power to intervene against them when necessary, these Socialists stop well short of anti-clericalism.

The rest of the anti-partition front are extreme Republicans, able to arouse the feelings of the younger voters, and often liable to challenge the orthodox candidates, but there is little that is constructive in their programmes. As the senior and most influential party, the Anti-Partition League has appeared tired in leadership, lacking the vigour and enthusiasm to be expected of an "oppressed minority" bent on redress. Its performance in Parliament in the last fifteen years has been irregular and even now it does not accept the title of official Opposition. Questions like education and the actions of the police may occasionally bring the members to the House in a body, but otherwise they act individually and seldom take part in the debates on economic affairs or the ordinary functions of government. Their lack of vitality, however, is no more than a reflection of the state of mind of many of their constituents. Time has shown that there are great material advantages in a Northern Ireland that remains part of the United Kingdom. Election figures have clearly established that some Roman Catholics, whose religion is nominally co-terminous with Nationalist sentiment, have been ready to vote for the Unionist Party. Among them, too, are some who have felt that the Irish Republic was mistaken in severing all connection with the British Commonwealth, if only because its action reinforced the division of the country.

For the most part Nationalists vote conscientiously for their ideal of a free and united Ireland, but while hopes of its early attainment have faded, they have been recompensed by prosperous conditions and by peace. As a result interest in politics has sunk to a relatively low level. The periodic revivals are best seen at elections when bolder Republicans are apt to awaken a response from young men without always being successful in securing the nomination. Save where the Irish Labour Party has made an incursion and in some remote areas, Nationalism is in control. Nor is there yet evidence that even a mild degree of Irish Socialism will take root in rural areas where a majority of the voters are small farmers and the influence of the Church is at its strongest. The division most likely to arise is between peaceable men and those attracted to militant attempts to end Partition; yet, at least while there is no economic distress, republicanism does not find much effective outlet. Despite the efforts by the Governments in Dublin to make Partition a world issue, the minority generally have little genuine belief in any arbitrary action in their favour. As a long-term hope, they have the faster rate at which the Roman Catholic population is increasing, but some changes of mind are possible before this natural process runs its course. The immediate question would seem to be whether the present attitude towards Parliament will be followed by a fuller acceptance of the Constitution and, what is most desirable, a greater co-operation in welfare and everyday affairs. Yet if at times a hint can be seen of this, progress is slow and below the surface.

The history of the orthodox Labour movement in Northern Ireland is not a happy one. In the battle of loyalties its mind was for long uncertain and its position correspondingly insecure. It has failed, too, to draw its support through the trade unions which, although generally led by Socialists, have never been able to count on their members at election times. The Ulsterman does not take easily to the political side of trade unionism, and few have been drawn away from their first allegiance to the Unionist Party and its offshoots whose constitutional aims are un-equivocal and answer far deeper stirrings in their being.[1] The Protestant workman never quite forgets that since the Plantation the Roman Catholics have been the principal threat of undercutting in the labour market. Thus the Labour Party has been marginal, seeking support from the fringes of both sides and standing only against Unionists. In so doing it has often been inclined, however much it has sought not to commit itself, to favour a united Ireland. During the war the issue was brought to a head when a section broke away to form a Commonwealth Labour Party which failed to survive, and at the next crisis in the move-ment the rest of the Labour Party freed itself from active anti-Partition influence, decided that the standard of living of the workers could best be raised by Northern Ireland's continued membership of the United Kingdom under a (then) Socialist Government, and stood forth as a branch of the British Labour Party. The conversion was too quickly followed by the Ulster General Election of 1949 at which all three of the seats held by members of the newly constituted Northern Ireland Labour Party were lost, together with one held by a member previously expelled from the ranks of Ulster Labour and later admitted into the Labour Party of Eire. Since that time the Northern Ireland Labour Party has been making a conscientious attempt to re-establish itself on the lines of British Socialism. At the General Election of 1953 its poll was increased but it again failed to win a seat. In the event of any considerable trade depression it will certainly regain a representation; on the other hand, the sounding of any fresh alarm concerning the Border will always mean that the Unionist majorities will be restored.

Experience has shown that Parliament is the poorer for the exclusion of Labour members willing to undertake, with the Independents, the

[1] The Trades Disputes and Trade Union Act, 1927, repealed by the Imperial Par-liament, is still on the Statute Book in Northern Ireland. This enables trade union members to contract into the paying of a political levy instead of contracting out as in Great Britain.

duties of Opposition and to bring forward the social questions which some Unionists pass over more lightly. Except where they may be charged with splitting the official Unionist vote in the working-class areas of Belfast, the party has made good its pledge to support the Union, and as loyalty becomes less urgent it is capable of becoming a third force. On living conditions it makes, despite the existence of the Government's policy of parity with Great Britain, a strong appeal, but otherwise its programme tends to be over-doctrinaire. This is particularly true of the belief that the land should be nationalised, an unhopeful proposition in a country owned by small farmers.

The Labour movement obviously suffers from the lack of the solid trade union backing which is given in Great Britain. Not only do trade union members vote independently, but the unions themselves are without a central organisation. They are represented in a Northern Ireland Committee of the Irish T.U.C., which the Northern Ireland Government declines to recognise on the grounds that a Dublin-based body opposed to Partition is not suitable to negotiate on wages and conditions which have to be kept as close as possible to British standards. It would appear that the interests of Northern Ireland and its workers, the majority of whom belong to British unions, would better be served by the formation of a Northern Ireland Committee of the British T.U.C., but any effort that has been made towards this end had been defeated by unions in which anti-Partitionists have control. In general, industrial relations in Ulster have shown a lag in development, and while there may be direct contact between the Government and individual unions the absence of a representative body like the T.U.C. is not in keeping with the times. As has been observed elsewhere in this chapter, working men, though among the strongest supporters of Unionism, have little say in the direction of domestic policy, and the fact that even organised labour has yet to take its proper place in public affairs may be regarded as a weakness of the same order. The problems of Northern Ireland eminently demand all the economic co-operation which trade unionism in Great Britain has shown to be possible.

Of Communism, there is only nominal evidence on the surface, although in Northern Ireland, as elsewhere, its activity in the unions is out of all proportion to its numerical strength.

Unhappily, it cannot be denied that sectarianism continues to dominate politics. Between Unionist and Nationalist there exists a gap that is broadest at the point where the one is Protestant and the other Roman Catholic. Even the drift by which some Roman Catholics vote Unionist, and some Protestants come to avow themselves Nationalist, does not serve to lessen the differences between one religion and the other. Elsewhere their historic struggle for supremacy may appear to have lost its intensity and its hold on human passions; in Northern Ireland, where the balance of power is more evenly poised, it has been, and is, the fundamental issue. Protestant objections to the Roman Catholic system do not require elaboration, but whereas they are matters of conscience, and whereas Roman Catholics for their part cannot be expected to rebel against their faith and morals, there are on both sides people of little or no piety at all whose instinctive racial antagonisms are primarily expressed in terms of religion. Many Unionists will say that the root of the trouble lies in the political ambitions of the Roman Catholic Church, and it is true that the hierarchy discourages co-operation on both the religious and secular planes. The divisions to-day are still deep, deeper even than in the last century, and they will take time to be diminished. But where the purely religious aspect is allowed to be obscured, the possibility of better things is not so remote. Already there has been observed a readier acceptance of the constitutional position by Roman Catholics as individuals and even a respect for the achievements of Northern Ireland as an area of self-government. For this the sharing of material benefits has been largely responsible, but with it is the fact that special recognition has been given to the minority's position. Though friction may persist in local authority areas where control is being contested and where the letting of houses is liable to be carried out on a political basis, the Roman Catholic population has undoubtedly received, as the Government of Ireland Act expressly provided, equal treatment before the law, and in certain fields something inclining towards liberality.

One of these fields is education, the focal point of many of the current issues in Ulster. Almost from the date of the first meeting of the Parliament of Northern Ireland, religion and politics have converged on the schools. These have witnessed controversies not only between Church and State, and Protestant and Roman Catholic, but between Unionist and Unionist. For it is here that tolerance has been at stake and the liberal ways of the Ulster people have been weighed in the scales. Briefly, it may be recorded that in the beginning the Government planned a non-denominational system of public education which was mostly accepted by the Protestants but was defeated by the refusal of the Roman Catholic Church to allow its children to attend schools outside its care. Thus there arose the question of what claim the Church schools had upon public funds. A compromise was reached, as in England, in 1923, but only after the Government had incurred the anger of the more extreme Protestants;

and the fires burst out again after the war when the time came to implement the pledge of a new plan of educational advance. At this point, in
the Education Bill of 1948, the Government, in acknowledgment of the
burdens which the Roman Catholic community, by their abstention from
the public system, were called upon to bear, provided that the rate of
grants for capital expenditure should be raised to a level of 65 per cent,
or 15 per cent above that in England. (Nearly all running costs, including
teachers' salaries, have always been paid by the State to denominational
schools.)

In the storm that followed this proposal the debate on the Unionist side
was indicative of the issue that lies before both the Party and the Ulster
people. On the one side the more inflexible Protestants strenuously
opposed the Bill; on the other moderate opinion urged it forward in the
name of fair and realistic dealing and with the ultimate purpose of
rebutting charges of intolerance and of consolidating a period of peaceful
progress. The Government prevailed, and although a recrudescence of
opposition forced the resignation of the Minister of Education early in
1950, the principles of the Act emerged intact. The measure therefore
stands as an example of liberal policy, but it remains to be decided
whether the Unionist Party is prepared to make it a precedent for appeals
to the minority on an even broader front. The choice before the Party is
to restrain its propaganda against Anti-Partition and to concentrate on
a positive domestic programme or, in declining to play its hand from the
strength which it now undoubtedly possesses, to rely upon a constant
regeneration of the differences that divide the people. The liberal course,
unfortunately, is made the more difficult by the attacks upon the Constitution emanating from the Irish Republic, and by the sporadic outrages of the Irish Republican Army. The effect of these, in turn, is to
intensify the demands from the more vehement Protestant and Orange
elements for an aggressive attitude towards minority as a whole. Insufficient credit has been given to the Government for its resistance to
such pressure, and for its defence of impartial administration of the law.
Not until Northern Ireland can be left to itself can the desire for peace
and good feeling grow of its own accord and the democratic mind of the
Protestant majority be fully exemplified.

When religion rather than class so appears to predetermine party
allegiance, those qualities which Unionism draws from the essential
character of its adherents and antecedents are often forgotten. Constitutional and religious loyalties perforce remain supreme issues that serve
to emotionalise the more normal approach to welfare politics. Yet the
fact is not to be underestimated that these loyalties embrace the same

G

attachment to civil liberty as Great Britain enjoys without challenge from within its borders, and that this deep-rooted sentiment is reinforced by the conviction that the Union stands also for the attainment of the highest level of material well-being. It is, therefore, of secondary importance whether Unionists are Conservative, Liberal or Socialist. Their situation demands the synthesis that, behind the conventional ties between the Unionist and Conservative parties, continues to be evolved. For events have shown that Unionism, in undertaking the task of self-government, has been ready both to adopt Imperial legislation whether of the Right or the Left and to devise measures of its own. The test, after all, is not the emergence of a new political creed so much as the practical results of such government and these, as have been shown, compare not unfavourably with those in the rest of the United Kingdom. They have been, first, the maintenance of law and order and of fiscal stability, a substantial expansion of industry and agriculture, the building up of a new educational system, and the development of social services at a rate which, in view of initial leeway, has been faster than that in Great Britain. Good government, too, is dependent upon an efficient Civil Service and in this respect the highest British standard has been maintained. Northern Ireland has thus responded to the need for constructive political thought and practice in a way that might not have been confidently anticipated when the Government of Ireland Act was passed; and if the criticism is made that it has usually followed the lead of the Imperial Parliament, what has been done independently in some departments gives promise that once the "leeway" has been eliminated even more originality will be introduced. The principle of parity in expenditure will then require to be somewhat freely interpreted. Another condition that has at last been satisfied is that of internal security; for although disorders may break out from time to time the Constitution is now seen to be established on a permanent basis. But at the same time it may be considered that nearly all the initiative in legislation must continue to be taken by the Government and its advisers. So long as the Unionist Parliamentary Party is divided between businessmen and farmers of Conservative leanings and others who are more Orangemen than political theorists, strong leadership is essential. To this the rank and file of the electorate can usually be relied upon to respond, but a study of administration fails to show many legislative innovations brought about through force of public opinion. To this extent devolution, while associating the people more closely with the work of government, has yet to create a political consciousness on modern lines. For the lack of this consciousness the Partition struggle is of course primarily responsible. When, if ever, this ceases, the instincts of the Ulster Unionist, which can best be described as a blend of Conservatism, Liberalism and moderate Socialism, will be given fuller play. Possibly the time will come when, during a period of more extreme Socialist rule at Westminster, the Parliament of Northern Ireland will decline to go further along the same road and will begin to make the maximum use of its own powers. Yet, as has been seen, finance will always exercise a restraint, in which case the danger will be one of estrangement from Britain rather than a flight to dominion status. Enough has been seen of the rise of a "provincial nationalism" to suggest any such development would leave a deep mark on the Unionist mind. Even in recent years the absence of National Service and the passing of the Safeguarding of Employment Act (which requires even British subjects born outside Ulster to have permits to work), have tended to put Northern Ireland in a position of being in but not of the United Kingdom.

With this reservation, and it is one with a great deal of relevance to the future, it can be said that the Union has been upheld for more than thirty years in face of the severest of political and physical pressures, and that more broadly Ulster has been able to prove the value of what in the beginning was a British constitutional experiment embarked upon with little guidance from the past. In an age of centralisation its form of devolution has been demonstrated as having advantages over a wide field of government, and it has been practised without any material weakening of the unity of the kingdom or any direct repudiation of national obligations. If the system has shown itself to be fundamentally sound and flexible enough to keep pace with the many changes produced by thirty years of peace and war, the subordinate Parliament and Executive may also be said to have succeeded because of the stability, responsibility and moderation found in the community. The qualities of good sense, industry and perseverance which characterise the majority in Northern Ireland have enabled them to undertake the conduct of their own public affairs while keeping intact their faith in the Union. That many pitfalls have been avoided in the acquisition of power and the administration of a deeply divided area is seen in the rarity of appeals against actions as being *ultra vires* the Government of Ireland Act. It is the attempted balancing of inlook and outlook, of regional and national duties, that is probably the best creation of this political reform, and one that has given weight to the demand for its application to Scotland. The wonder is that it was first planned as a compromise and accepted as an unavoidable alternative to the merging of Northern Ireland in an Irish Free State. Few can then have foreseen that a solution of such a kind reached under the stormy circumstances that then existed would be so enduring and so practical in its benefits. The merits of the devolutionary system of government, however, cannot be fully assessed in the absence of a greater degree of political unity among the population as a whole.

As has been said, public and social co-operation between Protestants and Roman Catholics is a plant of tender growth. Its development is consistently retarded by the pressure brought by the Irish Republic against the Partition settlement and by periodic outbreaks of violence on the part of extremists North and South. These campaigns serve to keep alive the defensive attitude of the great body of Unionists and to encourage the party organisation and the Orange Order in confining politics to issues of loyalty and, inevitably, of sectarianism. And so long as the best efforts of moderates on both sides are frustrated in this way, so long will Northern Ireland be a dual society, a prey to suspicion and friction, and unable to realise its fullest potentialities in human welfare and culture. Mr W. B. Maginess, Q.C., Minister of Finance, has defined the spiritual basis of Partition as "freedom, loyalty, dissent" and the Unionist belief as "the right to think, to debate our opinions, to differ from our neighbours". But this creed, containing as it does the ingredients of liberal philosophy, has yet to be adopted as a positive Unionist policy to be preached at home as much as it is declared abroad. Northern Ireland's material progress has already done much to commend the British connection to those of Irish national sentiment: it remains to be seen whether it can or will be made the basis of a reconciliation and an identity of interest that will save Ulster from another half century of political conflict detrimental both to the system of local self-government and the peace and prosperity of its people.

CHAPTER 4

NORTHERN IRELAND AND THE DEFENCE OF THE BRITISH ISLES

By CYRIL FALLS

AMONG the subjects reserved for control and legislation by the Parliament of the United Kingdom and thus beyond the purview of that of Northern Ireland are the waging of war, the making of peace, the attitude of neutrality, the raising and control of armed forces. The Northern Ireland Government is thus excluded from initiative or responsibility in the matter of defence, either in preparation or in action. When conscription for military service was introduced in Great Britain the Northern Ireland Government requested that it should be extended to Northern Ireland. The British Government refused on political grounds. It considered that conscription for service in a cause which they repudiated would so exasperate a considerable proportion of the population of Northern Ireland that it could be enforced only with great difficulty, and that the effort needed to enforce it would be so heavy that the extra military man-power thus recruited would not compensate for it. This exclusion of Northern Ireland from the application of conscription furnishes a good example of the complete control of the British Government in the most vital feature of defence.

This statutory reservation need not be taken to imply that the Northern Ireland Government has no relation to matters of defence or that it is not consulted about them. In practice its views and its advice, which may be useful because of its local knowledge and experience, are sought, and its suggestions are when possible met, as regards, let us say, the quartering of troops. In the Second World War the Government took an active part in the encouragement of recruiting on a voluntary basis within its own territory. The links between it and the Service commands which dealt with Northern Ireland were always close. Yet these are affairs of convenience and courtesy which do not involve the attributes of government. Constitutionally, the Northern Ireland Government possesses no rights or responsibilities in such business.

Thus, excluding civil affairs, the action of Northern Ireland in defence on the strictly military plane is confined to obedience to the behests and observance of the regulations of the British Government. Yet Northern

Ireland can and does render valuable service through its very existence, by reason of the fact that it forms part of the United Kingdom, and its capacity to do so has notably increased in the past thirty years.

Ireland has repeatedly caught the eye of hostile strategists as a potential stepping-stone to England. "He that will England win, let him in Ireland begin." Their theory was that the direct invasion of England might prove an insuperable task, whereas it would be easier to gain a foothold in Ireland. Once the expeditionary force, which would have brought with it a large supply of arms, had established itself, the task would be to organise an Irish army for service against England. One Spanish strategist, writing early in 1602, foresaw that in such a situation the majority of the available English forces would be attracted to Ireland. The next step would be the invasion of England by the main Spanish forces. Another, less ambitious, had previously urged that a base should be secured in southern Ireland for the purpose of intercepting English shipping in the Atlantic. The doubtful factor in such calculations was command of the sea. Any expeditionary force would require periodically fresh supplies and probably reinforcements. The evasion of a superior fleet was always a possibility—particularly, of course, in the days of sail—but a grave disaster might be incurred if the superior fleet encountered a convoy.

The first instance in modern history of a serious invasion of Ireland directed against England was the landing of a Spanish force at Kinsale, at the mouth of the Bandon, on September 23, 1601. This would have constituted a far more serious threat than it actually did but for the fact, unknown to the Spaniards, that Tyrone's rebellion, alive in Ulster, was to all intents and purposes dead in Munster. In this case there was no direct trial of strength with Spain, since the Spaniards, heavily outnumbered, shut themselves up in the town to await the arrival from the north of their allies Tyrone and O'Donnell. The latter were routed by the Lord Deputy, Mountjoy, whereupon the Spanish commander obtained honourable terms under which his force was shipped back to Spain with its arms and colours.

The second threat was that of 1689, when James II, driven from England and deposed, arrived in Ireland with French aid. His friend and patron Louis XIV provided him with money, experienced officers, and a relatively small force of French troops.

The French King might have gained much better results with a larger contingent, but, as a diversion from the strength which he had to face on the Continent, this proved exceedingly effective. All but a handful of the English and foreign troops available were drawn to Ireland, so that not only was the aid of William lost to his allies but England herself was almost denuded.

The campaign in Ireland is famous for its dramatic episodes, but one event outside Ireland, though of the highest significance, has failed to grip the public imagination to a similar extent. On June 30, 1690 (o.s.), the very day before the Battle of the Boyne, was fought the naval battle of Beachy Head. The Anglo-Dutch fleet suffered a heavy defeat at the hands of the French commander, Tourville. Command of the sea passed to France, and her fleets rode the sea in triumph all that summer and autumn. The peril of invasion was in the end averted, but it is worth while to emphasise how great it was at a time when there were less than 8,000 regular troops in England.

In 1796, when the great French expedition sailed to Bantry Bay, the French did not possess command of the sea. It was a slack British blockade of Brest and the bad choice of Spithead as the base of the Channel Fleet, when the French fleet was at Brest, far to windward, which rendered the expedition possible. There can be no doubt that if the powerful French force carried with the fleet had landed it would have overrun Ireland. Bad weather prevented it from doing so, though had the frigate carrying the admiral, Morard de Galles, and the general, Lazare Hoche, not become separated from the rest of the fleet, it may be assumed that they would have had the strength of mind to overcome the difficulties. In 1798, in the midst of the Irish rebellion, a thousand French troops, landing in Killala Bay, achieved astonishing success before they were defeated and forced to surrender.

In the First World War the danger of an invasion of Ireland was never pressing, though during the rebellion of Easter Week, 1916, the German ship *Libau*, laden with arms for the rebels, was captured off the Kerry coast. On the other hand, the part played by the Irish bases was of vital importance in the maintenance of transatlantic communications at their eastern terminals and in the prosecution of the anti-submarine campaign.

Before the end of 1914 twenty-three "patrol areas" were established in home waters, and of these eight had Irish bases: Kingstown and Belfast, Larne, Lough Swilly, Blacksod Bay, Galway Bay, Queenstown and Berehaven. Of these Queenstown was the most important. Between July and August 1915, all the western patrol areas, from the Hebrides to Ushant, were placed under a single command, with headquarters at Queenstown. In 1916 and 1917 the port was used as a base for the submarine-decoys known as Q-ships, and it was off the Skelligs in February 1917 that there occurred the most famous incident in their career, when the *Farnborough*, after allowing herself to be torpedoed by the *U83*, sank her unsuspecting opponent with a sudden burst of fire. It was at Queens-town that the American Admiral W. S. Sims took over command in June of the same year.

One of the lessons of the war was that Irish bases would always be invaluable in the defence of the approaches to the chief English and Scottish ports in the event of a war against an enemy employing sub-marines in strength in the Atlantic; that for shipping passing south of Ireland Queenstown was vital; and that in general it was the most im-portant Irish base. As time passed, and the range, reliability and striking power of aircraft increased, it also became apparent that Irish air bases might play a big part in any future war. The loss of the ports, anchorages and airfield sites which were included in the territory of Eire, under an agreement made in April 1938, was therefore viewed with foreboding by those who best understood ocean strategy. Northern Ireland remained available, but the ports within the area it comprised had not played a prominent part in the naval operations of the First World War.

In the Second World War Eire adopted a policy of neutrality and protested against the stationing of British forces in Northern Ireland territory and the use of Northern Ireland ports as naval bases. It lodged another protest when United States forces arrived at the beginning of 1942. The Government of Mr de Valera never yielded to persuasion on this matter, even when that persuasion was strongly reinforced by the voice of the United States. He himself, when asked whether he would be prepared to abandon neutrality if partition were brought to an end and the six counties were united with the rest of Ireland, replied that he would not; to do so, he contended, would be to barter Ireland's right to freedom for the purpose of securing her right to unity. It must be added that Eire behaved generally as a benevolent and friendly neutral. Petty and un-intentional infringements of the border by troops who did not know the country well were frequent, but when they occurred the commonest procedure was for a policeman to request the offenders to return to their own side. British airmen who made forced landings were treated with particular consideration. Catalina aircraft of Coastal Command flew over Donegal or Leitrim to reach the Atlantic from Lough Erne, and it was one of these, Z/209, which rediscovered the German battleship *Bismarck* on May 26, 1941, after she had once evaded pursuit. Though the fact has not been officially revealed, there is no doubt that the intel-ligence services of the United Kingdom and Eire established relations. All this came far short of counter-balancing Britain's inability to make use of southern and western Irish bases but it is none the less worthy of record.

Before the war, the Navy's only official connection with Belfast, a commercial port, apart from the shipbuilding yards of Harland and Wolff, was the maintenance of the Ulster Division of the R.N.V.R. There were no establishments at Londonderry or Larne. In late August 1939 a Flag Officer in Charge was sent to Belfast, and the other two ports were selected as bases for patrol and auxiliary craft. From the summer of 1940 the Germans were able to establish submarine bases closer to the Atlantic trade routes. The importance of the three ports in Northern Ireland then increased—as did the handicap caused by the loss of Queenstown and the potential airfields in Eire. Shipping from the east coast of England had to be diverted from the Channel and sent north about round Scotland. Incoming shipping could use only the North-west Approaches, the bulk making for the Clyde and the Mersey. "All had to come in around Northern Ireland," writes Mr Churchill. "Here, by the grace of God, Ulster stood a faithful sentinel. The Mersey, the Clyde, were the lungs through which we breathed."

As the struggle grew more intense the work of the Northern Ireland bases for the support and replenishment of the escort forces expanded. The number of anti-submarine vessels based on the Belfast area increased from four on June 14, 1940, to 80 on October 11 of that year. Belfast became in particular a trawler base of great importance. Escort groups for convoy protection were based on Londonderry and, from being a minor base, it developed into the main advanced fuelling base for escort forces of the Western Approaches Command.

In March 1941, Gare Loch, on the Clyde, and Londonderry were selected as American destroyer bases in the event of the United States becoming involved in the war. The construction, carried out by an American firm, was financed under lend-lease, but the materials had to cross the Atlantic in British ships, since it was illegal for American ships to enter war zones. The United States approached Mr de Valera in an endeavour to obtain the use of Lough Swilly also, but without avail. Work on the base was well on its way to completion when the Japanese attacked Pearl Harbour in December. The first United States warships to visit a British port during the war were five destroyers which, after providing the escort for a convoy, arrived at Londonderry. The "U.S. Naval Operating Base" was formally established as part of the command of the Commander-in-Chief, United States Atlantic Fleet, on February 5, 1942.

"The green Irish countryside", writes the historian of the United States Naval Operations in World War II, Professor Samuel Eliot Morison, "was heaven compared with the barren wastes of Iceland.

Repair facilities also were superior, since Londonderry was already an important base of the Royal Navy, and the main British centre for anti-submarine training. The British 'dome teacher', in which personnel were trained in the use of anti-aircraft guns in a sort of planetarium, was of immense value to American gunners, as were the British 'tame submarines' on which escort vessels practised both day and night attacks."

In the same month, February 1942, the eastern terminal of the mid-ocean groups of the Newfoundland Escort Force, Royal Canadian Navy, was changed from Iceland to Londonderry, and this run was continued until the end of hostilities. Like the United States historian, the Canadian, Mr Joseph Schull, comments on the pleasant nature of the new terminal as compared with the old. Now, he remarks, the groups had to look forward to "the smile of the green Foyle rather than the scowling crags of Iceland greeting them at the end of each voyage." In such circumstances the nature and surroundings of the final haven are not without moral effect upon the crews reaching it after a voyage entailing constant watchfulness and stress amid deadly danger and high responsibility. It was, however, above all on the purely strategic side that Londonderry proved its value as a naval base.

The narrow-guage railway to Lisahally, on Lough Foyle, was brought into use in February 1943 for the supply of fresh water, stores and provisions to ships alongside the jetty. Cranes and other facilities were installed, and from March onward destroyers and other vessels were berthed and given the necessary service. Lisahally camp was opened as part of the United States base.

During the year 1943 the facilities at Londonderry were expanded to keep pace with the developments of the Battle of the Atlantic. It may be recalled that the phase of the submarine war during the last five months of 1942 and the first five of 1943 was characterised by the organisation of small fleets of U-boats, working in co-operation with aircraft, in "wolf packs". Their principal area of action was the central Atlantic, where the loss of freighters, especially in the earlier part of the period, was enormous. The next phase, from late May to mid-September, was costly for the allies but highly successful. At last equipment and tactics were becoming adequate to meet the peril. Among the new facilities at Londonderry were a gunnery school, a signal school, aircraft-recognition and anti-aircraft lecture rooms, and arrangements for drill with depth charges. The changed situation in the submarine war brought about the closure of the trawler base at Belfast in August 1943, but the United States base at Londonderry remained in service until September

2, 1944, when it was "decommissioned" after playing a vital part in the war.

During 1943 naval air stations, taken over from the Royal Air Force, were opened in the Northern Ireland Sub-Command. That at Eglinton was commissioned as *H.M.S. Gannet* and Maydown as *H.M.S. Shrike* for the accommodation of naval air squadrons forming and training with fighter aircraft of American type. Belfast Airport became *H.M.S. Gadwall*. Its main function was the provision of accommodation for squadrons disembarked from the merchant aircraft—carrier ships and the escort carriers. Berths alongside were available for these ships, and a maintenance yard was constructed.

The problem of the army in Ireland for at least eighteen months after the fall of France in the summer of 1940 was anxious and difficult. It provided the garrison of Northern Ireland, which consisted in the main of two divisions and an independent brigade, to begin with indifferently equipped. Yet Northern Ireland did not appear altogether likely to be the object of direct attack, except from the air. (Belfast was attacked four times, three times heavily, in April and May 1941, and there was a little bombing outside it; but on the whole Northern Ireland came off better than might have been expected.) The land forces in the Northern Ireland district had to act—it might, indeed, be argued that this constituted their main function—as a garrison for the whole country, while precluded from entering four-fifths of the territory. And this four-fifths was exposed to the risk of invasion to a much greater degree than Northern Ireland itself.

Plans were worked out for an immediate crossing of the border in the event of a German invasion. Intelligence was fairly good. There was no doubt that the Government of Eire and its armed forces would defend their territory with all their might. It was to be expected that, were their territory violated, they would co-operate with the British forces in attempting to expel the invader. This had been the policy of Norway, Holland and Belgium, which had, like Eire, carefully preserved their neutrality as long as they could, but none of them provided a promising precedent. Nor could there be any guarantee that elements of the Irish Republican Army would not prove hostile. The forces of Eire itself were gradually expanded several times over, but they lacked modern equipment as well as experience.

The first United States troops arrived in Northern Ireland in January 1942, and there carried out training for the expedition to French North Africa. In preparation for the invasion of Western Europe, large American forces began to come in in October 1943. Northern Ireland, in fact, became one of the main stations and training-grounds of American land forces in the United Kingdom. Belfast was the assembly point for the bombarding ships of the United States Western Forces under the command of Rear-Admiral A. G. Kirk, United States Navy. This force sailed from Belfast on June 3, 1944, to support the landing in Normandy on June 6.

In the early stages of the war the weakness of the Royal Air Force in Northern Ireland was in part due to inability to provide greater strength, in part to the fact that convoys and ocean shipping were then routed south of Ireland. A single squadron of Ansons of Coastal Command (a native squadron, No. 502 Ulster Squadron, Auxiliary Air Force) was stationed at Aldergrove, employed on anti-submarine patrols north of Ireland, in the North Channel, and the northern part of the Irish Sea.

After the fall of France the same factor applied to air forces in Northern Ireland as to naval forces. Hostile air and naval forces based in northern France and the Biscay coast made the South-west Approaches, in the absence of bases in southern Ireland, too dangerous for ocean convoys. These now had to be routed through the North-west Approaches. Northern Ireland at once became of prime importance. It was now the natural and the indispensable base for aircraft engaged in the protection of transatlantic shipping, just as it was for surface vessels engaged in that task. Construction of new airfields was undertaken. Coastal Command anti-submarine and long-range fighter squadrons were drafted in. Soon Hudsons, Ansons and Blenheim fighters were operating from Aldergrove, while No. 502 Squadron, re-equipping with Whitleys, was working from a new airfield at Limavady. The Whitleys carried the first long-range radar for the detection of U-boats on the surface. As short-range fighter protection for Belfast, Fighter Command provided a squadron of Hurricanes.

Serious shipping losses that winter led in February 1941 to the decision to devote the maximum naval and air resources to countering the enemy's attack in the Atlantic. Particular stress was laid upon the rapid completion of airfields still under construction. By midsummer 1941 five squadrons of anti-submarine aircraft and two of long-range fighters were in operation, and a flying-boat station with two squadrons of Catalinas was established on Lough Erne. In the late autumn two Spitfire squadrons and a Defiant (night-fighter) squadron were added.

Thenceforward little change occurred until the appearance of the "wolf packs" in mid-Atlantic in August 1942. This demanded air support at ever-increasing distances from base. Now, indeed, Northern Ireland, in conjunction with Iceland, became the outpost without which defeat in the Battle of the Atlantic would have been practically certain. Northern Ireland and Iceland became extreme advanced bases for Coastal Command Liberators, Flying Fortresses, Catalinas and Sunderlands. Convoy battles raged with increasing violence all through the winter of 1942. At moments the shadow of defeat seemed to hang over the ocean. Yet by about May 1943 the U-boats had suffered so heavily that victory was assured. Throughout this crucial period there were always three squadrons of long-range land-based aircraft operating from Ballykelly and three of flying-boats on Lough Erne. The most important work of all was that of the "Very Long-range" Liberators of No. 120 Squadron and later also Nos. 59 and 86 Squadrons based at Ballykelly and Aldergrove, with detachments working from Reykjavik in Iceland, in co-operation with surface convoy escorts. They were called upon for a fresh effort when, in October 1943, an attempt was made to resuscitate the convoy war. Never numbering more than from forty to fifty, the deepest debt is due to these very long-range aircraft and their crews. They faced a situation as desperate as that which confronted Fighter Command in the Battle of Britain. Documents from hostile sources prove that without their co-operation with naval craft around the convoys the struggle could not have been successfully maintained. Nor could they have accomplished what they did without the bases of Northern Ireland.

From November 1943 only routine escort and support was necessary for the Atlantic convoys. Another call, though one of less urgency, came in the summer of 1944, when the inshore attack phase, with U-boats fitted with the Schnorkel breathing-tube, developed. Then the flying-boat squadrons on Lough Erne, which had been reduced to two, were again raised to a strength of three, and other reinforcements were sent over. The Schnorkel phase, however, proved far less menacing than the Germans had hoped.

The object of this chapter is to explain the strategic value of Northern Ireland in the defence of the British Isles and in particular in the protection of the Atlantic routes, without which Great Britain cannot exist, in peace or in war. Only the briefest mention will therefore be made of Northern Ireland's contribution to the war effort by its industrial and agricultural production and then only from the military point of view. The value of this production of manufactured articles and of food was very great in the Second World War, but it hardly comes into the field of strategy. It does not depend upon the strategic situation of the territory, except in so far as the industries of Northern Ireland stood in less danger from air attack than the majority of those of Great Britain. At the same time it must be borne in mind that, though the shipyards, the mills and the farms would have existed had Northern Ireland been neutral, and their goods would probably have been available to British purchasers and to them alone, neutrality might well have had an adverse effect on war production. In such a case the British Government would have been unable to apply the regulations considered necessary, while a neutral Government in Dublin might have applied restrictions. Secrecy, ease of consultation and supervision, and other considerations, make production on home soil generally preferable in time of war to production through neutrals.

A great share of the military production was represented by the firm of Harland and Wolff. At the outbreak of war the cruiser *Belfast* had just been completed; the aircraft carrier *Formidable*, the submarine depot-ship *Adamant*, the aircraft-repair ship *Unicorn* and the minesweepers *Bangor* and *Blackpool* were under construction. Among the important ships built during the war at Belfast for the Royal Navy were the cruiser *Black Prince*, the Canadian cruiser *Ontario* and the light fleet carrier *Glory*. Several frigates and smaller craft also came from these yards. To a remarkable extent, however, Harland and Wolff's establishment became a general arsenal, with relatively small departments in considerable numbers making arms and equipment of the most diverse kinds. About 1,500 bomber aircraft and hundreds of flying boats were constructed by it. Its repair facilities for both naval vessels and freighters were invaluable. Its primary task, however, was the production of merchant shipping, and it built about one-tenth of the total war output of the whole of the United Kingdom. Two large liners built during the war, the *Campania* and the *Pretoria Castle*, were used by the Navy as escort carriers.

The machinery for the protection of ocean routes against the combined attacks of submarines, long-range aircraft and surface raiders is complex and highly technical. It is also in constant development. The principle is, however, simple, and it is by looking at the principle that the vital importance of Northern Ireland can best be realised. The aim must be to project—that is, to base—the defences as far out into the ocean and as far away from the terminal ports as possible. On the western side of the Atlantic such outposts were readily attainable, and it was to provide them for her own needs that the United States established the Caribbean bases. The bed of the eastern side of the North Atlantic Ocean is of a different type, and there are no ready-made facilities in the form of islands. Yet Northern Ireland, in conjunction with Iceland on the flank of the northern routes, fulfils a double function. It provides close naval and air cover for the terminals, in approaching which shipping, whatever deviations it has made in the wide ocean, must converge; it also provides a springboard for air cover over the central Atlantic, the most difficult part of the ocean to reach. In this respect it is not ideal because not situated far enough to the westward; yet the flying-boat base of lower Lough Erne lies about 175 miles west of any English airfield and 100 miles west of any Scottish, giving a saving of 350 to 200 miles on a flight out from and back to base. Northern Ireland provides a measure of protection against invasion of Ireland as a whole while it remains a base for British sea, land and air forces. Finally, as has been shown, it provides a convenient terminus for vessels employed on convoy duties. It does not altogether compensate for the loss of the southern Irish bases, but it affords the only substitute for them at present available.

It is not the present intention to enter the political field; but one small feature of it must be briefly surveyed, since it cannot be divorced from the strategic subject of the chapter. Suggestions have been made that the defence of the Atlantic routes need not depend entirely upon Northern Ireland; if, it is argued, Northern Ireland were to be incorporated in the Irish Republic, that State would in return be prepared to participate in the North Atlantic Treaty; in that case all Ireland would be available as it was in the First World War. To this proposition Northern Ireland replies that the Republic of Ireland has no right to impose such a bargain, that, if it desired to take part in the defence of freedom, it might be expected to do so without imposing terms which Northern Ireland would regard as a denial of freedom.

Another and more strictly military answer is to be found. The obligations of the North Atlantic Treaty, important as they are, are considerably looser than those which form part of the duties—as also of the rights—of membership of the United Kingdom. The former allow even in theory, and still more in practice, a latitude in interpretation which might create grave embarrassment and heavy handicaps in warfare. It might well prove that a limited participation of the Irish Republic in defence was gained at the expense of a serious weakening in the participation of Northern Ireland—and the extent of the participation of Northern Ireland would then be decreed and controlled from Dublin, not from Whitehall. There would be no guarantee that the facilities afforded by Northern Ireland in the Second World War would again be available in like quality in Ireland as a whole or even in Northern Ireland itself. Setting aside all political and sentimental considerations, the United Kingdom would be accepting a great risk in entering upon such a blind bargain. It is notable how clearly defined this feature of the situation has become since the Second World War to senior officers of the armed forces of the United States, who had previously no comprehension of it.

The stress has been laid upon the historical aspect because it illustrates the strategic importance of Ireland in various circumstances. Most attention has been paid to those of the Second World War. It can be said with confidence that the strategic importance of Northern Ireland there revealed has been little altered and in no way decreased. If the service rendered by it had to be described in a single word, that word would be "anti-submarine". There is no sign that the submarine threat has diminished since then; it may indeed be found to have increased owing to the far higher submerged speed of the modern submarine. While that is so Northern Ireland must continue to play a vital part. It remains as valuable a factor as ever in the defence of the Atlantic routes and their traffic and ultimately, in the widest sense, in the defence of the British Isles.

CHAPTER 5

ULSTER'S ECONOMIC STRUCTURE

By K. S. ISLES and N. CUTHBERT

NORTHERN Ireland is economically so interwoven with Great Britain that, looked at broadly, it is not a separate economy at all but an un-differentiated part of a single economic system embracing the whole of the United Kingdom. This economic unity is closely bound up with political unity. On the one hand, natural conditions promoting economic interdependence with Great Britain form one of the main foundation stones on which political union rests; and, reciprocally, this natural tendency to economic integration has been greatly strengthened by the fact of political union. As a result of political union, and its implied recognition that economic union is desirable, the main policy decisions affecting economic conditions in Northern Ireland are made by the central government and apply indiscriminately to the whole of the United Kingdom; and, likewise, the main economic and financial institutions are common to the whole. Thus Northern Ireland and Great Britain are served by the one monetary and financial system and are both subject to the same monetary policy. Again, though Northern Ireland's fiscal system is not wholly common with that of Great Britain it is very largely so, and even where differences are formally permissible the scope for effective independent action by Northern Ireland is not very great in practice. Then again, social services are in all important respects on the same footing as those in Great Britain; for even though they are formally separate, economic integration is too close in other ways to permit of significant differences. Even more important, between Northern Ireland and Great Britain there is no restriction whatever on the passage of goods or the transfer of capital in either direction; and people are free to move from one to the other without let or hindrance and to live and work wherever they please.[1] Moreover, most of the other economic institutions, such as trade unions, trade associations and wage-fixing machinery, are either unified with those in Great Britain or are run on parallel lines; many of the trade unions, for example, are national bodies with their headquarters in England.

[1] Owing to the existence of heavy unemployment, the government of Northern Ireland has in recent years imposed a system of employment permits in certain occupations with the object of giving preference to local workers. But this restriction does not affect the migration of Northern Ireland workers to Great Britain or their subsequent return.

Because of this close integration, industrial growth and economic stability in Northern Ireland are subject to the same general conditions and the same general measures of control as they are in Great Britain. There is therefore a similar trend in economic development. But, as in other regions, production is largely concentrated in the kind of industries most suited to the particular environment; and since the economy of Northern Ireland is therefore not simply a small-scale model of that of Great Britain, important differences can also occur both in the rate of economic development and in the degree of economic stability. Differences do in fact occur mainly because the industries which have become traditionally established in Northern Ireland are very limited in range. It so happens that the pattern of industry suited to the environment is such that some of the general factors retarding growth, and some of those causing instability, tend to bear on Northern Ireland more heavily than they do on the British economy in general. In this respect the province is closely akin to the Development Areas in Great Britain— those areas in which the government gives special encouragement to industrial development because they contain pockets of unemployment. For, like the Development Areas, it is differentiated from the rest of the British economy by having a very specialised industrial structure and unemployment much above the average.

Northern Ireland is set apart from the Development Areas, and is further differentiated economically from Great Britain, by the fact that it is a separate area of subordinate government. It is thus in the unique position of having control over its own domestic affairs. This, however, is not to say that its economic differentiation from Great Britain would inevitably be less marked than it is if this constitutional difference did not exist: the pattern of industry would not necessarily be either more or less varied than it is, nor would the general economic state of the province necessarily be more satisfactory or less satisfactory. For, on the one hand, there is no reason in principle why a central government should feel itself debarred from singling out the problems of any particular area for separate treatment; indeed, the Development Areas have already been singled out in this way. On the other hand, while a provincial government might find the limitation of its powers a serious handicap in dealing effectively with certain provincial needs, a central government might be expected generally to be less well apprised of what the changing provincial needs are. It must therefore not be taken for granted, as something which is self-evident, that domestic autonomy has been a dominating factor in causing Northern Ireland's present economic position to be what it is. Nevertheless, the Government of Northern Ireland certainly does possess considerable powers of control over the rate and pattern of industrial growth and, as we shall see, it has in fact made a good deal of use of them. Hence, notwithstanding the difficulties, some attempt will be made to see how far the course of economic development has been due to the particular constitution, and how far it has been determined by the basic economic facts.

Provincial self-government has had an important indirect effect by focusing attention on the differences which exist between economic conditions in Northern Ireland, looked at in total, and those in the whole of the United Kingdom. Since the care of industrial development within its own borders is one of the provincial government's chief functions, governmental authorities and the public alike have had it thrust upon their notice that industrial growth in Northern Ireland is hampered by special difficulties, requiring special treatment, apart from those affecting the whole country. Separate statistical data relating to economic conditions in Northern Ireland, and bearing on those special problems, are therefore regularly collected and published. Although these data are disappointingly inadequate for a thorough study of the provincial economy, they do contain information not available for other regions of the United Kingdom. Moreover, apart from the official statistics, which are collected for the province as an entity because it is a separate area of government, certain other economic statistics relating to the whole region can be collected, more readily than for specific regions in Great Britain, because it is separated from them geographically. For these two reasons many of the data required in the study of economic conditions in Northern Ireland can be obtained even by the private investigator.

Economic conditions in Northern Ireland illustrate some of the main difficulties by which industrial development is hampered in the more outlying parts of the United Kingdom generally. It is therefore important that the factors responsible for these conditions should be understood, outside Northern Ireland as well as inside. For regional diversity within the United Kingdom is so pronounced that it may significantly affect the way in which some, at least, of the general economic measures work out on balance in the country as a whole. It is specially liable to distort the effects of measures for controlling the general level of employment. Modern employment theories, and the general policies based upon them, are largely derived from a consideration of the mutual dependence which exists between various aggregate quantities for the whole country. Thus budgetary policy (formulated with an eye to the effects on levels of income, prices and employment for the whole country) takes account of such entities as the total national income, total expenditure on consumption, total savings, total exports, imports and the balance of payments, and the total amount of investment (replacing and increasing the country's stock of capital goods) that would consequently be great enough to sustain a high level of employment without promoting a cumulative rise in prices. It is recognised that in any region or regions with persistently heavy unemployment investment in new industry may need to be given special encouragement. But in considering how much additional investment would be required at any time in order to give some desired fillip to total employment, it is implicitly assumed that the total effect would be the same whichever region received the initial stimulus of the investment. Although this is a natural assumption to make in the absence of greater knowledge than we at present possess about the factors governing employment in individual regions, it is one which obviously needs to be checked as soon as possible through regional studies.

Moreover, in deciding how best to bring about a desired increase in employment in any particular region in which there is heavy unemployment, as there is and always has been in Northern Ireland, it is important to know how employment (and income) in the region would respond to different stimuli. It is important, for example, to know how far employment (and income) would increase altogether if the government succeeded in bringing about an initial increase, of a given size, by inducing business men to establish new undertakings. Through the expenditure of the additional income associated with it, the direct increase in employment, in or for the new undertakings, would induce some secondary increase in employment (and income) in other industries; but compared with the initial increase this indirect increase might be large or small. It is therefore necessary to study the particular region, and its economic relations with other regions, in order to find out what is the normal ratio for it, between the direct effects on employment and income, caused by an increase in investment, and the direct and indirect effects taken together. It may be that, if the people of the region are very thrifty, induced effects are largely prevented through additional saving. Again, it may be (as it seems to be in Northern Ireland) that they are largely spilled over into other regions through the expenditure of much of the initial increase in income on goods imported from outside. If that is so, and if at the same time employment in the rest of the country is running at a very high level, investment in industrial undertakings in the particular region will not only be so much the less effective in raising the level of employment there, but will also aggravate the inflationary tendencies which will consequently exist in the economy as a whole. Likewise, in these conditions, the steps taken to curb general inflation will aggravate unemployment in the particular region. There seems no doubt that the monetary and fiscal policies of the early fifties have had effects of this kind on Northern Ireland. The inference is that the central government should supplement its general data for the whole country with regional studies; since, if it did, it might consider it undesirable to apply all general measures to the different regions indiscriminately.

That provincial self-government has not been extended to other parts of the United Kingdom might seem to imply that it has not worked well. Such an inference would be over-hasty. The system was devised for Northern Ireland not for economic reasons but as a political expedient, as part of the arrangements for settling the Irish constitutional question. In Great Britain it appears still to be regarded essentially in that light. At any rate the central government has shown no inclination to regard it as a serious experiment for testing how well this alternative technique for handling the economic problems of a region works in British conditions. Nevertheless, the control of internal economic matters (within its limited constitutional powers) is among the provincial government's most important functions. The question therefore arises whether, in economic matters, this form of government is more effective than control from the centre—and might with advantage be extended to other clearly-defined regions such as Scotland and Wales—or whether it is a handicap and should be abandoned even for Northern Ireland. There is also the important supplementary question whether in the light of experience there appear to be any significant respects in which the powers exercised by the provincial government could with advantage be modified. A full discussion of these questions would be out of place in a general work like the present, especially as it would involve detailed comparisons with other regions whose data would have to be specially collected and analysed; but some of the relevant considerations will be briefly touched upon in Chapter 7.

Since Northern Ireland is merely a sector of the British economy, subject to the same general conditions as the rest of the country, its economic position can best be discussed in relation to that of the United Kingdom in general. In what follows, therefore, the complex of external conditions and internal policies which are common to the whole will be taken for granted, and the discussion will be confined to the special economic problems and policies of Northern Ireland regarded as a region with limited powers of self-government. This means that the object will be to indicate the nature, causes and effects of those features of its economic structure which cause the trend of economic development to diverge somewhat from the common trend. Hence in assessing these various conditions in the economic life of the province the method will be to relate them to, and measure them against, their counterparts for either Great Britain or the United Kingdom as a whole, whichever is the more relevant in each particular case; for only in this way can their significance be judged.

The present chapter, on Northern Ireland's economic structure, will examine the main features of the provincial economy and their mutual dependence; in Chapter 7, on economic policy, an outline will be given of the provincial government's powers and the chief policies which it has pursued; some comments will be made on the effectiveness of these policies and on the possibilities of making use of other devices which formally come within its existing powers; and attention will be drawn to the possible need for enlarging its effective powers by making its financial relations with the central government more flexible and more liberal.

(a) *Area and Population.* Northern Ireland has an area of 5,238 square miles. At the time of the 1951 Population Census it had a population of 1,371,000. There was an average population density of 262 per square mile, compared with 755 per square mile in England and Wales and 172 in Scotland. Within Northern Ireland itself, however, the population is very unevenly distributed, about 53 per cent of the total living in urban areas. What is even more striking is that about two-fifths of the total are in Belfast and the surrounding towns and villages; a fact which emphasises that this compact region must play a highly important part in the social and economic life of the province. The age distribution of the population differs somewhat from that of Great Britain, partly, at least, because there is a somewhat higher rate of natural increase. Thus, at the 1951 Census, there was a smaller proportion of the population than in Great Britain (72·4 per cent compared with 77·5 per cent) who were over 15 years (i.e. of working age or above it) and a correspondingly higher proportion under 15. On the other hand, the difference in the proportion of the population gainfully occupied is small.

According to the Census figures the proportion of the total population gainfully occupied is practically the same as in Great Britain. On the one hand, the proportion gainfully occupied, taking males and females separately, is lower than in Great Britain in the main working-age group, 15-65. But, on the other hand, the proportion is considerably higher, for both sexes, in the age-group 65 and over; it is also higher in the age group under 15, since in Northern Ireland the school leaving-age is still 14.

Northern Ireland is an area from which there is a fairly large migration of people. Between 1926 and 1951 there was a net emigration of about 10 per cent of the total size of the population at the outset.

TABLE 1

NET LOSS (OR GAIN) BY MIGRATION PER 1,000 OF POPULATION

	Scotland	United Kingdom	Northern Ireland
1921–31 ..	−80	−15	−82
1931–39 ..	− 7	+11	− 4
1939–49 ..	−21	+ 4	−35

Source: Registrars-General.

Table 1 shows that, over the past three decades taken as a whole, emigration from the United Kingdom has been about balanced by immigration. By contrast, Scotland and Northern Ireland have both lost fairly heavily, the rate of loss in Northern Ireland being rather higher than in Scotland. Between 1926 and 1937 about one-third of the net loss was to European countries, including Great Britain—principally, no doubt, Great Britain. This net emigration to Great Britain (or continental Europe) during the eleven years taken together amounted in total to only about 20,000 people. But from estimates which we have made for the individual years, it appears that the annual net flow, in or out, was in most years quite large in comparison with the net movement during the whole period. The evidence goes to show that there is a fairly large mobile section of the population which moves to and fro between Northern Ireland and Great Britain in response to changing conditions of employment.

(b) *The Industrial Structure.* The industrial structure of Northern Ireland has three outstanding features. These are: firstly, the predominance of agriculture, which is by far the biggest single industry whether judged by the number of persons gainfully occupied or by the value of net output; secondly, the almost complete lack of extractive industries apart from agriculture; and, thirdly, the high degree of concentration of industrial workers in a very few industries. These features are shown up, with varying degrees of clarity, by the following table, which gives the industrial distribution of the 470,000 employees insured under the National Insurance Acts at May 1954.

Table 2 greatly underrates the real importance of agriculture since it covers only employees and not family workers. It is estimated that of the 603,000 persons gainfully occupied in Northern Ireland, almost 105,000

TABLE 2

INDUSTRIAL DISTRIBUTION OF INSURED WORKERS IN NORTHERN IRELAND AT MAY 1954

Industry	Percentage of all insured workers
Production:	
Agriculture	4·0
Forestry and fishing	0·4
Mining and quarrying	0·9
All production	5·3
Manufacture:	
Building and contracting	8·1
Treatment of non-metalliferous products (other than coal or oil)	0·9
Shipbuilding	3·6
Engineering	5·0
Vehicles	4·0
Linen	9·9
Other textiles	5·5
Clothing	7·6
Food, drink and tobacco	5·3
Manufactures of wood and cork	1·1
Paper and printing	1·2
Other manufacturing industries	1·6
All manufacturing industries	53·8
Services:	
All Service industries	40·8
Unclassified	0·1
Total	100·0

Source: Ministry of Labour.

or about one-sixth, are engaged in agriculture. This compares with about 5 per cent for the United Kingdom as a whole. As regards male labour the contrast is still more striking. At the Northern Ireland Census of 1951, 24 per cent of all gainfully occupied males were engaged in this industry, while the comparative figure for Great Britain, as shown by the Census of the same year, was only 6 per cent. But, as Table 2 shows, agriculture ranks among the most important industries of the province even when judged by the number of insured employees.

The predominant form of agricultural organisation in Northern

Ireland is the small farm worked mainly by the farmer and his family, and only calling on outside labour at busy seasons of the year. The Census of the Ministry of Agriculture taken at June 1952, for example, shows that, of the total of 145,000 persons gainfully occupied in agriculture in any capacity, paid workers formed less than one-sixth. Of late years the tendency has been for this proportion to fall. At the same time there has been a noticeable decrease in the amplitude of the seasonal variations in employment of insured agricultural workers. For the three years 1937–8 to 1939–40 the average amplitude of these seasonal variations, away from the employment trend, was about 29 per cent of the average volume of employment represented by the trend figures. For the years 1942–3 and 1943–4 the average variation was only 11 per cent of the trend. Although it has risen somewhat since the war it still lies well below the pre-war average; thus, for the three years 1947–8 to 1949–50, it was less than 20 per cent.

Small-scale farming is much more typical of agriculture in Northern Ireland than in Great Britain. In 1952, for example, 78 per cent of farms in Northern Ireland were under 50 acres in extent, compared with 64 per cent in Great Britain. At the other end of the scale, only 2·4 per cent of Northern Ireland farms were over 150 acres, compared with 12·1 per cent in Great Britain. In fact the contrast is even greater than these figures suggest. For "rough grazing" is excluded from the figures for Great Britain but is included in those for Northern Ireland. But even though the figures for Northern Ireland do contain this bias, the mean size of holding is only about 36 acres compared with 100 acres in Great Britain.

There are two other general points of contrast between farming in Northern Ireland and Great Britain apart from the size of holdings. Firstly, owing to such factors as the difference in soil fertility, the greater distance to the main British markets, and the smaller range of climatic differences, Northern Ireland has a different pattern of production and a smaller range of products. Because of these physical differences, the tendency has been towards proportionately more livestock farming than in Great Britain and proportionately less arable farming. The second point of contrast is that, by and large, Northern Ireland suffers from a deficiency, compared with Great Britain, in agricultural equipment. Although this relative deficiency cannot be accurately measured, it is well authenticated and has been officially stressed, as recently as 1947, in the Report of the Agricultural Inquiry Committee. In that report it was pointed out that, in many parts of Ulster to-day, farmers and labourers are working with implements which show little advance on those used a century ago. This comment refers more particularly to the position on the smaller farms, where the deficiency has been largely due to the farmers' lack of capital. Nevertheless, there has been a considerable increase in mechanisation of late, even on the smaller farms, especially since the beginning of the war. Between 1939 and 1945 the number of tractors increased ninefold, and there has been an increasing tendency for small farmers to make use of up-to-date equipment by getting work done on contract. However, the relative lack of equipment still persists. There is evidence for this in the greater number of persons per acre engaged in farming in Northern Ireland than in Great Britain. A strict comparison is not possible in this respect, both because of the greater proportion of part-time workers on Northern Ireland farms and also because of differences, noted above, in the composition of the total output. But even if only regular male workers are taken into account, the difference is still very marked. In 1951 there were 30·2 regular male workers per thousand acres in Northern Ireland, compared with 21·5 in Great Britain.

The dominance of agriculture in Northern Ireland is shown not only by the large share which it takes of the working population but also by the large proportionate contribution which it makes to the total income. We estimate that in 1951 the total income earned by all persons gainfully occupied on farms was £37·6 million, or 17 per cent of the total private civilian income of the province. In the United Kingdom in the same year the corresponding proportion amounted to about 6 per cent. In view of the much greater dependence of the population on agriculture in Northern Ireland than in the United Kingdom as a whole, both for employment and income, it is not surprising that the provincial government has made special efforts to increase agricultural income. As we shall see in Chapter 7, it has done so by improving both the standard of husbandry and the methods of marketing the produce.

The second important feature of the industrial structure indicated by the distribution of man-power in Table 2 is the small proportion of the total engaged in extractive industries. The reason is that there are no important mineral deposits that can be profitably worked. Although small deposits of coal are to be found here and there, they are all unworkable (except on a very small scale in one or two places) because of severe faulting. The chief products of the mining and quarrying industry are limestone, sand, gravel, road metal and granite. These provide materials for the building and construction industries and for the manufacture of cement and bricks, though not in sufficient quantities to provide for all the needs of the province. The lack of domestic sources of coal and of the principal minerals required in the basic heavy industries is one of the greatest handicaps to industrial development, It greatly narrows the range of industries which can be profitably carried on in the province—in particular, the range of industries which employ men. At the same time, by raising the cost of power to all industries, it reduces the profitability, and hence the vitality, of those industries which are nevertheless able to take root.

Owing to these effects, the lack of mineral resources is itself one of the main reasons for the third distinctive feature of the industrial structure—namely, the concentration of a large proportion of the workers in a very few industries. Another important reason for this specialisation on a few industries is that the domestic market for many varieties of goods is too small to permit of production on a profitable scale unless part of the output can be exported, either to Great Britain or abroad. Production even for the local market therefore tends to be limited to goods which, being light and valuable in proportion to their bulk, can compete successfully in Great Britain—that is, to light industries with comparatively low costs of transport. The textile industries form the most important group, accounting for about 30 per cent of the total number of workers engaged in manufacturing. Another unified group consists of engineering, vehicle building and repairing, and shipbuilding. This group provides employment for about another 20 per cent of the total. Thus the two groups, each composed of closely related industries, together employ about half the total workers engaged in manufacture. A feature of the two groups is that from the point of view of employment they are complementary rather than competitive. In the textile group almost two-thirds of the workers are women, while in the engineering, vehicle and shipbuilding group there is a preponderance of men.

For purposes of comparison we have roughly classified manufacturing trades into two groups, according to whether they produce instrumental goods or consumption goods. The industrial subdivisions used by the Ministry of Labour are not detailed enough to enable this to be done accurately. But it appears that about one-third of all insured male workers in Northern Ireland are employed in instrumental trades. This figure represents about two-thirds of the total males insured in manufacturing industries, which is a substantially higher proportion than in Great Britain. The industrial distribution of insured women workers, on the other hand, is very different. Slightly more than half of the total (or 90 per cent of those insured in manufacturing) are engaged in consumption-goods industries.

These facts indicate much of the weakness in Northern Ireland's industrial structure. Since industries producing capital goods are subject to wider variations in employment than consumption industries and services, depression tends to strike Northern Ireland with unusual severity, causing heavy unemployment, particularly among men. Moreover, though most of the female workers are employed in consumption-goods industries, this does not have as great a stabilising effect as might be expected *à priori*. The reason is that employment in this group is heavily concentrated on a few industries which do not enjoy as much stability as most consumption industries, particularly those producing necessaries for a sheltered home market. For the goods produced are largely of a luxury or semi-luxury type, and a large proportion of the output has to be exported. Easily the most outstanding industry in this group is the linen industry. This industry alone employs about three-eighths of all the women engaged in manufacture, and if we include in the linen industry the making up of linen goods, the proportion is still higher. The industry has experienced the usual fluctuations of employment associated with textiles; but since linen is one of the more expensive fabrics, and since Northern Ireland specialises in the finer grades of linen, the demand is subject to greater variations than is the demand for textiles in general.

(c) *Dependence on Exports.* An important result of the high degree of specialisation on a few manufacturing trades is that economic prosperity is to a very great extent dependent on external trade. For the provincial markets of the three main industries—agriculture, textiles, and shipbuilding and engineering—and of others making very specialised products, only absorb a small proportion of their total output; and the surplus has to be sold outside the province, as a means, in effect, of paying for imports into it. Official estimates are made of the quantities and value of goods exported annually to all places outside Northern Ireland's own borders; but because of differences in the way in which these external-trade statistics and those of the Census of Production are grouped it is impossible to estimate with any precision, what proportion of Northern Ireland's own production is thus exported. From an examination of the figures it appears, however, that the goods exported from Northern Ireland embody between 60 and 70 per cent of the value of the total net output of goods produced in the province.

Whatever their final destination, most of these exports are sent initially to Great Britain. Some go there as sales to merchants, others as consignments on their way to foreign purchasers. Many of those which are sold in the first instance in Great Britain are eventually exported to destinations outside the United Kingdom by the export houses which buy them. But exports of Northern Irish goods to places outside the United Kingdom (exports in the international as distinct from the interregional sense) cannot be ascertained, at any rate not from published statistics. On the one hand, few direct exports to places outside the United Kingdom are recorded in Northern Ireland's own trade statistics. For few foreign-going ships call at Northern Ireland ports—fewer, indeed, than before the war, a fact which has weakened Northern exporters relatively to their competitors in Great Britain. On the other hand, exports passing through Great Britain, even those consigned to foreign countries, cannot be distinguished from goods produced in Great Britain itself, since in the trade statistics of the United Kingdom exports are classified according to port of shipment. Though exports across the land border with Eire are recorded separately, they include re-exports of goods produced in Great Britain. Hence for an indication of the importance of exports abroad it is helpful to supplement the official statistics by private inquiries. According to a small sample inquiry among business men which we made in 1946, exports to foreign countries accounted for about 45 per cent of the total output of linen and for about 40 per cent of that of engineering products.

The great dependence of Northern Ireland's chief industries on markets outside its own borders has important consequences for the stability of both employment and total income. Between exports and employment there is a direct physical relation. So much of the total production is for export that one would expect an increase in the physical volume of exports to be associated, either as cause or effect, with an increase in employment, and a decrease in exports to be associated with a decrease in employment. One would likewise expect exports and unemployment to be correlated inversely. When the three series are compared with each other over a period—we have examined them for the period since 1924—the expected relationships are clearly discernible, notwithstanding the many conflicting forces which tend to obscure them.

The dependence of total money income on the total value of exports (including those to Great Britain) stands out even more clearly. A comparison which we have made of the two series for the period since 1935 shows that, notwithstanding the great change that has occurred in money values in the meantime, the ratio of the value of exports to money income has been remarkably stable both from year to year and over the whole period: total income has generally been a little more than half as great again as the value of exports. It is not surprising that there should be a fairly close relationship between the value of exports and income earned in producing for export. What is noteworthy is that there has also been a fairly constant ratio between the value of exports and total income, and therefore between the value of exports and income earned in producing and supplying goods and services for the domestic market. In other words, variations in income earned in export production have generally been accompanied by roughly similar proportional variations in income earned in producing for the home market.

Such changes in the volume and value of exports, together with the associated changes in income and thence imports, are the media through which alterations in economic conditions, either in Great Britain or abroad, are transmitted to Northern Ireland; they are the means by which the provincial balance of payments is kept in equilibrium. When a change in external conditions reduces the amount of income earned in the production of goods sold outside the province, the balance of external payments is equilibrated through a reduction in total income sufficient to bring down imports to a level at which they can be paid for by the reduced value of exports. This adverse effect may be partly offset through an increase in industrial efficiency stimulated by the resulting fall in the rate of profit. In so far as it is not, the reduction in income required to effect the necessary reduction in imports may be brought about either through a fall in rates of wages and profits—relatively to those in Great Britain—or through a relative increase in unemployment.

This explains how Northern Ireland's great dependence on external markets (both for getting raw materials and selling finished goods) acted as a major cause of its depressed state during the period between the wars. It explains the operation of one of the principal sets of forces responsible for the greater severity of the depression in Northern Ireland than in Great Britain. The unemployment rate among insured workers in Northern Ireland was substantially greater than the annual average for Great Britain in every single year throughout the interwar period—and, indeed, it has consistently maintained a higher level right down to the present time. In the very first year for which statistics for Northern Ireland were collected separately, 1923, it averaged almost 18 per cent, whereas in Great Britain it was only about 12 per cent. Though the divergence has tended to be rather smaller in years of comparatively light unemployment than in the worst years, it has been quite appreciable even in the best of times. Thus in 1927 the annual unemployment rate was lower than in any other year from 1923 right down to the early years of the war, and yet it only fell to 13 per cent compared with 9 per cent in Great Britain. In 1938, one of Northern Ireland's worst years of unemployment on record, the divergence was much greater, the corresponding percentages being 28 and 13. The average amount by which the annual average rate for Northern Ireland *exceeded* that for Great Britain during the years 1923–39, taking the simple arithmetic averages of the annual rates, works out at an unemployment percentage of 8·5. During the interwar period the unemployment rate was substantially higher than in any of the Ministry of Labour's administrative regions in Great Britain with the exception of Wales. Since the war it has been substantially higher than in Wales also. Notwithstanding the great reduction in unemployment throughout the whole of the United Kingdom since 1939, the differential rate in Northern Ireland has continued to be fairly high; from 1945 to 1952 it averaged between 5 and 6 per cent. The pre-war figures of unemployment for Northern Ireland—as, indeed, those of other relatively depressed areas—may in some years have been swollen by the inclusion of returning migrants who were last employed in other regions. For, under the reciprocal arrangements relating to unemployment insurance, unemployed workers may draw their insurance benefit at any employment exchange, at which they are registered, anywhere within the United Kingdom. Considerable numbers of workers do, in fact, migrate from Northern Ireland to jobs in Great Britain, and when trade becomes slack many of them return to their homes in Northern Ireland and register as unemployed there.

(*d*) *Transport Costs.* Where there is neither undue harshness of climate nor deficiency of people willing to work and capable of working efficiently, the problem of location of industry tends to resolve itself into a problem of transport. As we have pointed out above, Northern Ireland is highly dependent on its external trade because of the limited size of the home market and the need to import a high proportion of the raw materials used. In comparison with competing firms in Great Britain, producers in Northern Ireland therefore tend to be at a twofold disadvantage. The extra cost of transport on raw materials, over and above the amount paid by competitors in Great Britain, tends to make their costs of production relatively high; while the corresponding extra cost of transporting the finished goods to market tends to make the net price obtained—the price at the factory—relatively low. This narrowing of the gross margin means that, unless the efficiency of industry in Northern Ireland is maintained at a higher level than in Great Britain, less will be available for distribution among the various factors engaged in production.

The full extent of the transport disadvantage is hard to gauge. On some materials that are imported from abroad the difference is slight or non-existent. This is so where the price of the materials includes transport to any British port. In a few instances materials produced in Great

Britain are consigned to manufacturers throughout the United Kingdom at a uniform price, the transport charges being in effect pooled. But in most cases the additional transport cost to Northern Ireland has to be borne by the producers. Coal is a most important example, since in one form or another it enters into the costs of nearly all manufactures. In the linen industry the average cost per ton of the coal actually used in 1935 (still the last year for which these figures for Northern Ireland and Great Britain can be compared) was about 43 per cent higher than the corresponding average in Great Britain; in textile finishing it was 36 per cent higher than the average cost in the same industry in Great Britain; in engineering it was 29 per cent higher; in gas production 14 per cent higher, and in electricity generation 20 per cent higher.[1] The greater the importance of coal in comparison with the value of the net output of the goods concerned—i.e. the value added to the raw materials by the work done on them in Northern Ireland—the more significant are these percentage differences in raising the total costs of the goods. Thus the effect of the additional cost of coal is to restrict industrial development, so far as unsheltered production is concerned, to those industries in which the proportion of coal costs to the value of net output is low. In some industries, it is true, the additional cost amounts to upwards of 10 per cent of the value of net output. But, in general, such large differences in total cost make production in Northern Ireland impossible except in industries which produce wholly for the local market, are thoroughly sheltered from outside competition, and are therefore able to charge higher prices to cover the extra costs. There is no doubt that this factor dictates a very strict limit to the range of unsheltered industries which it is profitable to locate in Northern Ireland. In all the industries which have developed on a fairly large scale—notably linen, engineering and ship-building—the cost of coal forms such a small proportion of total costs that the extra cost of it in Northern Ireland amounts to a fairly insignificant percentage of the value of net output—in none to more than 2 per cent and in some to much less.[2]

Outward transport costs vary greatly according to the class of goods and their packing qualities. In most of the unsheltered industries which have thriven in Northern Ireland, the actual freight charges form only a small percentage of the selling value of the goods—often less than 1 per cent. But there are some industries which have managed to survive even though their outward freight charges exceed those paid by manufac-

---

[1] Source: Census of Production, United Kingdom, 1935.

[2] It is difficult to compare the transport costs on raw materials other than coal, because the data in the Census of Production (1935) are not sufficiently defined.

turers of the same products in Great Britain by as much as 8 to 10 per cent of the selling price. On the other hand, on some products the total outward transport charge is under 0·5 per cent. In addition to the direct charges, however, the packing of the goods in such a way as to enable them to survive the risks of cross-channel transport is often a sizeable item in itself. For this reason the introduction since the war of a ferry service capable of dealing with loaded road vehicles has meant a considerable saving to many manufacturers. Even so, the handicap due to distance from the main markets in Great Britain is intensified by the handling costs and damage of goods in transit, and there is room for improvement in port facilities.

So far as can be judged, internal transport charges do not differ greatly from those for similar hauls in Great Britain. Both rail and road transport rates are controlled by the Transport Tribunal provided for in the Transport Act (Northern Ireland) 1948. In sharp contrast is the lack of control over the rates and charges for cross-channel shipping services. These are fixed by the Chamber of Shipping, a body which is composed of members of the industry and which effectively prevents competition on the basis of rates.

(e) *Wage Rates*. Where transport costs are higher than for competing industries in Great Britain, the difference is generally taken into account in wage-bargaining, as a reason for a somewhat lower wage than in Great Britain. Though, in general, wages tend to be rather lower than in Great Britain, they are by no means uniformly so. In some industries skilled workers are paid at rates higher than the average rates paid to similar workers in Great Britain, while the wages of unskilled workers are generally lower. In occupations in which wage rates are lower, the differential is greater, as a rule, for women than for men. During the war and early post-war years the percentage margin between wage rates in Northern Ireland and Great Britain tended to become narrower. A wage index which we have calculated for Northern Ireland (on a comparable basis to that of the official index for the United Kingdom) shows a rise between September 1939 and May 1948 of 100 per cent. The rise in the United Kingdom as a whole during the same period was 75 per cent. Since 1948 the two indexes have risen at about the same rate. One reason for the faster rise in the index for Northern Ireland is that agricultural wages, which form a larger proportion of the total than in Great Britain, rose from their very low starting-point in 1939 more rapidly than industrial wages. But another and important reason is that there also occurred a considerable decline in the differential in industrial wage rates themselves.

I

Northern Ireland's future industrial prosperity may well depend on the exercise of wage restraint. In the absence of higher productivity, complete wage equality with Great Britain could, in adverse conditions, ruin the competitive position of many of its industries. The danger here is that trade unions, many of which have their headquarters in Great Britain, may be over-zealous in getting and preserving parity; they may, in doing so, undermine the economy by stifling new investment. It is fairly clear that the reduction which has occurred in the differential in wage rates during the past decade has not been so damaging to employment in Northern Ireland as it might have been if employment in Great Britain had been less buoyant. For many firms in Great Britain, owing to the greater scarcity of labour there, have to pay more of their workers at overtime rates, and have to offer more generous scales of bonus payments (than are paid in Northern Ireland) as a means of retaining their workers; so that the additional labour cost there is probably a good deal greater than the difference in wage rates. But if selling becomes difficult an increase in the wage difference may be the only way of maintaining Northern Ireland's competitive position.

The fundamental reason why rates of wages, particularly those of unskilled workers and women, have tended generally to be lower than in Great Britain is that the supply of labour has been (and still is) more plentiful than in Great Britain in relation to the demand; or, to express the difference the other way round, the demand has been weaker than in Great Britain in relation to the supply. This contrast was even more marked before the war than it is now. On the one hand, because of the natural handicaps already mentioned, industrial employment did not increase as fast as in Great Britain. On the other hand, workers generally were unwilling to migrate to Great Britain, in search of work there, merely because rates of pay in Northern Ireland were lower and unemployment was heavier; some workers did migrate, particularly from among the unemployed, but not enough of them did so to bring down the unemployment rate, and raise wages, to equality with Great Britain.

During the early years of the war, however, when war needs were causing the demand for labour to increase generally throughout the kingdom, employment expanded a good deal faster and farther, proportionately, than in Great Britain, since there was more slack in the form of unemployment to take up. This was the main reason for the tendency for wage rates in Northern Ireland to catch up with those in Great Britain. But there were also contributory causes operating from the side of the workers. In particular, though the regulations governing the wartime direction of labour did not apply officially to Northern

Ireland, the Ministry of Labour co-operated effectively with the Ministry of Labour in Great Britain, and many thousands of workers were placed in jobs in Great Britain through its agency and were given financial assistance in getting to their places of work there. In addition, many workers migrated to jobs in Great Britain on their own account. The resulting decrease in the supply of labour in Northern Ireland, compared with what it would have been otherwise, enabled the trade unions to bargain more effectively for higher wages.

The strengthening of the bargaining power of the workers due to this cause, and the resulting tendency for wage rates to rise faster than in Great Britain, has been reinforced by the agricultural and food policy adopted by the United Kingdom as a means of dealing with the general food shortage.[1] For this policy tended to cause a greater rise in the cost of living in Northern Ireland than in Great Britain. It did so because of the arrangement under which the Ministry of Food, in order to stimulate the production and to control the distribution of rationed foods, bought the main agricultural products at uniform prices throughout the kingdom, accepting delivery in the various agricultural districts, and also, through the medium of distributors, sold at uniform (and lower) prices to consumers. Before the introduction of this system the surplus produced in Northern Ireland above local requirements had to be sold in Great Britain at whatever price it would fetch there. Hence, under competitive conditions, the local price was forced down below the price in the principal markets in Great Britain, by the amount of the direct and indirect costs of transport from the place of production in Northern Ireland. This price differential was, indeed, an important cause of the pre-war disparity in wage rates, since it was generally recognised that workers in Northern Ireland *pro tanto* had the advantage of a lower cost of living. By removing the differential, the system of uniform agricultural prices tended to reduce real wage rates in Northern Ireland compared with those in Great Britain, and by so doing it tended to promote a greater rise than in Great Britain in money wage rates.

(*f*) *Output per worker.* The obstacles which natural conditions have put in the way of industrial development in Northern Ireland show their effects in practically every aspect of the economy. Directly, they take the form of a lack of indigenous raw materials and a remoteness from markets; and indirectly, in consequence, they exert a powerful control over the industrial structure—both the pattern of industry and the technique of production—and also over the rate of industrial growth and the level of incomes. Since they involve for most industries some

[1] *Cf.* below, chapter 7 (*a*).

additional transport costs above those borne by the same industries in Great Britain, they tend to confine industrial growth to a fairly narrow range of light industries requiring a comparatively small investment of capital per worker and a large number of women in proportion to men. Average wages earned per worker are lower than in Great Britain partly for this very reason—that women form a substantially larger proportion of the labour force—but also because rates of pay themselves tend to be rather lower and because the lack of heavy industries means that there are proportionately fewer of the high-wage jobs. No doubt rates of profit on the average are affected in a like manner, but it is impractical to verify this point statistically.

These and other adverse effects of Northern Ireland's natural industrial handicaps show themselves collectively in the difference, between the province and the United Kingdom as a whole, in the average value of net output per person engaged in manufacturing industries. It is therefore instructive to compare net output in Northern Ireland and the United Kingdom, in order to see how great the difference is on the average and how far it is due to a difference in industrial structure and how far to other causes.

The average value of net output per employee, measured over the whole of industry covered by the 1949 Census of Production, was £515 in the United Kingdom and £369 in Northern Ireland. Thus the value of net output per employee in Northern Ireland was only 73 per cent of that for the United Kingdom as a whole. But when a comparison is made of the individual trade-groups the difference is not so great as it appears when output is looked at in total. In only nine trade-groups out of thirty-nine was the figure for Northern Ireland lower than 73 per cent of that for the United Kingdom, and these nine together accounted for about 5 per cent of the total employment covered by the Census. The result looks worse in total than in the individual trade-groups because these groups are very differently weighted (according to their employment) from what they are in the United Kingdom. In Northern Ireland, because of the natural disadvantages already discussed, there is a greater tendency to specialise on industries in which there is no need for enormously heavy and expensive capital equipment and in which, in consequence, the value of net output per head is fairly low.

We can get an idea of how much of the difference in the average net output per head was due to Northern Ireland's different pattern of industry by calculating what its average per head would have been if—net output per head in each separate industry being what it was—the workers had been distributed between the different industries in the same

proportion as in the United Kingdom: that is, by weighting the net output in each of Northern Ireland's industries in accordance with the relative sizes of these industries in the United Kingdom as a whole. We
cannot in this way allow for industries not represented in Northern
Ireland at all—some of them high-productivity industries—or for
Northern Ireland industries which did not possess true counterparts in
Great Britain. But taking the 39 trades which can be compared, the
effect of the reweighting process is to raise the average value of new output in these trades from 72 per cent of that of the United Kingdom to
77 per cent. This suggests that Northern Ireland's greater concentration
on industries with a low value of net output accounts for only a minor
part of the difference in the average value of net output over all industry.
But the full effect is not shown by these figures. For it appears that
Northern Ireland tends to concentrate, more than the United Kingdom
as a whole, on low-productivity industries within each trade-group. An
adjustment based on a finer subdivision of industries, in the limited
number of trade-groups which it is possible to break up for this purpose,
shows that some part of the remaining disparity can be explained in
this way.[1]

But there are other differences between the province and the kingdom
which must also be taken into account. It has already been shown that
transport costs both on raw materials and on the finished goods, in
excess of those borne by the same trades in Great Britain, have the
effect of reducing the value of net output per head. We must also bear in
mind that relatively few of Northern Ireland's industries are engaged
in the production of goods bearing trade marks which give them a distinct and secure market to themselves. In industries which do produce
such goods there are specific selling costs, particularly advertising costs,
and—if these accomplish their purpose—also high profits; and the
value of net output is inflated on both counts. In Northern Ireland, on
the contrary, a very large part of the total output of manufactured goods
is sold in highly competitive markets by comparatively small producing
units which have no power to charge a price much above production
costs.[2] In the linen industry, for example, the many individual producers
in Northern Ireland not only compete keenly among themselves, but in
addition have to sell their wares in competition both with linen manufactured abroad and with other fabrics. In other industries the position
is similar. The goods are sold on the basis of high quality and low price,

[1] *Cf.* Leser, *Journal of the Royal Statistical Society*, Part II, 1950.
[2] An examination of the Report of the Census of Production of 1949 shows that,
in thirty-five trade-groups represented in Northern Ireland, the average size of firm

not on that of expensive advertising and monopolistic control. Moreover, in many trades, owing to the lack of coal and minerals, only the less-capitalistic stages of production are carried on in Northern Ireland, and in these the value of net output per head is generally lower than in those which require a large amount of capital per worker. Finally, as noted above, most of the industries which can be carried on profitably in Northern Ireland employ a large proportion of women, who earn low wages compared with men and who consequently depress the average value of net output per worker.

It follows from what has just been said that it would be quite wrong to attribute the disparity between Northern Ireland and the United Kingdom, in average value of net output per worker (often loosely called productivity), to a difference between them in the average efficiency of the workers. If such a difference in efficiency does exist, it is not indicated by these figures, still less measured by them. The best guide to the relative efficiency of labour as such is the opinion of industrialists who have had experience as employers in Great Britain as well as Northern Ireland. We have personally discussed the question with a considerable number of employers of this kind. All those whom we have asked have been unanimous in their answers. Their experience is that, once workers in Northern Ireland have been trained for the specific work which they are to do, they are in every respect as efficient as workers in Great Britain in the main centres of the particular industries concerned, and, in addition, they are generally more adaptable, have more aptitude for improvisation, and show a greater willingness to work.

(g) *Income per Head.* A useful index of the level of economic prosperity in Northern Ireland compared with that in the United Kingdom as a whole is the relative volume of the income flow in the two regions, a flow which, for this purpose, can most conveniently be represented by the average amount of income per head. It must be emphasised, however, that income statistics are principally of use in observing the direction and causes of change, through time, in economic conditions and welfare within the country to which they refer, not in comparing the level of economic welfare in different countries, or even different regions of the same country; they are mainly useful as a guide to domestic policy. Comparisons between the level of income in different countries are notoriously difficult to interpret correctly. If the countries compared are

---

(measured by the number of workers) was in general much smaller than in Great Britain. This was not true, however, of a few of the individual trades, namely, timber, building and contracting, bread and cake baking, linen and hemp, and tailoring and dressmaking.

very different from each other in their industrial structure—and hence in the composition of total production and income—or if for this or other reasons the money prices of the goods which they produce are not brought into very close relation with each other and with those in other countries, the comparative figures of money income per head may give a false impression of the comparative level of real income. This difficulty is encountered even when comparing Northern Ireland with the United Kingdom as a whole. The most awkward complication is due to the much greater relative importance of farming than in Great Britain. For in Northern Ireland, as in every country, agricultural incomes, as measured in money, are lower than industrial incomes; and yet it is not clear that real incomes are lower in anything like the same proportion. Hence, in comparing the figures of total money income in Northern Ireland and the United Kingdom, we must not take them as being strictly accurate; in particular we must bear in mind that, for the reason stated, the figures for Northern Ireland probably underestimate its comparative position. There is a further reason, however, for keeping the comparison broad in the present case; namely, that there are no official estimates of income for Northern Ireland. We have therefore had to make our own estimates, and in doing so have been forced to indulge in even bolder assumptions than generally have to be made in compiling official statistics.

Owing to the type of statistics on which we have had to depend, the last year for which an estimate can at present be made is 1951. In that year total Private Civilian Income, on our estimates, was approximately £250 million.[1] This amounted to 1·85 per cent of the corresponding Private Civilian Income of the United Kingdom, the latter being adjusted to allow for certain items that could not be separately estimated for Northern Ireland. Expressing the total income as an average income per head of the civilian population, the comparative figures were £182 for Northern Ireland and £267 for the United Kingdom; which means that the average for Northern Ireland was only about 68 per cent of that for the United Kingdom. Taking 1938 as the base year, since it was the last full year before the war began, we find that by 1951 income per head in the United Kingdom had risen by about 150 per cent, whereas in Northern Ireland it had risen by over 200 per cent. Hence the two outstanding facts about income per head in Northern Ireland, as shown up by the comparison, are: firstly, that it is appreciably lower than the average for the United Kingdom; and, secondly, that since the beginning of the war

---

[1] For details and methods of calculation, see article by Norman Cuthbert in *Journal of the Statistical Society of Ireland*, 1951.

it has grown at a somewhat faster rate. These facts are indicative of the extent to which Northern Ireland differs economically from the United Kingdom as a whole, and of the relative changes that have occurred since just before the war.

The relative improvement in income per head in Northern Ireland has been due, in the main, to the very factors which have caused the increase in income per head in the United Kingdom as a whole during the same period—factors which have affected the whole economy but some regions more than others. Owing to the great increase entailed in the demand for goods and services of all kinds throughout the whole economy, the level of employment has risen to the point at which labour has become generally scarce. For this reason the percentage rise in employment, and therefore in income, has tended to be greatest in those regions which, at the outset, had the highest percentage of unemployed workers on whom to draw. Northern Ireland at the outset had more slack of this kind than any other region. In 1938, our base year for the comparison, the annual average unemployment rate was nearly 30 per cent, which was even higher than in 1931. With the great increase in industrial activity during the war, wage rates rose faster and farther (from their somewhat lower starting-point) than in Great Britain, and profits also rose steeply. At the same time, the policy of uniform agricultural prices, by transferring the cost of transport to the Ministry of Food, raised farmers' incomes more than it did those in Great Britain.

But in spite of the relative improvement since 1938, income per head is still considerably lower than the average of the United Kingdom, and there does not appear to be any factor in operation which is likely to raise it to the average in the near future. The industrial handicaps due to the climate, the lack of fuel and other raw materials, and the remoteness of the chief British markets, are hard facts to overcome.

CHAPTER 6

DEVOLUTION AND PUBLIC FINANCE

By THOMAS WILSON

1. THE establishment of a regional Parliament such as that of Northern Ireland raises at once a number of difficult and important financial questions. The new assembly, wide though its powers may be within the province, can have no say in such matters as foreign policy or defence to which the term "Imperial Services" is usually applied, for we are dealing here with devolution, not dominion status, and these services must remain with Westminster. Thus the work of government is shared between two Parliaments, and the people so governed can be required to contribute on an equitable basis to both. It is here that the difficulties begin. The taxes collected in, say, Yorkshire go into the exchequer pool from which come both the funds to be spent on common Imperial purposes and those to be spent locally in each county; there is no question of dividing up the taxes paid by Yorkshire between such items of expenditure as warships on the one hand and, on the other, the health services provided by Westminster for the benefit of the people in Yorkshire. But it is obviously a different matter when there are two Parliaments. Both have some claim on the revenue of the province, and means must be found of sharing it that will be "fair"—in some sense of the word—to the two claimants. Now it is here that devolution in Northern Ireland is often held to have been a failure.

The complaint that Northern Ireland is subsidised has been made repeatedly since the new Parliament came into existence. In its more extreme form the argument amounts to saying that the little state of Northern Ireland is a foolish and artificial creation that can be kept alive at all only by the injection of powerful subsidies from Great Britain. This is described as the cost of partition, but not very convincingly, for even if it were true that Ulster was helped in this way by London, it would not follow that in a united Ireland subsidies would be unnecessary to maintain comparable public services; on the contrary, there may be reasons for believing that the Province would be worse off[1] if separated from Great Britain, and subsidies would still be needed—but would clearly not be provided by the other twenty-six counties which are poorer

[1] *Cf.* chapter 8 on "Economic Policy", by K. S. Isles and N. Cuthbert, especially p. 181.

than the North. Indeed the upshot of the argument, if followed through as it rarely is to the end, would be that Ireland, whether united as a republic or divided as at present, cannot maintain unaided public services on the British scale. But the assertion with which the argument begins is fortunately untrue: it is not the case that Westminster has had to make continuous subventions to Stormont to keep the Parliament going; taking one year with another, the Ulster taxpayers have not only paid in full for their own devolved services but have made a net contribution to the cost of the Imperial services as well.[1]

Much more serious is the argument that, although Ulster may have contributed on balance to Imperial expenditure, she has done so on far too small a scale. If not actually subsidised with regard to her domestic expenditure, she has not, so it is held, fulfilled her obligation as part of the United Kingdom to pay a fair share of the common costs of government. This, it must be noted, is not merely an extreme republican argument; it seems to be accepted by people who are far from being republicans.

Ulster contributes much less per head to Imperial expenditure than does Great Britain as a whole. That must be conceded at once. But is it proper to infer that the Province is therefore defaulting on its obligations as part of the United Kingdom and thus, in an indirect way, receiving a subsidy? The answer must surely be in the negative, for it is not true that equity requires equal contributions irrespective of the conditions of the contributors. Equity means that like should be treated as like, and that is a very different matter. In discussing financial relations between Scotland and the rest of Great Britain, the Cato Committee was careful to point out that a lower contribution per head to Imperial expenditure would not necessarily mean that Scotland was being improperly subsidised,[2] and the same conclusion applies to Northern Ireland which, notwithstanding its local Parliament, is as much a part of the United Kingdom as Scotland or Wales, or England herself. In a modern State where, on the one hand, progressive taxation and, on the other, expenditure on local purposes according to need are accepted as canons of public finance, an area can be described as subsidised only if it receives some peculiar benefits that allow it to make a smaller net Imperial contribution than other areas would have to make if their level of prosperity were the same. This is the definition of a subsidy from which we shall start. Is there, then, any reason to suppose that Northern Ireland is sub-

---

[1] There have been *individual* years of which this was not true, but it is true taking one year with another.

[2] Cmd. 8609, para. 219.

sidised in this sense of the term? The present chapter will be largely concerned with this question and further statistical evidence will be advanced by Robson in an appendix. It will be seen that Ulster has made a somewhat larger net contribution to the Imperial Services than equity would strictly require—larger, perhaps, than would have been made if the Province had not been given its own Parliament.

The view that Ulster is subsidised is without foundation, but there are some other financial questions which, if less closely related to the debate on partition and therefore less politically exciting, are nevertheless of basic importance in trying to decide whether devolution has been a success. The first question is whether the powers of expenditure and taxation accorded to Stormont have led to a harmful conflict of policies with Westminster; this, it will be appreciated, is part of a broader issue. Within the field of public finance, great harm could clearly be done if the two governments were pulling in opposite directions. Moreover, even if a major conflict were in the end avoided, petty friction between the two governments is an obvious danger, and relations could become particularly strained in negotiating the allocation of public funds between their respective responsibilities. On general grounds the danger is undeniably a real one, but it can be said at once that it appears to have been successfully averted in the case of Northern Ireland. The policies adopted by Stormont have not conflicted in any harmful way with those of Westminster, and the financial negotiations between the two governments appear to have been smooth and harmonious—even when there were Socialists in power at Westminster and Unionists at Stormont, as Sayers has observed.[1] Stormont's budgetary proposals are discussed each year with the Treasury before being presented, and a report is submitted to a Joint Exchequer Board; for many years this Board has not been called upon to exercise its statutory power to settle any matters that may be in dispute, a clear indication that the machinery has worked smoothly.

The second question is whether the financial arrangements are such as to allow Stormont to make sufficient use of the independent powers conferred by devolution. This, in a sense, is the opposite danger to the one we have just discussed, and for my own part I do not feel that quite such a confident answer can be given. The question will occupy the latter part of the chapter, and we need not anticipate what is said.

The last question to be raised now—and one which will not hereafter be discussed in this chapter—is whether devolution adds significantly to the costs of government. The view that the local parliament is a costly

[1] Chapter 3.

extravagance seems to be firmly held by most people in Ulster, whether Protestant or Catholic, Loyalist or Republican, and complaints are constantly made about the burden of taxation. Such complaints are very natural and indeed very proper—but dislike of the tax-collector is by no means a peculiar Ulster characteristic! The vast bulk of the taxes collected in Ulster, as elsewhere, go to pay for the social services, education, defence and the like, and devolution in itself will add to the burden

TABLE 1

REVENUE IN 1952–53

TRANSFERRED REVENUE		£ million
Tax revenue:		
Estate, etc. Duties	2·2	
Stamp Duties	0·7	
Excise Duties	1·0	
Motor Vehicle Duties, etc	1·6	
	5·4	
Non-tax revenue (land annuities, interest, etc.) ..	2·4	
Total transferred revenue		7·8
RESERVED REVENUE		
Tax revenue:		
Customs and Excise	23·9	
Purchase Tax	5·6	
Income and Sur-Tax	26·3	
Profits Tax ⎫	6·2	
Excess Profits Tax ⎭		
Other Inland Revenue	0·1	
	62·1	
Non-Tax revenue (Post Office, etc.)	3·5	
Total Reserved Revenue		65·6
TOTAL REVENUE		73·4

(Note: Minor inaccuracies have been caused by rounding up the figures.)

only if it raises the cost of administration. It is true that something could be saved if the Northern Ireland Civil Service could be disbanded, but this would be offset by an increase in the number of imperial civil servants who would then have to take over the work. Indeed if it is true that a decentralised administration is more efficient, the country as a whole may actually save some small sum as a result of devolution. The remaining cost is that of the Provincial Parliament itself, consisting of the salaries of its members and the upkeep of the two chambers; by modern standards of State expenditure this is too trivial an item to detain us.

2. As a preliminary to the discussion of these questions, the financial relations between Westminster and Stormont may be briefly summarised. The powers retained by Westminster include the Crown, defence, war and peace, foreign policy, foreign trade, coinage and bank notes, food subsidies and some agricultural subsidies, and the National Debt; these reserved matters are usually referred to as the "Imperial Services". There are also a number of other matters, described as the "reserved services", that are performed by London for Northern Ireland and are paid for in full by the people of the Province: the Supreme Court, the Post Office, the B.B.C., the Revenue Departments and certain other items. With regard to taxation, the Government of Ireland Act (1920) prohibits the Northern Ireland Parliament from levying customs duties, excise taxes on commodities, income tax, sur-tax or any tax on profits. Apart from these reserved matters, Stormont is free to pass its own legislation and has, in fact, been responsible for a wide range of activities including social insurance, health, education, industry, agriculture, internal transport, the preservation of law and order, town and country planning. The list of transferred services is impressive on the expenditure side, but, on the revenue side, the Provincial Parliament is narrowly restricted to some relatively small taxes: stamp duties, death duties, entertainments duty, motor vehicle duties, and certain minor items. These taxes, together with some non-tax revenue, finance only about one-tenth of the cost of the transferred services at the present time, and Stormont is therefore dependent upon money received from London if the obligations transferred to the local legislature are to be fulfilled.

An estimate is made of the proceeds of reserved taxation levied in the province, and this is divided into three parts:

(1) the full cost of the reserved services performed for Northern Ireland;
(2) the Imperial Contribution;
(3) Northern Ireland's share of the reserved taxation estimated to have been paid by the Province.

This third part, together with transferred revenue, goes to meet the cost of transferred expenditure incurred by the Northern Ireland Government. (The social insurance fund will be referred to below.) Thus the disposal of the revenue attributed to the Province in 1952-3 can be illustrated as follows:

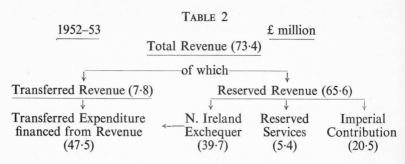

TABLE 2

1952–53   £ million

Total Revenue (73·4)

————of which————

Transferred Revenue (7·8)   Reserved Revenue (65·6)

| Transferred Expenditure financed from Revenue (47·5) | N. Ireland Exchequer (39·7) | Reserved Services (5·4) | Imperial Contribution (20·5) |

Over and above the fraction of reserved taxation returned by Whitehall to Northern Ireland, a payment is made to the social insurance fund under an important reinsurance agreement designed to spread the risks so covered over the United Kingdom as a whole. In 1952–3 this sum amounted to £4·3 million.[1] It should be noted that the reinsurance payment is not related to the proceeds of reserved taxation, which implies that the principle on which the agreement was based was not identical with that governing the finance of Stormont's budgetary expenditure.

3. The figures above illustrate the ways in which revenue is divided between Imperial and Provincial services, but the guiding rules by which the division is made have still to be examined. In successive Home Rule Bills, various formulae were proposed, and since the coming into force of the Act of 1920 itself, the procedure has been substantially modified in the light of experience. These historical developments are illuminating and will receive some passing references in due course; but at the outset it seems more convenient to describe the present method of allocation from which the figures already quoted have emerged.

The negotiations between the Treasury and the Northern Ireland Ministry of Finance take place behind closed doors, but the guiding principle in their deliberations has been stated clearly enough. The "principle of parity", as it is usually called, implies that Northern Ireland, as an integral part of the United Kingdom, should contribute to Imperial purposes on the same basis as other areas; at the same time devolution should allow the people of Northern Ireland greater freedom of choice to determine the volume and composition of public expenditure and taxation within the province. In order to elucidate the meaning of parity it is convenient to take the most simple example which is also, as it happens, fairly realistic. It will be supposed, then, that the Government of Northern Ireland makes no use whatsoever of its power to levy taxes,

---

[1] Thus total transferred expenditure in 1952–3 (£51·8 m.) = £47·5 m. from revenue *plus* £4·3 m. from the reinsurance fund.

other than those reserved by Westminster, at rates of its own choosing, but prefers to impose the transferred taxes at the rates prevailing across the Channel. These taxes, together with some non-tax revenue, meet only about one-tenth of estimated provincial expenditure; if the budget is to be balanced, Westminster must provide sufficient funds to offset the discrepancy between Stormont's narrowly limited power to impose taxation and its wide obligations on the side of expenditure. Parity of treatment requires that Westminster will, in fact, make up the difference *provided* Northern Ireland is not spending at a more liberal rate than Great Britain. "Parity in taxation means parity in the public services." The reserved taxes collected in the province by Whitehall are levied at the same rates as across the channel, and we have assumed that the transferred taxes are also at the same rates. Stormont can then fairly claim from Westminster whatever sum is needed to supplement its own revenue and maintain the transferred services at the level prevailing in Great Britain.

Naturally if the transferred taxes were at a lower level than the same taxes in Great Britain and the difference were not made good by some new taxes peculiar to Northern Ireland, Stormont's claim on Westminster would have to be correspondingly reduced. If the Ulster people are allowed to carry a lighter burden of taxation, they must face the consequence in the form of less public expenditure. Nor will the principle of parity allow them to embark upon more lavish schemes of public expenditure than those adopted in Great Britain unless it is possible to pay for the excess out of their own transferred revenue. Parity does not mean uniformity: within the limits set by the constitution, Stormont should be free to adopt its own policies with regard to both transferred revenue and transferred expenditure. But parity does imply that revenue and expenditure must move in harmony: the consequences of lower taxation or higher expenditure cannot be evaded by claiming more assistance from Whitehall at the expense of the Imperial Contribution. The latter, it will be seen, should emerge as a residual:[1]

[1] The portion of reserved taxation handed over to Stormont is still referred to as "the residuary share". This is now an anachronism.

As has been indicated above, the "reserved services" performed by Westminster for Northern Ireland are a prior charge that must be met in full. The remainder is divided between the Imperial Contribution on the one hand and transferred expenditure on the other. Originally the Imperial Contribution was planned as a specific sum "fixed more or less in advance of provision for transferred expenditure" (*Ulster Year Book* for 1950, p. xxv). So long as this principle was accepted, Stormont's share could appropriately be termed "the residuary share". But this principle was soon abandoned as impracticable and thereafter account was taken each year of Stormont's "necessary" expenditure. It will be appreciated that if the principle of parity is consistently

Imperial Contribution=Reserved Taxation—Cost of Reserved
Services—Stormont's Claim for Transferred Expenditure.

The payments under the Social Services Reinsurance Agreement do
not enter directly into the calculations just described and are not, as
has been remarked above, related to the proceeds of reserved taxation; it
is apparent, nevertheless, that these payments are in harmony with the
principle of parity. Unemployment insurance, which was a reserved
service in the Act of 1914, was transferred in 1920, with serious consequences for the finances of the Province that were not apparently foreseen at the time. Throughout the inter-war period Ulster suffered from
particularly heavy unemployment and the solvency of the insurance fund
depended upon budgetary assistance. The burden was a heavy one, and
it was recognised in 1925 that Westminster should come to the assistance
of the Provincial Government. The assistance then afforded was on a
limited scale which left the province to bear rather more of the cost of its
own unemployment than was borne by the other relatively depressed
areas in the United Kingdom; moreover unemployment assistance was
not included till 1936. With the introduction of the new schemes in 1948,
an agreement was made for full reciprocal aid between Great Britain
and Northern Ireland with regard to national insurance; in the case of
national assistance, non-contributory pensions, family allowances and
the health services rather less than full reciprocity was provided. Since
the end of the war unemployment in Northern Ireland has been heavier
than in any other region in the United Kingdom and Stormont has therefore received special reinsurance payments in addition to her share of
reserved taxation. These receipts have complicated the accounts and
have, unfortunately, led to some misunderstanding.

Given the principle of parity, there appears to be little need for any
special agreement relating to the social services. For Stormont is fully
entitled to ask for whatever is required to maintain the social services,
or any other form of transferred expenditure, at the same level as in
Great Britain. If no such reinsurance agreement were in existence the
province's claim on reserved taxation could be correspondingly increased
and the Imperial Contribution legitimately reduced. The origin of the

---

adopted, it is the Imperial Contribution that becomes the residual. It may be that even
to-day that principle is not always so applied: that is to say, some regard may be paid
to the effect on the Imperial Contribution of claiming from Whitehall the full amount
to which parity of taxation would entitle the province. An element of compromise may
well be present with the result that neither the Imperial Contribution nor transferred
expenditure can be simply described as the residuary legatee. The fact remains that
the official terminology is somewhat misleading.

first reinsurance agreement of 1925 was understandable; for at that time the method of determining the Imperial Contribution by deducting "necessary" provincial expenditure from total revenue was comparatively new and its implications may have been insufficiently appreciated. But it would seem that, by 1948, the arrangements could have been simplified.

The disadvantage of doing so would be the consequential reduction in the sum described as the "Imperial Contribution". It is true the *net* payment from the province would be unchanged and some critics have held that the sums received under reinsurance should always be deducted in determining the true "Contribution". The argument in defence of the existing practice is not very frequently heard but could perhaps be put in the following way. It will be agreed that, whether there is a separate reinsurance agreement or not, social insurance, in particular unemployment insurance, is designed to cover risks that should be shared together by all parts of the country. Areas such as Northern Ireland that are heavily dependent on foreign trade and thus contribute large sums per head to the United Kingdom balance of payments can reasonably expect the more sheltered areas to come to their assistance when times are bad. No one would challenge the validity of this argument as applied to inter-regional financial relations inside England, and it can be legitimately extended to cover any area inside the United Kingdom which has a limited measure of self-government. The next step would be to contend that, in so far as economic ill-fortune can be covered by insurance schemes, the finances of these schemes should be isolated from the other budgetary accounts in estimating the Imperial Contribution; for the latter will reflect more fairly what the region is achieving if its size is unaffected either way by the cost of risks that are insurable and can be fairly spread over the whole country. How much weight should be attached to such considerations? The argument may be felt to be not unreasonable, but it may be held that, since so many risks cannot be covered by such schemes—which are themselves only dubiously entitled to the term "insurance"—it may not be worth while to distinguish in this way between transferred budgetary expenditure and the insurance funds. Moreover, as will be suggested at a later stage, the reinsurance agreement has the incidental disadvantage—from the point of view of those who believe in devolution—of restricting the province's freedom to experiment with the social services. It will be clear that the real case for separating the accounts in the present fashion is political: it keeps up the size of what is described as the "Imperial Contribution" and has so far prevented it from becoming negative. Admittedly some of Ulster's

K

critics are sufficiently sophisticated to deduct the reinsurance payments in order to arrive at a net figure—even if they are not sophisticated enough to understand the principle of parity—but a small or negative figure bearing the official title "Imperial Contribution" would attract much more widespread attention and undeniably cause embarrassment even if it could be defended as fully equitable. For this reason the attitude of the Stormont Government should not be unsympathetically dismissed.

4. Ulster's Imperial Contribution has fluctuated a great deal: in 1934–5, a year of deep depression in Ulster, it fell to a negligible amount; in 1944–5, a year of prosperity and high employment, it amounted to £36 million; the average Contribution since 1921 has been about £10 million. If it is felt that in order to arrive at the net amount provided for Imperial purposes a deduction should be made for the special social security payments, the figure so obtained will be smaller and will be even negative for some years. Thus for 1953–4 the gross Contribution is estimated at £8·6 million, but the net figure at only £4·6 million. But this is not surprising in view of the abnormally high level of unemployment in the area. Scotland's implicit "Imperial Contribution" is less than that for England and Wales together,[1] and it may well be that the contribution of some areas, say South Wales, has been negative in bad times: at all events, there is no reason whatsoever to suppose that Ulster has been treated more favourably than any of the depressed areas of Great Britain.[2] On the contrary, Ulster appears to have been worse treated than the rest of the United Kingdom during the greater part of the

---

[1] *Report of the Royal Commission on Scottish Affairs*, Cmd. 9212, chapter 3.

[2] There have, it is true, been some special payments from Westminster to Stormont apart from those provided under the social security agreements; but these are of insufficient importance to have any material effect on the verdict.

(1) When the new Ulster Government was established, a capital sum was contributed to the cost of inaugural expenses, including buildings. This, of course, has long since ceased to be relevant to the accounts.

(2) A further sum was paid to cover the cost of damage to property during the disturbances—a liability that would have accrued anyhow if devolution had not been accorded.

(3) A sum that still accrues annually to Stormont was also transferred in the form of the old land annuities due to the State against the capital sums previously expended in buying out the landlords. In view of the republican attitude to the land annuities in Eire, it would be difficult for Ulster's critics to maintain that this was an improper subvention. In any case the sum is small (about £650,000 a year).

(4) There were large special payments for war expenditure which arose from the fact that Stormont acted as an agent for some imperial ministries during the war and thus incurred expenditure of a quite abnormal kind. There was clearly no element of subsidy in this: the expenditure, which lay outside Stormont's constitutional competance, was incurred on behalf of Westminster solely for reasons of administrative convenience.

period of devolution, for it was only in the late thirties that the principle of parity was fully accepted[1]: prior to that parity in taxation gave Ulster less than a full claim to parity in expenditure. The reinsurance scheme for the social services was also inadequate.

It would be out of place in this context to discuss in any detail the nature of these earlier arrangements, but it seems worth while to compare the modern parity arrangements under devolution with the regional implications of central government finance within Great Britain itself. On the revenue side, the sums levied by the Inland Revenue in Scotland or Wales or Kent reflect the income of the area and the value of its capital; the indirect taxes paid by the area reflect, in turn, its expenditure. Thus the contribution of each area bears some sort of rough relationship to its prosperity. There is a corresponding reflection of regional needs in the apportionment of expenditure between different areas on items corresponding to the transferred services in Northern Ireland. A region where income per head is lower than the average and the volume of unemployment higher will make a smaller contribution per head to the Exchequer and the National Insurance Fund and will receive larger payments per head from both these sources. The implicit "Imperial Contribution" per head of such an area will clearly be less than that of the more prosperous parts of the country, and this would be generally regarded as a fair arrangement—even if its "Imperial Contribution" were negative. It will be appreciated that these remarks relate only to the broad principles of public finance, in practical administration some discrepancies may be unavoidable and may affect either way both the respective contributions of the regions in Great Britain and the contribution of Northern Ireland. But, administrative difficulties apart, it can be said that the principle of parity is an attempt to accord to an area with regional self-government the same treatment as that accorded to other parts of the United Kingdom. Devolution is not regarded in Ulster as a half-way house to dominion status or complete independence, but a permanent arrangement for limited provincial autonomy that does not involve any disintegration of the United Kingdom. This seems to be the most appropriate interpretation of the term, and if so much is conceded, the principle of parity in financial matters can be regarded as a natural corollary. The gradual adoption of this idea in dealing with the affairs of Ulster can be compared with similar developments in the relationship between central and local governments in Great Britain. In the federal States a comparable tendency can be discerned. Or, to look at the matter from a different angle, "parity" can be described as the

[1] By what is known as the Simon Declaration.

inter-regional application of the idea that taxation should be progressive and that expenditure should vary with need.

5. Strictly speaking, it is unnecessary to estimate reserved taxation at all in order to apply the principle of parity. Stormont has been made responsible for maintaining services that cost much more than can possibly be raised from transferred revenue, and Whitehall must in fairness make up the difference provided (a) the transferred expenditure is agreed to be no higher than is sanctioned by parity, and (b) the transferred taxes are not less heavy than corresponding taxes in Great Britain. The balance required can thus be estimated by examining transferred taxation and transferred expenditure and comparing them, respectively, with comparable figures for the rest of the country; the estimates of reserved taxation are wholly unnecessary for this purpose. If, indeed, it were held that the application of parity must be restricted by the condition that the sum handed over to Stormont should never exceed the amount of reserved taxation paid by the province, reserved taxation would then have to be estimated; but such a restriction would have little to commend it. An equally heavy burden of taxation justifies equally good public services; this is what parity means. The Imperial Contribution that emerges from the application of this principle could be negative if economic conditions in the province were particularly bad. A ruling that the Contribution must never be negative would imply a departure from equitable treatment in such circumstances. It would mean that the area with self-government was being more harshly treated than other areas that were governed direct from Westminster and were unembarrassed by any estimates of their "Imperial Contribution".

The existing method of setting out Ulster's financial relations with Westminster is the partly anachronistic consequence of some earlier proposals for the determination of the Imperial Contribution that have now been abandoned. Thus the first Home Rule Bill of 1886 provided for a fixed Imperial Contribution of £3·6 million to be derived from customs and excise duties collected in Ireland by the London Government; the proceeds of these taxes, which were to be imposed by Whitehall, would have had to be estimated because the variable balance was to be payable to Ireland, where it would have been used, together with the transferred revenue, to pay for local services.[1] The Second Home Rule Bill (Committee Form) provided that for six years, during which nearly all taxes were to be reserved, one-third of the proceeds would form the Imperial Contribution; once more an estimate of reserved taxation would have been

---

[1] Cf. the essay on Financial Relations by J. I. Cook in *Devolution of Government* (Institute of Public Administration).

essential. The Bill of 1912 differed from its predecessors in that Ireland was not to be required to make a positive Imperial Contribution initially; on the contrary a net payment from Great Britain was anticipated—a fact which might, perhaps, have been borne in mind by subsequent critics of Ulster, the only part of Ireland in which devolution eventually became effective. It was hoped that at a later stage Ireland would become solvent and an Imperial Contribution, the variable excess after Irish needs had been met, could then begin; the calculation of "Irish needs" was to be made by a Joint Exchequer Board. In the Act of 1920, the Imperial Contribution became once more a fixed charge, and this implied that the total amount of reserved taxation paid by each part of Ireland had to be calculated in order to determine the residues to be returned to Belfast and Dublin respectively. The charge was fixed initially for only two years, and it was soon apparent that a constant figure could not reasonably be demanded. Ulster's contribution of about £8 million was calculated in the post-war boom; in the ensuing slump and the doldrums of the 'twenties, a figure of this size could have been maintained only by cuts in expenditure within the province of a severity greater than those suffered by the rest of the United Kingdom. These difficulties were taken into account in determining the contributions of 1922–3 and 1923–4, and the final Report of the Special Arbitration Committee (Colwyn Committee) laid down some of the principles that have governed our subsequent relations with Great Britain and bear a rough resemblance to those proposed in 1912. It was established that the Imperial Contribution was to be a variable sum obtained by deducting Ulster's necessary expenditure from the proceeds of taxation in Northern Ireland, provided that, if transferred taxes were lower than across the Channel, the claim on reserved taxation would be correspondingly reduced.

Once the Colwyn formula had been accepted and the idea of a fixed contribution abandoned, it would have been possible to dispense with the estimates of both reserved taxation and the Imperial Contribution, for Stormont's claim on Whitehall was fully determined by taking account of "necessary expenditure" and transferred taxation.

The accounts could be simplified in this way, but it is necessary to ask whether any other advantages or disadvantages would follow. To some economists it would no doubt appear a retrograde step to give up the separate calculation of the yield of reserved taxation; for these figures are valuable in estimating the total volume of incomes, public and private, that are earned in the province and may thus facilitate the formulation of policy. Indeed it has been urged that estimates of regional incomes are badly needed within Great Britain itself and fuller information is now being provided by the Board of Inland Revenue, though on a less complete scale than that available for Ulster. The figures for the Imperial Contribution are of interest in a different way to the people of Ulster; for they show that the six counties are providing something towards the cost of the Imperial services and are therefore a sign of common citizenship with people in other parts of the United Kingdom. In wartime in particular, when the Imperial Contribution absorbed about two-thirds of reserved taxation, Ulster could take a legitimate pride in what she was doing. In peace-time the matter may be viewed differently, and estimates of the Contribution may then be a source of embarrassment if local industry happens to be depressed.

It is a fact that the Ulster Government does not like to see the Imperial Contribution decline. It has even been suggested[1] that Ministers are reluctant in good years to expand the transferred services to the full extent warranted by parity lest, in bad years, the cost of maintaining these services should drag down the Imperial Contribution to a negligible, or even a negative, figure. It is not easy to say whether this suggestion is well-founded. It would certainly be ironical if the claim that Ulster is subsidised, so often advanced by the anti-English party, had led to our paying more to England than parity would strictly require us to do!

If reserved taxation and the Imperial Contribution were no longer estimated, it would be held that the subsidy was so large that it had now to be concealed. But it is doubtful whether the likelihood of unfair charges of this kind should be allowed to affect the decision. The object of abandoning these calculations would not be to silence the unfair criticism but rather to mitigate the effect of such criticism on those who take serious economic decisions.

6. So far attention has been largely confined to considerations of equity, and the verdict on the arrangements at present in force in Ulster has been, on the whole, favourable. It is now necessary to consider whether in other respects the arrangements are equally satisfactory. In particular it may be asked whether devolution gives the province genuine self-government on a sufficiently important scale to justify the existence of a separate parliament. A reasonably comprehensive answer to this question would involve the discussion of many topics that lie outside the scope of the present chapter, but some reference must be made to the effect of the financial arrangements.

While Stormont is fully entitled to receive whatever sums can be justified on the basis of parity, there is an obvious danger that this dependence on the Treasury may in practice make it more difficult to take an

[1] *Cf.* Isles and Cuthbert, pp. 163-4 below.

independent line and may foster centralising tendencies that detract from the value of devolution. At the same time it must be borne in mind that too much independence in public finance could lead to a harmful conflict of policies within the United Kingdom. Would it be feasible to accord greater powers of taxation to a provincial government than those exercised at present by the Parliament of Northern Ireland? For what purposes could such powers be usefully employed?

There are obvious limits to the extent to which taxation can differ between areas that are not separated by a tariff barrier. Northern Ireland is within the United Kingdom customs unit, and this is as it should be. Control over the *customs* would imply a much greater degree of independence than can reasonably be expected from devolution, and would involve the disintegration of the United Kingdom. The harmful economic effect of erecting barriers to trade within so small an area need not be stressed; common sense requires that free trade should be maintained within the United Kingdom. There are therefore limits to the extent to which *excise* duties on goods can be imposed at different rates in different parts of the county. If, for example, cigarettes were taxed more heavily in Ulster than elsewhere, smokers would find it worth while to order their supplies from cross-channel shops; with no customs barrier, such evasion could not be prevented. The scope for evasion would no doubt differ from one commodity to another and would reflect differences in the extra cost and inconvenience of buying in distant markets. Since Northern Ireland is separated by sea from the rest of the country, there would presumably be more scope there for differences in excise duties on transportable commodities than would be the case in any other part of Great Britain, and it may be concluded that the ban on the imposition of such taxes imposed by the Government of Ireland Act could be safely relaxed a little if this was thought, on other grounds, to be desirable. (The petrol tax appears to be a good example of one that might be transferred.) In the case of, say, Scotland, excise taxes on commodities need not, perhaps, be excluded altogether, but it would be unwise to suppose that wide differences in rates could, in practice, be maintained. "Freedom and whiskey gae thegither." But devolution means rather less freedom than that!

On the face of it, provincial taxes on income would seem to be somewhat more promising. In the U.S.A. some States levy their own income taxes, and Northern Ireland could presumably do the same. But the administrative cost would not be negligible, and the task of assessment would be particularly difficult in the case of profits of companies that operate in different parts of the United Kingdom.

There is perhaps a temptation to give too much weight to the administrative inconvenience of extending the scope of transferred taxation. Such scepticism, if carried too far, may lead to doubts about the desirability of having any transferred taxation at all. Ulster can finance only a tenth of its expenditure from its own revenue, and it may be asked whether there is any advantage in having direct control over this small fraction of what is required. Would anything be lost if the Provincial Parliament were entirely dependent upon Westminster for its revenue?

There are substantial advantages in transferring some control over taxation as well as control over expenditure, and these advantages may be grouped under three headings.

(i) A Provincial Parliament should be free to exercise, albeit within limits, some independent control over the volume of expenditure and taxation in the area. The local electorate may favour more elaborate public services than those sanctioned for the rest of the country, but parity of treatment clearly precludes the financing of excess expenditure at the expense of the Imperial Contribution, whether the latter is explicitly calculated or not; in such circumstances, the Provincial Parliament must be able to raise additional revenue on its own account. No doubt this is an academic possibility at the present time. If the burden placed on the English taxpayer is more than he can carry without seriously harmful economic effects, it would be unwise for the poorer parts of the country—Scotland, Wales and Northern Ireland—to weigh their people down with even heavier loads. More relevant to-day is the possibility of reducing both taxation and expenditure; for it may reasonably be held that taxation at rates that can be borne by the wealthier regions may crush those that are less fortunate. That is to say, in addition to the adjustment of its "Imperial Contribution" to an area's taxable capacity, already provided for by the principle of parity, it may be thought desirable to spend less on the transferred services themselves with corresponding benefit to the local taxpayer.

In fact the Northern Ireland Government has made little or no use even of its present powers to reduce taxation. The transferred taxes include death duties which are a particularly onerous burden in an area where family business predominates, and the Unionist Government might therefore have been expected to hesitate before adopting public services on quite the same scale as that introduced at Westminster by the Socialists after the war. If transferred expenditure could have been kept down even by 3d. in every pound below its present level, death duties could have been lowered by the equivalent of 25 per cent of their yield. But socialist policy with regard to expenditure was in the main faithfully copied, and although in 1952 a very small easement of death duties was allowed, this was offset by another transferred tax.[1]

Stormont's power to reduce taxation is not confined to the transferred taxes, but is extended by a somewhat curious clause in the Constitution to two reserved taxes of great importance—income tax and sur-tax. Although precluded from levying such taxes itself, the Provincial Parliament can lower their effective rates by arranging for rebates. Section 25 of the Government of Ireland Act gives the Parliament of Northern Ireland power:

". . . to grant relief from income tax and sur-tax or either of these taxes to individuals resident and domiciled in . . . Northern Ireland . . . and such relief may be given generally to all such individuals or to individuals whose total income is less than such amount as may be determined by the Act granting the relief."

If an attempt were made to invoke this clause, the constitutional lawyers might well differ as to the precise nature of the power thus conferred by the Act. (The reference to "individuals" but not to "companies" is puzzling.) The intentions of those who framed the legislation may not be altogether clear; but it is relevant to observe that Westminster then contemplated the possibility of a subsequent transfer of very wide—perhaps too wide—powers over taxation should the two Parliaments of Northern and Southern Ireland agree to form a Council of Ireland (Section 36), and for this reason a generous interpretation of the clause quoted above may appear to be justified. It is also worth observing that when the Minister of Finance was asked in Parliament why the power to lower the income tax had not been used with the object of strengthening the economy, he did not, in his reply, shelter behind legal ambiguities but pointed out that the consequential cut in transferred expenditure would be unpleasant.[2] For the purposes of our present argument, at all events, it is more interesting to assume that the income tax could be lowered effectively to any level Stormont might choose; for the general possibilities of devolutionary finance are more relevant than the legal niceties of the existing Constitution of Northern Ireland.

The income tax and sur-tax paid by *both* individuals and companies amounted to £26 million in 1952–3 when expenditure on the transferred services came to £52 million; that is to say, income tax and sur-tax paid

[1] A further concession in 1954 was not so offset in an explicit way, but the sum involved was very small and the modest compensation required may easily have come on the side of expenditure. *Cf.* p. 67 above.

[2] H. C. Debates (Northern Ireland), April 21, 1953, cols. 897–99).

by *individuals alone* could have been reduced to zero if Stormont could have cut its expenditure by appreciably less than half. This, of course, is a wildly unrealistic example, but it is worth quoting these figures in order to indicate the wide range of choice that would lie before the Provincial Parliament if it were really free to reduce income tax and sur-tax on all individuals and companies.

In fact Stormont followed Westminster faithfully and adopted the Welfare State on the same scale as the Socialist Government at Westminster. Whether this course was right or wrong need not be discussed here, but the opinion may be hazarded that large differences in expenditure and taxation between different parts of the country are unlikely, apart altogether from legal restraints. The forces making for an extension of the Welfare State after the war were particularly strong and were not confined to one part of the country or one political party. Public opinion on these matters is sufficiently similar in the various regions of the country to make wide divergences in policy somewhat improbable.

More modest variations in taxation and expenditure should, however, be possible. No dramatic refusal to accept the new version of the Welfare State, but merely a little more caution, would have kept Stormont's expenditure 5 per cent below its present level; this would have made possible the equivalent of a reduction of about 1s. in the income tax—or a rather bigger reduction if applied only to individuals and not to companies. Or, as has already been indicated, a saving of 3d. in the pound in expenditure would allow death duties to come down by 25 per cent, and in this case no legal doubts about Stormont's competence would arise. In view of the fact that Stormont has made virtually no use of the powers at its disposal even when the Socialists were in office in London, some of the remarks made from time to time at Westminster about the social outlook of the Unionist Government may appear to be somewhat off the mark. But some supporters of devolution may feel—rightly or wrongly—that a more independent line should have been taken.

(ii) The second reason for granting a provincial government certain powers over taxation is to make possible some variation in the composition of taxation. The economic structure and the financial organisation of business is not uniform throughout the country, and certain taxes may be more harmful in some regions than in others. Given the amount of money to be raised, there is something to be said for raising it in slightly different ways if this can be done without too great administrative inconvenience. The economic limitations to regional differences in taxation have already been stressed, but it would seem that rather greater powers than those exercised by Stormont would be desirable. Direct taxation is particularly damaging to private firms, and firms of this kind play a larger part in Ulster's economic life than in that of the United Kingdom as a whole. But although Stormont has some power to lighten the burden, very little can be done without reducing transferred expenditure correspondingly because the power to impose alternative levies is so narrowly restricted. It may be held that a Provincial Parliament should not be obliged to choose to this extent between certain taxes imposed at damagingly high rates on the one hand and public services on a reduced scale on the other. For example, some modest rise in indirect taxes might permit a significant reduction in death duties in Ulster.

(iii) The final reason for allowing a regional Parliament to have a substantial volume of revenue of its own is more difficult to evaluate. Stormont is obliged at the present time to turn to Whitehall for nine-tenths of the money required to give the province public services comparable to those in the rest of the United Kingdom. It is true that Ulster's representatives need not go to the Treasury cap in hand. They are not asking for charity. The vast bulk of the taxation paid by the province is reserved taxation collected by London, and Stormont is fully entitled, on grounds of equity, to get what is needed to make good the disparity between its narrow taxing powers and its wide obligations to maintain the public services. Nevertheless the arrangement is such as to put the Treasury in a psychologically strong position, and in the course of the negotiations there is always a danger that regional experiments on the side of expenditure will be discouraged; for Whitehall may well have a bias in favour of uniformity that reflects nothing more sinister than a desire to avoid complexities and thus save time and trouble. With more revenue of its own, the provincial government might be inclined to take a stronger line. Even if the transferred taxes were imposed at exactly the same rates as those ruling elsewhere, their transference would not be pointless. It is over-facile to say that it does not matter who collects the taxes if the taxes are the same; in practice it may well matter a good deal. Admittedly the yield of transferred taxation is likely to be substantially less under any scheme of devolution than the volume of transferred expenditure. But the difference appears to be unduly great in the case of Northern Ireland at the present time, and is, of course, greater than was originally contemplated when devolution was first introduced, because, in Ulster as elsewhere, the yield of the reserved taxes has grown so much more than that of the transferred taxes.

7. In a previous section it has been explained that Northern Ireland is entitled to receive from Whitehall whatever sums are required to provide

public services at the same level as in Great Britain, but that any excess expenditure would have to be paid for, if it could be paid for at all, by Stormont itself. That is to say, transferred taxation would have to be made to bring in more than the comparable taxes across the channel.

This arrangement means that Stormont's expenditure is examined every year by the Treasury in order to ensure that it does not exceed what is sanctioned by "parity". How is this examination made? A simple comparison of expenditure per head between the two areas would clearly not suffice, for identical services may cost more in one area than in another. In view of differences in age composition, Ulster will expend less on the old but more on children. Industrial accidents will cost less but unemployment more. And so on. It is not actual expenditure per head, but the scale on which each service is provided, that should be taken into account. It is when some services are more generously provided and others less so that the calculations become really difficult. (A similar comparison must be made in dealing with transferred taxation, but this is likely to be very much easier.)

The Special Arbitration Committee (Colwyn Committee) dealt with this problem in 1923 in a very restrictive manner. It was laid down that: "In determining the necessary expenditure there shall be eliminated:

(*a*) All expenditure on any service in existence in both Northern Ireland and Great Britain incurred in providing Northern Ireland with a higher average standard of service than exists in Great Britain. . . .

(*b*) All expenditure undertaken by the Government of Northern Ireland on services which do not exist in Great Britain."

This formula, if strictly applied, would have made Stormont's control of transferred expenditure more apparent than real. One of the main objects of devolution is to permit legislation more specifically designed to reflect local requirements than would otherwise be possible. The Provincial Government should be free to spend more on service A than is being spent elsewhere and finance the excess by economising on service B; it should also be free to experiment by introducing new services not adopted in other parts of the country if it can save the money in other directions. The Colwyn formula would have prevented such variations in policy and would thus have tended to defeat one of the main purposes devolution is meant to achieve.

Fortunately the formula has not been strictly applied since 1931, and there are official assurances that these matters are now being worked out in a flexible manner. Just how flexibly it is difficult to judge, for the negotiations between Stormont and Whitehall are secret, but it is clear that Belfast has departed in some respects from the London pattern of expenditure.[1] Whether larger departures would have been made by Stormont but for pressure exercised by Treasury officials is a matter on which it is useless to speculate.

In this connection it is relevant to observe that the Social Services Reinsurance Agreement may tend to narrow the scope for independent action in dealing with a large part of transferred legislation; for this agreement is based on the assumption that contributions and benefits will be the same in Northern Ireland as in Great Britain. It is true that the arrangement was voluntarily accepted by Stormont, but its acceptance implied that, with regard to the future, the Provincial Parliament was willing to forgo the exercise of some of the powers conferred upon it by the Constitution.

8. The rate of expenditure in Great Britain on services corresponding to those transferred to Ulster is taken as a measuring rod in determining the province's claim to a share of the taxation collected by the central government. Two conclusions follow from this fact.

In the first place, it is clear that a different and presumably more complicated arrangement would have to be made if devolution were granted to all parts of the United Kingdom. Or, to make the same point differently, the Ulster formula could not be applied without modification in the fully federal States. If devolution were extended to Scotland and Wales, the fact that England's expenditure on non-Imperial services was the yardstick for the rest of the country would probably provoke a good deal of discussion, but the formula could undoubtedly be applied if England's leadership were, to this extent, accepted.

The second conclusion relates to representation at Westminster, described by Professor Mansergh as "the most difficult problem in any scheme for Devolution".[2] The Ulster electorate sends M.P.s to London who can speak and vote on any topic that comes up, notwithstanding the fact that a large part of the legislation applies only to Great Britain and not to Northern Ireland. At first glance this appears to be wrong.

The problem of representation caused a great deal of trouble in the past when Home Rule for Ireland was proposed. The bill of 1886 provided for no Irish members at Westminster; but it was rightly held that this would be unfair in the opposite direction, for the Irish people could have had no say in the determination of Imperial policies that affected them as much as the electors in Great Britain. When the second Home Rule Bill was introduced it contained the famous "in-and-out" clause that would have allowed Irish M.P.s in London to vote on Imperial

---

[1] *Cf.* the appendix by Robson.
[2] *The Government of Northern Ireland*, p. 52.

matters but not on matters affecting Great Britain only, and corresponding to those to be delegated to the new Irish Parliament. This clause, dubious in theory and certain to be troublesome in practice, was abandoned in its turn, and, in the end, the Act of 1920 allowed Irish members full participation at Westminster. Subsequently the difficulty was eased by the fact that only Ulster, not the whole of Ireland, was involved: the votes of Ulster's dozen M.P.s can have an important effect only in special circumstances, such as those obtaining after the election of 1951, when the major parties at Westminster are very evenly balanced. It would be a different matter if Scotland, with her seventy-one M.P.s, were given devolution as well.

On reflection, however, it does not appear that full representation at Westminster is as improper as it may at first glance appear to be. If the financial arrangements are such that Westminster's expenditure on non-Imperial services is taken as the measuring-rod in determining the financial claims of areas to which devolution has been accorded, it seems positively desirable that these areas should have some say in determining that expenditure. When Ulster's M.P.s in London vote on such matters as health and education, the bills before the House have an indirect significance that is of major importance for their constituents, even if the legislation applies directly only to Great Britain.

Moreover, in a more general way, London's policy has an important influence on public opinion in Ulster and thus, apart altogether from legal compulsion, constitutes the rough pattern that the provincial parliament will subsequently tend to follow. Such a conclusion may appear unduly cynical to those who expect devolution to lead to wide differences in policy and may be taken, wrongly, to imply that provincial self-government is useless. From a more realistic point of view, it would appear that wide differences are unlikely and would certainly be undesirable, although it does not follow that, in a less spectacular way, devolution has nothing to contribute to the meeting of the special needs of different parts of the country.

The full representation at Westminster of areas with limited self-government may not be in strict accord with the theory of parliamentary representation; but, on the assumption that "Home Rule All Round" is out of the question, it appears to be the best solution to what is undoubtedly one of the most difficult problems posed by devolution.

CHAPTER 7

ECONOMIC POLICY

By K. S. ISLES and N. CUTHBERT

BEFORE turning to examine the provincial government's economic policy, it will be helpful to recall the broad limits to its constitutional power to legislate on economic matters, and to note the further limitations on its freedom of independent action imposed by the basic facts of economic integration with Great Britain and the existence of common institutions. So far as constitutional limitations are concerned, the essence of the matter is that Northern Ireland is unable to make use of any of those techniques by which separate countries follow a policy of economic independence. On the one hand, it is precluded from establishing a separate tariff and from otherwise interfering with external trade, interregional or international: in its trade with other countries it is treated as an integral part of the United Kingdom, and between Northern Ireland and Great Britain the only restriction is the cost of transport. On the other hand, although a small degree of flexibility might conceivably be obtained through the banking system, Northern Ireland has no power to follow an independent monetary policy, involving separate rates of exchange, or to adopt an independent fiscal policy apart from minor concessions to adapt general fiscal policy to local needs. This means that it may not use any of the ordinary devices for stabilising employment through control of the economic climate. The economic integration with Great Britain arising from common policy in these matters, and from the existence of common institutions—in particular, the integration involved by the free transfer of goods and property rights and the free migration of workers to Great Britain and back—gives rise to two tendencies which are of vital importance both in assessing the provincial government's economic policy and in understanding the limited scope for usefully increasing its constitutional powers. Firstly, wage rates for any given class of labour tend to be adjusted in response to changes in the corresponding rates in Great Britain. The strength of this tendency was discussed in Chapter 5. It is due to the interregional mobility of labour and the integration of the wage-fixing machinery with that in Great Britain. Secondly, the new investment funds available each year for increasing the fixed and working capital of industry, anywhere in Northern Ireland or Great Britain, tend to be invested wherever it is expected they will earn the highest rates of profit; and hence new investment tends to be extended to the point at which the expected rate of return, on a given assessed risk, is about the same as in Great Britain at the margin reached. Thus, taken together, these two tendencies exert a powerful influence on the profitability of investment, the supplies of industrial capital and labour, the rate of industrial growth, the industrial structure and the volume of employment. Bearing them in mind, let us first briefly examine the government's policy towards economic development and then consider the scope for further independent action to stimulate development both under the existing constitutional powers and under various possible extensions.

(a) *Assistance to Agriculture.* Although its powers to legislate on economic matters are severely restricted by the Government of Ireland Act, especially by Sections 4, 9 and 24, Northern Ireland has nevertheless been able to take some effective action to increase employment, and otherwise to improve the economic position of the province, within the limitations thus placed upon it. The measures adopted fall into three main groups: firstly, measures designed to increase productivity in farming and value of agricultural production;[1] secondly, measures for increasing employment in manufacturing through the establishment of new industries; and, thirdly, measures for improving the efficiency and enlarging the scale of existing industries through the provision of capital. The first of these groups of measures will be considered in the present section, and the other two, respectively, in the two following sections.

Until 1932 the assistance given to agriculture consisted wholly of measures designed to improve the techniques of farming and the quality of the product exported to the English market. A Faculty of Agriculture was set up in the Queen's University of Belfast, with research divisions for investigating problems connected with soil and animal nutrition, animal and plant diseases, animal breeding, and so on. Educational facilities for farmers were greatly improved through the provision of winter classes at centres throughout the province, the establishment of residential schools for giving young men and women an intensive training in up-to-date farming methods, and the granting of scholarships tenable at centres outside Northern Ireland.

[1] For a discussion of these measures the reader may also wish to refer to an essay on "Agricultural Administration in Northern Ireland," by D. A. E. Harkness, published in *Devolution in Government*, (George Allen & Unwin, 1953).

Side by side with these research and educational projects, a system of grading was introduced to control the quality of agricultural exports. It was realised that farmers in Northern Ireland could successfully compete against agricultural imports, which in the 'twenties were flooding the British market, only by maintaining high and consistent standards of quality. Accordingly, between 1924 and 1933 Acts were passed which prescribed minimum standards of quality and packing to be observed by exporters of eggs, fruit, meat and dairy produce. These Acts required some modification of the powers of the Northern Ireland government under Section 4 (7) of the Government of Ireland Act, but this modification has been fully justified. For the success of the enactments in establishing for Northern Ireland's agricultural products a high reputation, and thereby an enhanced selling value, has been generally recognised. Progress was made at the same time in raising the quality of livestock. Assistance was given to farmers to induce them to keep, and to make available for service locally, good-quality rams, boars and bulls; while the Livestock Breeding Act of 1922, which required all bulls to be licensed, was instrumental in enabling the Ministry of Agriculture to improve the quality of cattle.

During the late 'twenties inquiries into the methods of marketing agricultural produce were being made throughout the United Kingdom. Those relating to Northern Ireland were made by the provincial government and were embodied in a report on marketing in 1932. It was recognised in the report that co-ordination would have to be introduced into the system through legislation; for voluntary co-operation would leave too many loopholes for spoiling the market. Although the Agricultural Marketing Act was passed in Great Britain in 1931, the Northern Ireland government waited till after the passing of the Import Duties Act of 1932, on the ground that action by the producers would be abortive unless accompanied by a restriction of imports. The Agricultural Marketing Act (Northern Ireland) 1933 enabled the Northern Ireland Ministry of Agriculture, in co-operation with producers' representatives, to formulate schemes for the marketing of agricultural products. These schemes all followed the same general pattern. A marketing board, composed of representatives of producers and nominees of the Ministry of Agriculture, had power both to require registered producers to sell only to the Board, or through its agency, and also to determine the prices and conditions of sale. Thus the procedure conformed closely to that adopted in Great Britain. It differed from it, however, in points of detail. For example, pig producers were not required to enter into contract to supply a given number of pigs to curers, as they were in Great Britain,

L

but could sell them at the standard price to the Pig Marketing Board. There were two reasons for this: first, since there were a great many small-scale producers of pigs, a contract scheme would have been difficult to administer; and, secondly, there was not a big enough demand for fresh pork in Northern Ireland to provide a local market for any excess production of pigs above the contract number. Under the scheme as adopted, the surplus pigs were exported to Great Britain by the Board. As regards milk marketing, also, the scheme adopted in Great Britain had to be modified to allow for special conditions existing in Northern Ireland. Owing to the large proportion of total output used for manu-facture, a pool scheme similar to that of Great Britain would have made the net price obtained for liquid milk unprofitably low. In order to raise the price of manufacturing milk to a profitable level without causing this result, it was therefore decided to supplement the proceeds of a levy on liquid milk by a government grant. At the same time, producers of milk for liquid consumption were required to be licensed, and all milk was graded and priced according to its quality. Prior to the war there were three grades, A, B and C, that were allowed to be sold for liquid consumption. But since 1944 grade C has been disallowed in the Belfast area, and, as pasteurisation facilities grow, the "safe milk" area is being extended throughout the province.

The problem of feeding the population of the United Kingdom during and since the war has caused important changes in Northern Ireland both in the general profitability of farming and in the relative amounts of output of the different products. Broadly speaking, these changes have come about through the general increase in the importance of domestic agriculture in the United Kingdom due to the interruption of normal supplies from abroad, especially during the war, and through an in-creased appreciation of the permanent importance of domestic agri-culture for the welfare of the nation. In Northern Ireland farmers have been relieved of much of the difficulty which they formerly experienced in competing successfully for markets in Great Britain, and they have readily been able to sell the whole of their output at a much more profit-able scale of prices. Indeed, for the most of the period since the begin-ning of the war the problem has not been to find an outlet for the surplus production in Great Britain, but to supply it with as much agricultural produce as possible. This change in the general position of farmers in Northern Ireland can be conveniently considered in two parts: firstly, the system introduced during the war and maintained until recently, under which the chief farm products were bought by the Ministry of Food at uniform prices throughout the United Kingdom; and secondly, the modifications made in this system with the partial reversion to the system of free marketing during the past two or three years.

Before the war the net prices received by farmers in Northern Ireland were the market prices obtained in Great Britain less the direct and indirect costs of transport in getting the products to their destination. But the introduction of the system of uniform agricultural prices put all farmers on much the same footing in this respect regardless of their distance from markets, and so it helped farmers in Northern Ireland more than the average. This is especially true as regards the transport of livestock. Before the system of uniform prices farmers in Northern Ireland were at a handicap not only because of the actual costs of transport, but also because of indirect costs due to loss of weight of the animals during transit and the greater uncertainties caused by distance when marketing was unorganised. The extra benefits conferred by uniform prices on Northern Ireland are reflected in the greater relative increase in the total net value of agricultural production than in Great Britain. Between the beginning of the war[1] and 1945, whereas the value of gross output rose by very little more than the average for the United Kingdom (122 per cent as against 116), the value of net output[2] rose by 205 per cent compared with the average for the United Kingdom of 176 per cent. But besides helping farmers in Northern Ireland relatively to those nearer the main British markets (by, in effect, pooling transport costs) the system of uniform agricultural prices benefited farmers throughout the whole country in two important ways. Firstly, it diminished the uncertainties of farming since prices were fixed each year in advance. Secondly, in determining prices the intention was to ensure that farmers generally could earn a reasonable profit. The subsidy in this respect, on each product, was the same for all producers. The difference between what the Ministry of Food paid the farmers (or foreign producers) and what it received from the sale of the goods to the public, through the ordinary trade channels, represented a subsidy partly to farmers and partly to consumers. Since it is unknown what the corresponding prices would have been in a free market, however, it is impossible to determine how much of the total amount of the food subsidies represented a subsidy to the farmers and how much a subsidy to consumers. But though farmers sometimes grumbled about the inadequacy of the prices fixed, there can be little doubt that farming has been much more profitable than it was

[1] The average of the three years 1936–37 to 1938–39.
[2] Gross output less purchases of feeding-stuffs, stores and seeds from abroad. The figures for Northern Ireland exclude the proceeds of the fattening of stores imported from Eire.

before the war, and particularly so in Northern Ireland, because of the uniform prices. During the past two or three years this system has been modified by the discontinuance of purchase by the Ministry of Food and the gradual re-establishment of a free market in agricultural commodities. But some elements of the system have been retained. Stated broadly, the position is that while in most products a free market has been restored farmers are guaranteed a minimum support price. If the price received in the market falls below this minimum the farmers get the difference as a subsidy. Farmers in Northern Ireland are treated in this respect equally with those in Great Britain. Their differential benefit from the uniformity of prices has disappeared in so far as the prices ruling in the market in Great Britain exceed the corresponding support prices by as much as the differential cost of transport, though it is retained in so far as the difference is less than that. To compensate for the loss, or partial loss, of this former benefit, an arrangement has been made with the central government for the Northern Ireland Ministry of Agriculture to pay out a total sum of £50,000 to farmers against transport costs. Hence while the relative position of farmers in Northern Ireland is not as good as it was under the system of uniform prices, it is better than it was before the war.

In spite of the limitations imposed by restrictions on the importation of feeding-stuffs into the United Kingdom during and after the war, the output of cattle, milk, poultry and eggs has risen considerably. These increases, which are shown in the following table, have been mainly due to an increase in the local production of feeding-stuffs, especially oats, brought about through an increase in the acreage under crops. But they have been partly due, as can be seen from Table 1, to a decrease in the number of sheep and pigs.

Northern Ireland's contribution to the food requirements of the United Kingdom during and since the war has been very considerable. Of special importance has been (and is) its production of animals which yield essential food products in scarce supply. In addition to meeting its own ration requirements of these products (during the period that rationing applied) it has produced an increasing volume for consumption in Great Britain. Animals and animal products exported to Great Britain in substantial quantities include fat and store cattle, sheep, meat, bacon, eggs, poultry and liquid and processed milk. There has been a similar growth in its surplus production of its staple crop, potatoes. Moreover, as a result of the policy of encouraging research and improving the quality of agricultural products, there has been a considerable increase in the export of seeds. An outstanding example is seed

TABLE 1

PRODUCE SOLD OFF FARMS OR CONSUMED IN FARM HOUSEHOLDS

	Unit	Quantity ('000 omitted)			
		1930–31	1938–39	1948–49	1950–51
Livestock:					
Cattle	Number	173	156	218	240
Sheep	Number	261	397	235	303
Pigs	Number	250	844	215	541
Poultry	Number	5,460	6,214	12,846	9,532
Livestock products:					
Milk	Gallon	90,078	83,000	114,702	117,726
Eggs	120	3,969	4,275	7,141	8,805
Wool	lb.	2,000	2,280	1,523	1,851

Source: Ministry of Agriculture.

potatoes, the shipments of which rose from 18,000 tons in 1939 to 136,000 tons in 1949. The following table shows the change in the net exports of some important food products since the beginning of the war. The figures do not, however, measure adequately the increase in net exports of cattle. In 1952 fat cattle exports formed a much larger proportion of the total than in 1940.

TABLE 2

EXPORTS (LESS IMPORTS) OF SELECTED AGRICULTURAL PRODUCTS FROM NORTHERN IRELAND

Product	Unit	1940	1952
Cattle	Number	66,000	90,000
Potatoes	tons	92,000	211,000
Eggs	cwt.	523,000	541,000
Milk (fresh)	cwt.	9,000	684,000
Milk (processed)	cwt.	45,000	674,000

Source: Ministry of Commerce: *Summary of the Trade of Northern Ireland*

(b) *Assistance to New Industries.* Ever since the problem of industrial development in the "depressed areas" came to be accepted in the United Kingdom as a matter of governmental responsibility, the shortage of jobs for industrial workers has formed one of the main subjects of the provincial government's economic policy. The chief means by which it has tried to overcome the shortage has been by offering to assist, financially and otherwise, any firms wishing to start new undertakings or to extend the productive capacity of existing establishments. Legislation empowering it to make concessions for this purpose is contained in two series of Acts: namely, the Loans Guarantee Acts, 1922–38 and 1946, and the New Industries (Development) Acts of 1932, 1937 and 1945.

The Loans Guarantee Acts had a very limited range: they were limited in respect of the form of the assistance that could be given, the type of undertaking to which they applied, and the length of time during which the power to make the concession was continued. Their object was to enable funds to be borrowed, at a low rate of interest, for the building of ships and other forms of capital equipment. The Minister of Commerce was empowered, subject to certain safeguards, to guarantee interest and the repayment of principal on loans made to or raised by corporations, local authorities, etc., for such purposes, so long as the use of the loans in the manner proposed was calculated to increase employment in Northern Ireland. Altogether loans to a total of £22$\frac{1}{2}$ million were guaranteed under these Acts, the chief industry to benefit being ship-building. The operation of these pre-war Acts ceased in 1940, and by 1950 all but about £7,000 had been repaid. Under the Loans Guarantee and Borrowing Regulation Act of 1946, the Minister of Finance is empowered to guarantee loans, up to a total of £2$\frac{1}{4}$ million in any one financial year, to facilitate the reconstruction or development of an industry, so long as he is satisfied that it is in the public interest to do so.

More far-reaching in their effects have been the New Industries (Development) Acts. These Acts were designed to give financial assistance to firms starting new industries or extending existing industries, provided these were calculated to increase employment in the province. The Acts of 1932 and 1937 had a limited success. Under the 1932 Act the government could make grants to undertakings established for the purpose of producing goods of a kind not then being produced in Northern Ireland. The assistance took the form of a grant equivalent to a reasonable annual rent over a maximum period of twenty years, and, in addition, local authorities were empowered to exempt such undertakings from rates. The 1937 Act went further and authorised the making of loans free of interest to cover the costs involved in building or adapting premises. It also authorised loans at interest for other capital requirements. Furthermore, financial assistance could be obtained for the extension of existing businesses. Altogether, fifty-four firms took advantage of the facilities provided under these two pre-war Acts, and by the end of May 1955 they were providing employment for 6,300 persons.

Under the 1945 Act the powers of the government to assist industrial development were greatly extended and made more flexible. The object was to adapt them to the changed conditions of the post-war period, so as to facilitate a quick reconversion to, and expansion of, peace-time industry. In the first place, the government was given much wider discretion than before in the kind and extent of financial assistance which it would give: the Act simply provides that grants may be made to assist industrial undertakings. In the second place, it was recognised that, after six years of war, one of the main obstacles to the peace-time development of industry was the shortage of suitable factory premises and of various basic services on which industry depends. The Act therefore empowers the government to acquire and develop land, to build and lease factories, to make grants towards the cost of basic industrial services—such as means of communication, power, lighting, water supplies and workmen's houses—and generally to assist industrial development in a more flexible manner than hitherto. Up to the end of May 1955, 143 firms had already been established with financial assistance under this post-war Act. Although many of them had not yet got fully going, they were employing between them at that date almost 21,000 workers, of whom 60 per cent were men. According to the plans for expansion which they individually submitted when applying for assistance, these firms will eventually, when fully established, employ a total labour force of approximately 28,000; in addition, 50 firms, employing 4,900 persons, have started production since the war with the co-operation of the New Industries branch of the Ministry of Commerce, though without financial assistance.

In sponsoring new undertakings, the aim has been not only to provide additional employment, but to widen the range of industries in order to secure greater stability of employment. Owing to the great concentration of manufacturing production in the textile industries, especially linen, and in the allied industries of shipbuilding and engineering, Northern Ireland is extremely vulnerable to industrial fluctuations originating outside its borders, particularly as the great bulk of the output of these industries has to be exported to markets in Great Britain or abroad. The aim has therefore been to diversify production as far as possible by encouraging the establishment of industries not liable to experience such wide variations in demand and employment as the staple industries. In this respect the Act has had a considerable measure of success. Of the total employment in factories established since the war (with or without financial assistance) over half is in industries which are new to the province, such as industries producing light and valuable consumption goods, processed food products, and goods for the domestic market. Besides, much of the additional employment in trade groups already strongly represented in Northern Ireland—about a third of the total being in textile industries—is really in new types of industries. For even where the industrial group to which new undertakings belong has previously been represented, the particular products manufactured by these firms often have not been. This is markedly so in the textile and engineering groups. Indeed, within the older-established sections of these industries there has since 1939 been a great increase in the range of products.

Notwithstanding these developments the employment position in Northern Ireland is far from satisfactory. Although employment in Great Britain has been running at a very high level ever since the war, unemployment in Northern Ireland has persisted on a substantial scale, the unemployment rate annually averaging between 5 and 10 per cent. Nor has there been any evidence of net improvement as the new industries have come into production. Indeed, the opposite has been true; for as a result of the textile slump, which was already beginning to make itself felt in the latter part of 1951, the position during 1952 was worse than at any time since the war. There were still, in early 1955, some 37,000 workers wholly unemployed. Moreover, the estimated peak eventually to be reached by employment in the newly established industries, proportionately to the number of workers unemployed, is low in comparison with that in other regions. In Scotland, for example, the estimated further expansion of employment in new industries in process of establishment (started after 1937) amounted at the end of 1950 to about 39,000 workers, or approximately the same as the number unemployed at that date. In contrast to that, the estimated further expansion in the corresponding undertakings in Northern Ireland amounted at the end of 1950 to slightly over 6,000, or only about a quarter of the volume of unemployment then outstanding. It seems clear that, in view of the growing population, the length of time required for new undertakings to reach maturity, the chance of contraction in existing industries, and the possibility that the estimated peak employment will not be reached in all the new industries, Northern Ireland's provision for employment has been far from adequate.

One of the great difficulties of the employment problem is that unemployment tends to be especially severe among men, particularly among unskilled men. Attention has been paid to this point in endeavouring to attract industries of a kind in which the ratio of males to females is high. The proportion of males employed in production and manufacturing industries at June 1954 was 64 per cent. But this figure does not provide a fair standard of comparison for judging how far the government, through the offer of differential inducements to potential new industries, has succeeded in raising the male proportion above what it would have been if an equivalent increase in employment had occurred spontaneously. For some of the old-established male-employing industries cannot reasonably be regarded as falling within the scope of the industries which the government might have tried to expand in this way. Thus it is reasonable to exclude building and contracting on the ground that it is a sheltered industry dependent purely on local demand, and shipbuilding and marine engineering on the ground that, in view of the existing level of these industries in the United Kingdom, any further deliberate expansion of them in Northern Ireland would not at present be justified. Farming also could reasonably be excluded, since the growth in mechanisation and the application of science to agriculture are tending to increase the economic ratio of capital to labour, thereby tending to make even the present labour force excessive. But even if we only exclude shipbuilding and engineering and the building industry, the male proportion in production and manufacturing industries is lowered from the 64 per cent stated above to 54 per cent. By comparison with this figure, the male proportion in those industries which have been started since 1945, with financial assistance from the government, was 60 per cent of the actual labour force employed in May 1955.

While the relative shortage of jobs for men has thus been slightly reduced, the position is still very difficult. Given the existing techniques of production and the existing difference between male and female rates of pay, the most economical labour force, in the vast majority of industries, consists of men for some kinds of work and women for others. Because of the lack of minerals and coal, most heavy industries which employ a high proportion of men are automatically cut out; and the industries most suitable for development in the conditions existing in Northern Ireland require, on the average, a fairly large proportion of women in their total labour force. This being so, one of the difficulties in securing further industrial expansion has been that the numbers of suitable women available (excluding those unemployed during the textile slump in 1952) have generally been too few to form an adequate backing for the unemployed men in a combined labour force. There are, however, several ways in which it might be attempted to meet this difficulty, and at the same time to expand employment as a whole. One would be to try to disperse industries more widely in rural areas, where it would be possible to tap supplies of female labour that are not revealed in the unemployment statistics. Another would be to try to develop industries which, though light, require a high degree of skill and which may consequently find it to be in their long-run interest to use male rather than female labour. A third would be to develop light industries which involve the use of such expensive capital equipment that it would pay to adopt shift working.

In this connection it is strange that more has not been done to develop the only important group of industries whose raw materials can be obtained locally—that is, raw materials produced by the local agricultural industry—especially those industries which employ chiefly men. During the past twenty years there has been a steady increase in the number of workers employed in the food-processing industries, but so far these have been restricted to the processing of milk, fruit, vegetables and pigs. Fat cattle, which form an important proportion of the total value of agricultural output (12·5 per cent in 1948–9) and which in the three years 1948–50 were exported to Great Britain at the annual average rate of 163,000, are slaughtered in Northern Ireland only in so far as they are required for local consumption. If those exported were slaughtered in Northern Ireland and were shipped to England in the form of carcase meat, the hides and offal would provide raw materials for a range of new industries capable of providing considerable employment, especially for men. Apart from this important gain in employment (of the kind which it is particularly difficult to arrange for) the appreciable loss of weight due to the transport of live animals by sea—estimated in the Babington Report to lie between 5 and $7\frac{1}{2}$ per cent—would be avoided. Moreover, according to members of the meat-processing trade, the carcase meat could easily be handled and transported in such a scientific way that its quality (as fresh meat) would not be inferior in any way to that slaughtered in Great Britain; indeed, it would be possible to ensure a uniformly high quality, and so to reap an advantage from being able to identify the meat as produce of Northern Ireland.

The failure of the government to take advantage of these potential benefits appears to be due, at least in part, to a fear that there might be adverse reactions on the farmers. It seems to be feared—notwithstanding the opinion of meat-processors stated in the preceding paragraph— that meat killed in Northern Ireland would be unable to fetch as good a price in Great Britain as home-killed meat. Moreover, under the system of uniform agricultural prices, the cost of transport and the loss due to shrinkage in weight and deterioration in quality while the beasts are in transit have been shifted from the farmers to the Ministry of Food at Westminster, and the provincial Ministry of Agriculture is probably anxious to avoid doing anything that might cause this benefit to its farmers to be lost. Against this cautious view, it can be shown that slaughtering in Northern Ireland would substantially increase the scope for industrial employment, both in the processing of food and in the manufacture of by-products, as well as providing an opportunity to build up a reputation for Northern Ireland as a producer of high-quality meat. Unlike some of the alternative projects for increasing employment, manufacturing based on fat cattle production promises to be capable of standing on its own feet as an economic undertaking. This view is confirmed by the success of the small experimental shipments of carcase meat to England made by the Government.

At the same time as particular food-processing firms have received governmental help in establishing new factories—as they have during the past decade—the policy of uniform agricultural prices, extended to Northern Ireland with an eye to the interest of its farmers, has put a handicap on manufacturing industries generally, and also a special handicap on those industries which depend on farm products, including the food-processing industries themselves. By raising farm prices to the same level as those paid in Great Britain, the system of uniform agricultural prices has tended to raise the cost of living more than in Great Britain, and, to that extent, to cause a relative increase in wages. Thanks to the great improvement in general conditions of trade and employment that has been going on, industrial development has not in consequence been held up absolutely; but it no doubt has been slower than it would have been if it had not been for these effects of removing the differential in agricultural prices. In addition, however, to this hampering effect on manufacturing of all kinds in Northern Ireland, the payment of uniform agricultural prices has weakened in a special way the competitive position of the particular group of industries which use the uniformly-priced agricultural products as their raw materials. For, with the exception of certain food-processors who have been working on a commission-basis for the Ministry of Food, manufacturers of goods from these products have lost the advantage of relatively cheap raw materials which formerly compensated, at least in part, for the greater cost (compared with that of favourably-situated competitors in Great Britain) of transporting their finished goods to market. The result may be seriously to retard progress in the only important group of industries which get all or most of their raw materials from domestic sources.

(c) *Investment and the Supply of Capital.* The failure of industry to grow fast enough to provide jobs for all the available workers, at market rates of pay, simply means that, given the amount of capital required per worker in the kind of industries best fitted to thrive in Northern Ireland, the rate of investment in industrial capital is not great enough to match the growth in the number of workers. *A priori*, this may be due to either, or both, of two general causes. First, it may mean that the expected rate of profit from investment on that scale does not provide sufficient inducement: even if investment in existing undertakings has been very profitable, further new ventures would not yield, or would not be expected to yield, such good returns on the capital as can be got elsewhere. Secondly, it may mean that industrialists, though wishing to establish new enterprises or enlarge existing ones (because they do expect to make at least the normal rate of profit on the investment), are nevertheless unable to do so because they lack the necessary funds and, for one reason or another, are unable to borrow them at current market rates.

Though the evidence is not conclusive, there is reason to believe that Northern Ireland is starved of capital in both of these senses. The main obstacle to industrial growth on a sufficient scale is the relative lack of openings for profitable investment; the margin beyond which further investment would be unprofitable (i.e. less profitable than alternative investments elsewhere) always tends to be reached while there are still too few jobs for all of the available workers. This is evident from the existence of heavy additional costs of transport in most lines of production, over those borne by competing industries in Great Britain, and from the narrow range of industries to which industrial growth, because of these additional costs, has been largely confined. But there is some indirect evidence that there is a shortage of capital in the other sense as well: it is generally more difficult than in Great Britain for old firms wishing to modernise their equipment, and for new firms wishing to make a start, to get hold of the necessary capital, even though on a reasonable assessment the expectations of profit on the investment are quite satisfactory. Evidence that this may be so will be examined below. Direct or indirect evidence is to be found in the following: in the existence of institutions which tend to drain off small savings to Great Britain; in the large export of capital to Great Britain (though this is certainly due in part to the lack of profitable openings for domestic investment); in the greater preponderance than in Great Britain of the small family firm, with its inherent difficulties in raising funds for expansion, especially in present conditions; and in the response to the provincial government's offer, through the Re-Equipment of Industry Act, 1951, of funds for the modernisation of equipment and techniques.

As regards the relative amount of producers' capital in Northern Ireland and in the United Kingdom as a whole, it is impracticable to make a direct comparison which would be meaningful because of the difficulty of estimating the total amount of invested capital on a comparable basis throughout. For this reason the best guide to the position in Northern Ireland is the flow of investment funds into and out of the province. Data are not available for measuring these flows year by year, but we can get figures which will enable us to estimate approximately the accumulated total amount invested outside the province by residents of Northern Ireland and the total invested in the province by outsiders.

Looking at the investment position from this point of view, the outstanding fact is that Northern Ireland is (or hitherto has been) on balance an exporter of capital. On the one hand, a large proportion of the total capital owned by people living in Northern Ireland is invested in government securities, business undertakings and other forms of property situated outside the province. On the other hand, a considerable proportion of the total capital invested in Northern Ireland belongs to outsiders. But the total amount of their holdings is very much smalle· than the total amount invested outside the province by residents. According to provisional estimates which we have made of these totals, residents of Northern Ireland collectively own investments outside the province valued at more than £400 million, while the counter investment in Northern Ireland by outsiders amounts to only about £60 million. Of the total amount invested outside the province, the bulk is situated in Great Britain. A large proportion consists of British Government securities; though, if we only take account of personal investment (as distinct from that made by banks and similar institutions), practically half consists of shares and debentures of companies. Again, just as most of the capital exported from Northern Ireland is invested in Great Britain, so, also, most of that imported from outside consists of investments owned in Great Britain. There is some evidence that the flow of capital both to and from Great Britain is tending to increase, and in this way Northern Ireland is being economically interwoven with Great Britain even more closely than before.

Since Northern Ireland is itself very short of capital, at least in the sense that not enough has been invested to bring industry up to the level at which there would be jobs for all the workers, it is important to consider why so much capital is exported. Measures for encouraging the investment of a larger proportion of the annual savings at home must be based on an understanding of the causes of the outflow. This does not mean that efforts should be made to counteract the effects of each and all of these causes. Some investment outside a region, particularly one as small economically as Northern Ireland, is natural and, from the point of view of the individual investor, desirable. What is required in order that industrial development in the province should keep in line with development in Great Britain is that the outflow of capital should be more or less balanced by a flow in the opposite direction. It is because the outflow is so much greater than the inflow that it is desirable to examine the causes in order to see how far (if at all) it is due to arbitrary and avoidable causes, and what action could therefore usefully be taken to diminish the outflow and increase the inflow.

The basic reason for the very large net export of capital, as of its counterpart, the lack of sufficient capital for investment in domestic industry, is the relative lack of openings for profitable investment within Northern Ireland. This means that, owing to the additional costs imposed by the natural handicaps, the expectation of profit from investment in industrial enterprises in Northern Ireland, if investment were raised to a level that would yield full employment, would be less than the corresponding rate of profit in Great Britain. To this extent investment would automatically rise to the required level if more business firms could be persuaded or induced to establish industrial enterprises in Northern Ireland; and from this point of view it would not matter greatly whether the funds were raised locally, which would presumably mean a similar reduction in capital exports, or whether they were obtained from the English capital market, which would mean a corresponding increase in capital imports. Thus in so far as the cause of the net export of capital is the lack of profitable openings for investment, there is no special problem of the supply of industrial capital over and above the problem of encouraging industrial development on a sufficient scale. The lack of capital is in this sense a result, not a cause, and will disappear automatically if sufficient inducement can be given, through the kind of measures outlined in section (b), to encourage new undertakings to be established.

But in addition to the lack of profitable openings for investment, there are special reasons for the large export of capital. Some of them are due to the nature of the particular institutions which happen to have evolved and which could be modified, without harm, in such a way as to facilitate the investment of a larger proportion of domestic savings in domestic industry. One such institutional factor, however, is a condition laid down in Northern Ireland's Constitution. In Section 9 of the Government of Ireland Act, one of the matters classified as a reserved matter is the Post Office Savings Bank and Trustee Savings Banks. The many small savings collected together by these banks, already included in the foregoing estimate of external investments, form part of the funds exported to Great Britain and represent a loss of potential capital for industry in the province. Some of these savings could no doubt be diverted to domestic industry if the Northern Ireland Government took steps to develop supplementary institutions of its own.[1]

That there should be a good deal of investment of Northern Ireland savings in British Government securities is not surprising. For there is an insufficiency of Northern Ireland trustee securities, both in variety and in volume, to meet the provincial demand for this type of investment. Thus the tendency for funds to be invested outside the province arises in part from the demand for gilt-edged securities. The heavy investment in the shares of outside companies, on the other hand, is probably due to three different reasons: a desire to spread risks over a greater variety of investments, a desire to participate in higher yields than those anticipated from the type of industrial investments available in the province, and a lack of opportunity for the small investor to buy shares of companies in Northern Ireland because very few are available to the general public. These reasons are a reflection of Northern Ireland's narrow industrial structure and they consequently tend to be self-perpetuating.

It does not necessarily follow that the individual entrepreneurs in Northern Ireland are more limited in outlook and enterprise than those in Great Britain. Rather, the concentration on a few industries (together with the geological and geographical facts responsible for it) tends in itself to discourage them from launching out into new industries, just as it discourages entrepreneurs in Great Britain from establishing in the province branches of their own industries. The other side of this is that an initial increase in the diversification of industry would help in getting further diversification. It would do so partly by creating a demand for ancillary products. Besides, entrepreneurs as a body would gain knowledge of a wider range of techniques, and there would be a greater chance of finding workers with the acquired skills necessary in any particular new venture. In this connection it is significant that some of the more important manufacturing industries in Northern Ireland owe their beginnings, and at least part of their vigorous later growth, to immigrants who brought a knowledge of the techniques of those industries with them. It is also noteworthy that factories established in Northern Ireland by companies registered in Great Britain are proportionately much less important in the textile, engineering and shipbuilding industries than in industries more widely dispersed geographically, such as those producing

[1] C.f section (e), below.

chemicals, precision instruments, non-metalliferous mining products, food, electrical goods, and leather goods.

Another reason why people in Northern Ireland hold such a large proportion of their wealth in Great Britain is that industry in the province offers little scope for the investor who wants to have his money in fairly liquid forms of investment and little scope for the small saver to invest in any industrial enterprise at all. This reason is closely related to those already mentioned; like them it is a reflection of the underlying conditions governing the industrial structure. In most of the light industries which thrive in Northern Ireland the unit of production, as we have seen, is fairly small. It does not follow that the business unit is also small, but in fact it generally is. The predominant form of business organisation is the private company, which as a rule is limited to family ownership. Compared with their importance in Great Britain, private companies are more important than public both in number and in paid-up capital. Of the total paid-up capital of companies registered in Northern Ireland, 60 per cent is in private companies, whereas the corresponding figure for Great Britain is only 35 per cent. Public companies not only form a smaller proportion of the total than in Great Britain, but are so few absolutely that they offer only a very narrow range of choice of investments. Besides, very few shares of public companies in Northern Ireland are regularly quoted on the Stock Exchange. The contrast with Great Britain in these respects is brought out by the following table:

TABLE 3

PUBLIC AND PRIVATE COMPANIES AT 31ST DECEMBER, 1953

Place of Registration	Private Companies		Public Companies	
	Number	Paid-up Capital £ million	Number	Paid-up Capital £ million
Northern Ireland	3,155	41·44	109	25·79
Great Britain	258,826	2,350	11,444	4,062
United Kingdom	261,981	2,391	11,553	4,088

Source: Central Statistical Office: *Annual Abstract of Statistics, No. 91*, and Northern Ireland Ministry of Commerce.

Whether the prevalence of family ownership and control of business in Northern Ireland has on balance helped or hindered economic development is hard to assess. On the one hand, by limiting the scope for industrial investment in the manner described above, it has encouraged the export of industrial capital which might otherwise have been profitably used at home. It may also have restricted expansion in certain industries by keeping secret the rate of profit earned. On the other hand, it has probably had an important stabilising effect on industrial employment. Thus there is reason to believe that during the worst years of the depression many family businesses continued to operate even when they were no longer earning enough to cover full managerial salaries. What does seem clear, however, is that when private companies, in order to overcome the difficulties of getting capital for extension or even maintenance, wish to convert themselves into public companies, it is in the public interest that they should have access to the appropriate institutions of the capital market on reasonable terms. As things are at present, the only choice open to most private companies is to sell out, lock, stock and barrel, to one of the large English finance companies.

But whatever may have been the net effects on industrial development resulting from the prevalence of the family business in Northern Ireland in the past, there is reason to fear that, owing to heavy death duties, they will be less favourable in future. For high rates of death duties are tending to limit the expansion and undermine the stability of family businesses more than they are those of public companies. On the death of an important shareholder in a public company the death duties can be paid, through the sale of some of his shares on the market, without endangering the continued existence of the company as such. But this is not true of the private company. The death of any of its chief shareholders is a contingency which sets it an awkward problem of policy. If profits are ploughed back into the business in order to expand its production, the testator's capital will be locked up. In that event the need suddenly to turn part of this capital into money may cause a severe shock to the business. It may even be forced to sell out. But even if it succeeds in maintaining its identity, it may only be able to do so by realising trading assets, or even part of its fixed capital, at bargain prices. In many family businesses policy is therefore dominated by the desire to avoid this contingency. Instead of using profits to expand production, they (or their principal shareholders if the profits are distributed) tend to hold large reserves in the form of bank deposits or gilt-edged securities. In so far as high death duties consequently restrict the expansion of family businesses more than that of public companies, Northern Ireland will suffer proportionately more than Great Britain: a larger proportion of investment funds than in Great Britain will either be held as idle balances or be exported to pay for marketable securities.

M

The effect on industry in Northern Ireland may also be adverse in so far as family businesses, instead of following this cautious policy, expand as fast as current profits allow. Already the high rates of death duties have forced a number of such businesses either to transform themselves into public companies (where this has been feasible) or to sell out to larger financial concerns or industrial concerns in Great Britain. Employment in businesses forced to sell out is liable to become less stable in consequence. As mere subsidiary and outlying factories controlled by firms whose main production is in Great Britain, they are more likely to be closed down in times of depression than are factories whose owners depend solely or mainly on their Northern Ireland production. While it may pay to buy factories in Northern Ireland, and to run them so long as there is a sellers' market and labour in Great Britain continues to be scarce, it must be expected that any contraction in output during times of depression will be concentrated in a firm's least economical factories; and depression, as we have seen, would tend to accentuate the cost disadvantages of location in Northern Ireland. The resulting danger of instability must not, however, be exaggerated. For there are several respects in which the transfer of ownership may work the other way. In particular, the factories concerned will stand to gain in strength from technical co-operation with a large organisation and from improved marketing facilities. In addition, some may gain in stability by being allotted processes which complement those of other factories in the same organisation. Nevertheless, in general, the danger of increased instability is real.

It is true that, since death duties form part of the transferred taxes, the government of Northern Ireland has the legal authority to fix the rates, if it likes, below those in Great Britain. It can only do so, however, at a price. For if parity of social services is to be allowed in calculating the amount of the Imperial Contribution, the Minister of Finance must be able to show that the general tax burden in Northern Ireland is not lower than in Great Britain. Such a complication arose over an amendment to the Finance Bill (Northern Ireland), 1951, relating to the length of time that gifts *inter vivos* must have been made in order to be exempt from death duties. It was then decided to revert from the five-year period adopted along with Great Britain in 1946 to the former period of three years. Since this change was made unilaterally, and since the loss of revenue therefore had to be made good by raising some other tax within the limited field of the transferred taxes, it was decided to impose a tax on pools.

Apart from trying to encourage business men to establish new industries, the most constructive action so far taken by the provincial government in the general field of investment has been to offer financial help to enable firms comprehensively to re-equip their factories. In the depressed state of industry in Northern Ireland in the pre-war years, profits were low and often negative. There was therefore a general shortage of funds, as well as a lack of incentive, for keeping capital equipment up to date. Although profits have been considerably higher during and since the war, funds with which to finance capital expenditure, on a scale sufficient to enable plants to be brought up to date, have often been lacking for other reasons. The principal causes have been common to the United Kingdom as a whole: in particular, high rates of taxation have made it difficult for firms to build up reserves, and the process of inflation has substantially reduced their ability to re-equip out of accumulated reserves. But, as we have seen, Northern Ireland's position is worse than that of Great Britain because of the greater prevalence of private companies and the consequent need for industry to hold larger liquid reserves as a safeguard against inopportune demands for death duties. In order to encourage and assist firms to overcome these difficulties by adopting comprehensive plans for bringing their plant and machinery up to date, the Parliament of Northern Ireland in 1951 passed the Re-Equipment of Industry Act. This Act provides for the payment of grants towards expenditure incurred in modernising industrial undertakings.

Compared with the New Industries (Development) Acts, which aim at increasing the total employment by subsidising new ventures, or the expansion of existing undertakings, this enactment is intended to encourage existing firms thoroughly to overhaul their equipment and so to get on a sounder basis by increasing their productivity. But where rebuilding, or even an extension of the building, is an unavoidable condition of the modernisation process, the expenditure on it may qualify for a grant on the same terms as machinery and equipment. Approved schemes are eligible for a grant of up to one-third of the total expenditure. Safeguards are provided against misuse of the grant through re-sale or letting of the equipment concerned within a period of ten years. The kind of assistance given under this Act is roughly similar to that provided for the cotton industry in Great Britain under the Cotton Spinning (Re-Equipment Subsidy) Act of 1948. In three important respects, however, it is more generous: the grant is for one-third of the total cost instead of one-quarter; all industries are eligible and not merely the cotton industry; and there is no lower limit to the size of firms or the amount of expenditure on re-equipment which may qualify for a grant.

Up to May 1954 about 160 applications had been approved, involving a total estimated expenditure on modernisation schemes of some £11 million. Grants of £1½ million on completed schemes had already been paid. Though not spectacular, these results indicate that the scheme has made a useful contribution towards a solution of the problem.

(d) *Some Economic Benefits and Drawbacks of Provincial Government.* Although limited self-government for Northern Ireland was not decided upon for economic reasons—at any rate not principally—the question whether or not it has in fact turned out well economically is clearly important to the people of Northern Ireland. Moreover, in view of the agitation for separate parliaments in Scotland and Wales, it is also important because it illustrates the kind of economic effects which regional autonomy might be expected to have in other outlying regions of the United Kingdom as well. But the question whether Northern Ireland is better off on balance as a result of having self-government, or whether it is worse off, cannot be answered definitely from the study of the economy made in the present chapter. What that question really amounts to is whether the province would be better off, from an economic point of view, if self-government were abandoned in favour of some arrangement for the devolution of certain administrative functions such as exists for Scotland and Wales. And for this purpose it would be necessary to assess and compare the effects of two different sets of governmental measures: namely, the measures actually adopted by the provincial government, and those hypothetical measures which, in the absence of self-government, would have been taken by the central government or its agencies. In this chapter, however, we have been concerned with the economy as it is, moulded as it has been by natural conditions as well as by governmental policy, and the comparisons with Great Britain have been made on that basis. The effects of self-government cannot be satisfactorily assessed by comparing the state of prosperity with that in other regions (such as Scotland or Wales) and attributing any difference to the fact of self-government; for part or all of it may have been caused by differences in the underlying economic conditions, whose influence cannot be distinguished. Nevertheless, some of the considerations discussed in this chapter do give rise to tentative conclusions, on both the economic benefits of self-government and also the drawbacks.

The economic benefits conferred by provincial government are those resulting from the increased flexibility which it gives to the economy. Greater flexibility is made possible in two different ways, the one legislative and the other administrative. The legislative advantage is that, at least in theory, economic and social measures adopted by the central government can be modified where necessary—within the limits set by the transferred powers—to suit Northern Ireland's special conditions, and, within these same limits, Northern Ireland can initiate legislation of its own in accordance with its own special needs. But while this adaptability must be admitted as a potential economic advantage, it would be easy to exaggerate its real significance. For Northern Ireland is economically so closely united with Great Britain that, notwithstanding its special features, the economic benefits accruing from its powers of independent enactment are probably not very important in practice.

The advantages accruing from decentralised administration have greater substance. One such advantage is that, within the limits imposed by Northern Ireland's share of capital expenditure, the provincial government can sponsor, or itself undertake, important developmental projects without having to wait for the central government to be convinced, in course of time, that they should take precedence over alternative projects situated nearer London and more favourably placed for pressing their claims. But the chief administrative advantage is that business men in Northern Ireland have much easier and quicker access to responsible officials—and so are able to obtain administrative decisions relating to their business more quickly—than would be possible if reference had always to be made to the central administration. They are thus able to avoid delays in production which administrative procedures would otherwise be almost certain to cause; indeed, from this point of view they are better placed than most of their competitors in Great Britain. With the establishment of governmental controls over the economy during and since the war, this advantage in many lines of production has taken on added significance. We have discussed its importance with industrialists who have established branch factories in Northern Ireland since the war, and who consequently have had experience of the administration of industrial-development measures in Great Britain as well as in Northern Ireland, They all value highly the ease with which they can get in touch with the responsible officials, and the speed with which, as a result, they can obtain administrative decisions and get industrial schemes under way. It is evident from their replies that in deciding to locate their new factories in Northern Ireland, in preference to alternative sites in Great Britain, some of them gave this factor a good deal of weight.

But from the point of view of Northern Ireland's economic development, separate provincial government also has very serious drawbacks.

The central government has, of course, a general responsibility for economic conditions and progress in Northern Ireland, which continues to elect representatives to the Imperial parliament. Nevertheless, having provided Northern Ireland with its separate provincial government, it tends to fix its own attention directly on affairs in Great Britain—since it has sole responsibility for them—and to concern itself with affairs in Northern Ireland only when, and in so far as, the provincial government makes explicit representations to it. In consequence, economic development in Northern Ireland is subject to a number of very severe handicaps. The most significant of these are set out below.

Firstly, in making policy decisions on economic and social matters for the whole of the United Kingdom, the central government tends to overlook any adverse effect which there may be on Northern Ireland (because of its special conditions) and hence any need which there may be to apply particular policies to it in a modified form. Though general measures must be determined in accordance with the interests of the whole country, the rules under which they are applied can often be adapted to suit the needs of particular regions. But owing to the very fact of self-government, Northern Ireland's special interests of this kind tend to be overlooked. An illustration is afforded by the rules adopted as an anti-inflation measure for restricting bank credit in recent years. These were adopted because of inflationary tendencies in the country as a whole. It so happened, however, that they came into force precisely at a time when, owing to the slump in the linen industry, unemployment in Northern Ireland, already heavy, was tending to increase. Probably the main trouble is that in central government policy making, especially in the early stages when the interests of different government departments in any proposed measures are being examined by inter-departmental committees, there is no one there, as a rule, whose overriding responsibility is to watch the interests of Northern Ireland.

Secondly, because the members of the government and their officials represent a subordinate authority, they tend to be at a disadvantage in dealing with ministers and officials in Great Britain, especially over any matters involving a conflict of economic interest. Certain kinds of industrial development tend, in consequence, to be heavily handicapped or altogether prevented. Some industrial schemes cannot be undertaken at all unless they have the approval or active co-operation of governmental authorities in Great Britain, as a means of obtaining licences, permits, essential supplies, etc. For this purpose they need the backing of the relevant ministers or officials in Northern Ireland, by whom their case must be urged. If, however, there appears to be any danger that they would significantly displace competing industries in Great Britain, the British officials are likely to show a reluctance to become embroiled. In order that they should be saved from embarrassment, the necessary backing in the province is likely to be withheld. It is particularly likely to be withheld if the relevant competing industries are run by the British Government or have any right to expect its special solicitude. In general, therefore, the provincial administration appears to be very reluctant to press for developments which would cause any disturbance in the economic structure of Great Britain, even when it is clear that in the absence of governmental control they would have no difficulty in attracting the necessary enterprise. Thus, it may well be that the unwillingness of the Ministry of Agriculture to encourage the processing of beef for export, by releasing enough fat cattle for the purpose, is partly explicable in this way.

Thirdly, the provincial administration is at a similar disadvantage in dealing with influential business interests in the province. In such a small business community as that of Northern Ireland there is inevitably a good deal of scope for the exercise of special privilege; and under self-government, therefore, it is difficult for the administration to be always thoroughly impartial. Two examples will suffice to show the nature and importance of this difficulty. The first relates to the location of new industries. There are various ways in which the Ministry of Commerce, like the Board of Trade in Great Britain, can influence industrial location. In particular, it possesses the power of the purse so far as financial assistance in the establishment of new enterprises is concerned; and it has had till recently control over building and permits to obtain certain raw materials. It cannot by means of these controls force new enterprises to accept a particular location, but it can usually prevent them from being established where it does not want them. This fact enables influential firms to exert pressure to restrain others from coming into a district as competitors for labour. Since the primary aim of the Ministry in seeking new industries is to provide additional employment where it is most wanted, rather than to permit alternative forms of employment where employment already exists, it is easy for it to convince itself that, in preventing the establishment of competing industries in such circumstances, it is acting in the interests of the community, especially as in some cases it may be. The other example relates to the import of coal. The price in Belfast is much higher than in most places in Great Britain. This is so partly because of extra handling and carriage. But there is some reason to believe that it may also be partly due to the existence of a ring in coal distribution which, like other rings, condones inefficient methods and permits of monopoly pricing.

Fourthly, so far as the capacity to attract new industry is concerned, self-government puts Northern Ireland at a disadvantage, in one important respect if not on balance, compared with the Development Areas in Great Britain, to which its economic conditions make it closely akin. Though the establishment of new industries in the Development Areas has been achieved partly through the offer of inducements, it has been partly achieved through deliberate pressure exerted by the central government through its control of materials, capital issues, licences to establish new undertakings, licences to build, etc. While the provincial government, acting as the agent of the Board of Trade, can use some of these powers to try to induce firms to establish new factories in Northern Ireland, it cannot use them, as the Board of Trade can, to dissuade firms from establishing factories somewhere else in the United Kingdom instead. The Board of Trade consequently has the pick of the new industries for the Development Areas. It cannot be expected to exert pressure on firms to locate their planned expansion in Northern Ireland so long as it is open to criticism for doing too little for these areas, the areas for whose development it is directly responsible.

The foregoing economic advantages and disadvantages of self-government cannot be quantitatively measured, and hence it is impossible to be sure whether the advantages outweigh the disadvantages or fall short of them. On the one hand, as we have seen, the provincial government has been responsible for enacting a series of measures designed to raise the level of employment and increase both agricultural and manufacturing efficiency. Agricultural production has considerably increased during recent years, largely as a result of this and other governmental action, and, according to the latest published figures, employment had already by mid 1955 been provided for some 21,000 workers in undertakings established after the war under the New Industries Development Act. But, on the other hand, as we have also seen, the planned increase in employment still to be made in factories established (or arranged to be established) with financial assistance from the government, or with the government's co-operation in getting supplies, etc., falls short of the amount required in order to get rid of the differentially high rate of unemployment compared with the average for the United Kingdom. Notwithstanding the considerable emigration of workers resulting from the relatively poor prospects of employment in Northern Ireland, and the relatively low average earnings, the unemployment rate has been consistently higher than the average for the United Kingdom by at least as much as 5 per cent unemployment, and in most years it has been substantially more than that. Thus, although unemployment is much less absolutely than it was before the war, there has not been a very large reduction in the differential rate, which, during the pre-war years 1923–39, amounted on the average to an unemployment rate of 8·5 per cent.

As regards the reduction of unemployment, Northern Ireland stands in fairly sharp contrast with the Development Areas in Great Britain; for in these areas there has been a large fall not only in the absolute amount of unemployment but in the differential rate as well. Nor is there much prospect that the relative deterioration in Northern Ireland will be reversed in the near future. The prospective increase in employment still to be made in factories already established or arranged for, in proportion to the existing deficiency in the number of jobs, is much smaller than in the Development Areas. Even before the increase in unemployment due to the slump in the linen industry, the planned increase, as we have seen, amounted to only about one quarter of the number of workers unemployed at that time, whereas in Scotland, for example, it was about the same as the number of unemployed workers. It does not necessarily follow that the expansion of industry and employment would have been greater in the absence of self-government, since it may be that the forces opposing expansion in Northern Ireland were harder to overcome. What is clear, however, is that the success of the provincial government in getting rid of unemployment has not been impressive in comparison with the central government's corresponding achievements in the Development Areas.

There is, however, one respect in which, as a result of having self-government, Northern Ireland almost certainly is worse off than it would be without it. There is a tendency for the provincial government to keep its expenditure on transferred services below the level which, having regard to the severity of taxation, would be allowed by the Joint Exchequer Board in calculating the amount of the Imperial Contribution. Under the existing financial arrangements there is no certainty that Northern Ireland will invariably have enough revenue, while taxing at the same combined rates as those applicable in Great Britain, to provide services of a comparable standard, even without making any contribution whatever towards the cost of the Imperial services. The fear of this possibility tends to make the provincial government reluctant, in years of expanding revenue, to commit itself to recurring expenditure on as high a scale as the Joint Exchequer Board would approve; and in years of sharply falling revenue there is always a danger, since the main tax-rates are fixed with reference to the needs of the United Kingdom, that it may prove impossible both to maintain all social and other public services

at a parity with those in Great Britain and also to contribute towards the
cost of the Imperial services. The Imperial Contribution never has, in
fact, fallen to zero; though occasionally, when Northern Ireland has
been specially depressed, it has not been much more than a token contribution. Indeed, if all services (including the provision of employment),
had always in fact been kept at strict parity with those in Great Britain,
the calculation of the Imperial Contribution for these particular years
would probably have given the result of a negative figure. Even now,
after more than a decade of consistently large Imperial Contributions,
the standard of services is not in all respects as high as in Great Britain,
partly because of a cautious attitude towards growing recurrent expenditure born of the experience of past difficulties in making ends meet.
Thus, as things are, self-government puts Northern Ireland in a position
in which reasonable financial caution impels it to stint somewhat on its
domestic services, in order, in effect, to contribute towards the cost of
Imperial services a larger sum than it would as an undifferentiated part of
the United Kingdom. This tendency to relative niggardliness in the
provision of public services is not, however, an inevitable result of self-
government as such, but is due to the particular financial arrangements
under which devolution operates. It is partly, and indeed largely, offset
by the reinsurance agreements relating to expenditure on social services.
It could be completely overcome by providing for the contingency of a
special grant from the Imperial exchequer in any year in which the
provincial government, though maintaining the same level of taxation as
in Great Britain, could not otherwise maintain parity of services even
when taking full advantage of the reinsurance agreements. Such a provision would merely represent an extension to Northern Ireland of the
right to parity of services (coupled with equality of the rates of taxation,
including local taxation, in effect adopted for the different parts of
Great Britain under the Local Government Act of 1929, and already
accepted in principle by the Joint Exchequer Board.

The payment of special grants for the purpose of equitably redistribu-
ting total revenue, on this principle of parity or on some modification of
it, is incidental to all federations as well as to central governments in
their relations with local-government bodies. It is, for example, an
accepted feature of the financial relations between the federal government and the governments of the member States in the Commonwealth
of Australia. Though provision was at first made for State grants only
till 1910 (as compensation for the loss of Customs revenue), it has been
found necessary to continue them ever since. Between 1910 and 1927 the
payments to the States were on a *per capita* basis, and, from 1927 to 1933,

according to a mechanical formula related to the States' public debts. From 1933 onwards, special grants have been accepted as a permanent feature of federal finance. Since it was recognised that the relative position of the Commonwealth and the various States is liable to vary, and that, owing to differences in natural resources or even past mismanagement, some States are likely to be much poorer than others, the Commonwealth Grants Commission was established to review the financial position of the different States year by year. In deciding upon the size of the grants to recommend for the claimant States, the Commission adopted as its criterion the relative financial needs of each State as seen against the background of conditions in the federation as a whole. It therefore laid it down that needy States, whatever the cause of their financial difficulties, should receive grants sufficient to enable them "by reasonable effort to function at a standard not appreciably below that of other States". No qualification was made that the rule should apply only if the grant required by a State for this purpose did not exceed the amount of taxation paid by the citizens of the State into the Commonwealth exchequer. Nevertheless, such a limitation would have been equivalent to the condition that Northern Ireland's right to enjoy parity of services only applies so long as the Imperial Contribution does not fall to zero. In this respect, therefore, Northern Ireland receives less favourable consideration from the United Kingdom than the Australian States receive from the Commonwealth.

In trying to reach a conclusion on the benefits and drawbacks of provincial autonomy for Northern Ireland, it is necessary to bear in mind that the system was devised for political rather than economic reasons. Furthermore, it was not actively sought by the majority of the people of Northern Ireland but—to put the matter bluntly—was forced upon them in an effort to appease the then embryonic Irish Free State. But with the withdrawal of Southern Ireland from the United Kingdom, together with its transition into a full self-governing dominion, and later (in 1948) its withdrawal as an independent republic from the British Commonwealth of Nations, these political reasons, even if they have not entirely vanished, have lost much of their force. Hence there is point in considering whether the benefits of self-government are great enough to justify its continuance, or whether it would be better for Northern Ireland to give up its semi-independent existence and return to (or ask to be no longer partially excluded from) the British fold. More weight than formerly, though perhaps less than due weight even now, can be given to the economic issues. And though it is necessary to rely on general impressions, it is hard to resist the conclusion, which has gradually been taking shape during the foregoing discussion, that Northern Ireland is worse off economically than it would be if the Government of Ireland Act were repealed and the semblance of self-government were thereby removed, especially as there would still be some devolution of administrative functions, presumably along the lines of that in Scotland. Whatever may be true of its non-economic effects, it appears that provincial autonomy has been a doubtful privilege economically.

Looking at the matter from an economic point of view, the existence of a provincial government encourages the expectation that effective action will be taken to improve economic conditions in the province. Yet the powers of the provincial government are not great enough to enable it to do anything very effective. It has too much power to be able to rest content to do nothing, but too little power to be able to take really effective action. It is true that it does not make continuously full use of all the powers which it possesses under its Constitution, and that ways have been suggested above in which more effective use could be made of some of them. But what appears to some of its critics to be slavish copying of legislation adopted by the central government for Great Britain does not denote an unimaginative approach to its problems, but a sense of realism. For, even within the confines of its transferred powers, the provincial government is often limited in its freedom to follow an independent course by the economic repercussions which such action might entail. Northern Ireland is linked with Great Britain not only economically, in the various intimate ways explained above, but also by ties of blood, of common language, of common nationality and of common traditions. In consequence, capital and labour are highly sensitive to regional differences in economic and social conditions. This is particularly true of capital, which is proverbially shy. But, with a somewhat longer time for reactions, it is also true of labour. Even during the period between the wars, when unemployment in the United Kingdom was wide-spread as well as heavy, workers moved to and fro between Northern Ireland and Great Britain, as relative conditions changed, in very considerable numbers. Any attempt by the provincial government to impose worse conditions on either labour or capital than exist in Great Britain—such as lower wages, less generous social services or higher taxes—would necessarily be limited by the danger of defeating itself by causing an outflow of either capital or labour as the case may be.

Moreover, regional self-government is only one method of achieving a devolution of the powers of government (above those of local government), and not necessarily in all circumstances the best. The main alternative method is that of the devolution of individual administrative functions. Instead of creating a number of subordinate areas of government (such as Northern Ireland) and transferring to each of them all the functions intended to be delegated, this alternative method is to subdivide the country differently for each of the different functions. The aim is to choose the particular kind of subdivision—the particular grouping of districts into administrative regions—which is the optimum from the point of view of the particular function concerned. This is the form which regional devolution (as distinct from local government) takes in England. In Scotland there are features of both methods. Thus the region selected for the purposes of devolution is generally the whole of Scotland; and though, unlike Northern Ireland, Scotland does not possess a separate parliament of its own, the Secretary of State for Scotland is generally responsible for Scottish affairs in the House of Commons. In the particular case of Northern Ireland, the province itself is almost certainly the optimum region for most functions. It is very doubtful whether, for any of the devolved functions, it could be usefully subdivided, and even more doubtful whether, for others, it could be effectively grouped with parts of England or Scotland. On the one hand, effective subdivision would be difficult because the industrial life of the whole province is dominated by Belfast and its neighbourhood; and, on the other hand, grouping with other regions would almost certainly be inefficient because of the Irish Sea. But even if the optimum size of region for the devolution of administration is, for these reasons, the same for all functions, i.e. the province itself, this is not sufficient reason why there should be a separate parliament for legislating on these devolved functions. In some respects a separate parliament may simplify the task of co-ordination. But it is a cumbersome way of doing this, and, as we have seen, there are some grave economic objections to it.

(e) *Some Economic Implications of an Increase in Legislature Powers.*
If the tentative conclusions on existing self-government are correct—namely, that since it does not enable Northern Ireland to take really effective steps to increase employment and income independently of Great Britain, there is not much to be said for it on economic grounds—the correct inference, even if there are no compensating benefits in other ways, may be not that self-government should be abolished, but that the economic powers of the province should be increased. The enlarged economic powers might, at the extreme, be as great as those of a self-governing dominion. Alternatively, they might represent a compromise between the existing position and this extreme, being much less than the economic powers of a self-governing dominion but substantially greater than the existing powers. The main distinction in this respect is between

self-government which would extend so far as to give independent control over customs duties and the monetary system (including power to interfere with the freedom of trade and of financial transactions with Great Britain), and self-government which would exclude these powers as distinguishing marks of an independent economy. An example of the first alternative is afforded by the Commonwealth of Australia, and of the second by the individual Australian States, though in recent years these have lost some of their former freedom to raise loans and levy taxes without consultation with the Commonwealth. Whether these alternative forms of self-government, and particularly the one involving the greater degree of independence, would be welcome in Northern Ireland (or in the United Kingdom for that matter) depends very largely on political issues. However important these may be, they lie outside the scope of this chapter, and all that is necessary here is to comment on the main economic issues.

In the lesser of the two proposals (which is also included in the greater) the main increase in powers would relate to fiscal matters other than customs and excise, and to financial institutions other than the monetary system. They would thus involve, as their main elements, greater powers of taxation and of freedom to dispose of revenue, and greater control over financial institutions.

As regards the financial institutions, which it is convenient to deal with first, we saw in section (c) that, even though the most potent cause of the net export of capital may be the relative lack of profitable openings for investment, there is another very potent cause in the nature of the institutions in which savings can be invested. For there are two institutional factors which supplement each other in promoting an outflow of capital, one of them indirectly and the other directly. On the one hand, because of the great preponderance of private over public companies, there is very little scope for small savers to invest in industrial enterprises at home even if they wished to. On the other hand, of the institutions which exist to collect the many small savings of the public into large aggregates, only the ordinary commercial banks can make them available, either as capital investments or as loans, to industry in the province. Two of the main institutions for collecting small savings are the Post Office Savings Bank and Trustee Savings Banks. Savings collected by them cannot be invested in industrial assets or lent to industrial firms in Northern Ireland, and so they go to swell the outflow of capital to Great Britain. A very substantial part (approximately half) of the total net saving is withdrawn from use in Northern Ireland in this way; and its withdrawal has no direct relation to the profitability of investment in the kind of industrial undertakings whose structure precludes investment by small savers individually.

It is doubtful, however, whether the growth of institutions which would enable these companion handicaps to be overcome would be greatly affected, in practice, by an increase in Northern Ireland's constitutional powers. It is true that the provincial parliament is precluded from interfering with the Post Office Savings Bank and Trustee Savings Banks, and from setting up competing banks of its own. But even if it had the constitutional power to establish corresponding savings banks, it is doubtful whether it would be able to divert very much more custom from these savings banks than it already could do, with its existing constitutional powers, in other ways.

Small savings can be invested in industrial capital either directly by the savers themselves, by buying industrial shares, or indirectly through banks and similar institutions. So far as the facilities for indirect investment are concerned, an improvement was made in 1946, when the Irish banks established, and provided the capital for, a special organ of their own, the Industrial Finance Company, to finance the development of small undertakings in Northern Ireland. No information is available on this company's transactions. But both from the continued outflow of small savings and from the continued need of small firms for additional capital, it is evident that it requires to be supplemented. Moreover, there are not many openings in Northern Ireland for the small saver to invest directly because of the lack of public companies whose shares can be bought on the market. In order to increase the number of these openings it would be necessary to create conditions in which private companies would be willing and able to convert themselves into public companies. Without any increase in its constitutional powers, the provincial parliament could do something, both to encourage this conversion and also to improve the facilities for putting small savings at the disposal of Northern Ireland industries, by establishing an official finance corporation. This would have the same general purpose as the Industrial Finance Company, but it would be on a much larger scale and one of its functions would be to co-operate with provincial firms in launching issues on the London money market, or even locally. With government backing such a corporation would probably be able to attract to itself an appreciable part of the flow of investment funds now directed abroad, and so be able to meet most of the demands for industrial capital likely to be made upon it—rather than directly upon the general public—without having to ask for funds from the government.

The other increase in powers sometimes proposed under the lesser of the alternative systems of self-government relates to fiscal matters. In discussing the effects of an increase in fiscal powers (other than customs and excise) it is important to bear in mind the broad distinction between powers of taxation and powers of expenditure. On the one hand, an increase might be sought in the provincial government's powers of taxation, involving a transfer to it of taxes at present reserved by the central government and thus enabling it to have greater freedom of choice regarding the combined rates, for the different income groups, at which the different kinds of taxation forming the tax system should be levied. On the other hand, an increase might be sought in its powers of expenditure, in the sense of greater freedom of choice regarding the uses to which the total revenue, whatever its amount, should be put. These two matters must not, of course, be treated as though they were unrelated: in general, the level of taxation is not determined in isolation but with reference to the need for revenue to perform the functions of government, and these functions are undertaken with reference to the capacity to obtain revenue. But an increase in powers of taxation might be granted without any change in the purposes for which revenue is required, and might therefore simply mean a greater freedom on the part of the provincial government to determine for itself at what general rate to levy taxation, or, as part of the same question, how much to spend on the given functions which it is permitted or is under obligation to perform. So, too, an increase in the provincial government's powers of expenditure could simply mean greater freedom in deciding how the given total amount of revenue yielded by taxation, as determined largely by the central government, should be allocated to the different purposes, including the reserved services, without any increase in the provincial government's functions. Hence, to state the matter with reference to the distinction between powers of taxation and powers of expenditure, it is necessary, in examining the implications of an increase in powers relating to public revenue, to consider the effects of an increase in powers of taxation, and an increase in powers of expenditure, according to whether the purpose is to make provision for governmental functions not formerly permissible or simply to control the severity of taxation in respect of given functions.

So far as an increase in powers of expenditure is concerned, most of the relevant fiscal considerations—as distinct from the economic effects to which the actual expenditure of additional revenue might give rise—are in essence the same as those relating to an increase in powers of taxation, and so it will be convenient to discuss them under that heading. The suggestion that an increase should be made in Northern Ireland's constitutional powers of expenditure can have meaning only if the idea is that the province should have the right to use part of its revenues in ways not at present permissible under the Constitution. Such an increase in powers would therefore imply either power to raise more revenue or power to reduce expenditure on some of the existing services provided out of the given revenue—i.e. power either to reduce expenditure on transferred services or to lower the Imperial Contribution. If what is involved is the first of these three meanings, namely an increase in the amount of revenue available to the provincial government, the fiscal effects are identical with those of either an increase in taxation or a sub-vention from the central exchequer—in effect a reduction in the net con-tribution to the Imperial budget. Again, if what is intended is that Northern Ireland should be entitled to reduce its expenditure on trans-ferred services, there is no formal restriction on its right to do so at present. It is quite free to deny itself the benefits of social services to any extent it wishes. But only in so far as it is able to lower comprehensive rates of taxation could there be any compensatory gain to the budget. Otherwise its action would be sheer self-denial, having the effect of swelling the Imperial Contribution, since this is merely the difference between revenue and actual expenditure on the permitted scale. Here again, as in the first case, powers of taxation are the important issue. Finally, if what is claimed is power to reduce the Imperial Contribution, this power already exists as a limited constitutional right. For while the existing constitutional arrangements would not permit Northern Ireland to reduce the Imperial Contribution by lowering taxation below the level in Great Britain, they would permit it, without raising taxation, to spend as much as would be required in order to raise the standard of the trans-ferred services—including those concerned with increasing the level of employment—to equality with the standard in Great Britain. Thus what is required for this purpose is not an increase in powers but a more liberal use of those already possessed. Nevertheless, for reasons already noted, the formula for calculating the Imperial Contribution does tend to depress the standard of social services below the British standard by making it dangerous to allow recurring expenditure to rise to that level; and hence there does appear to be need to make the formula more flexible. But apart from this the question of additional fiscal powers relates to increased powers of taxation rather than to increased powers over expenditure.

Turning, therefore, to the question of powers of taxation, it may first be noted that power to charge lower comprehensive rates of taxation than those applicable to Great Britain exists already. In the first place,

N

on transferred taxes Northern Ireland is free to charge whatever rates it pleases. It is true that, since these taxes form only a minor part of the whole tax system, it would not be possible by lowering them to make a large percentage reduction in total taxation. That fact, however, is unimportant. For, in the second place, under section 25 of the Government of Ireland Act the Parliament of Northern Ireland is empowered to grant relief from income-tax (and super-tax), to individuals resident and domiciled in Northern Ireland, by way of repayment to them of part or the whole of the tax levied upon them by the central government, on behalf of Northern Ireland, at the rates fixed for the whole of the United Kingdom. Constitutionally, therefore, Northern Ireland has the power to make a very large reduction in total taxation. But since a reduction could be made at the cost of having a correspondingly lower expenditure on transferred services (not at the expense of the Imperial Contribution) there is a serious risk that it would do more harm to the provincial economy—through its effects on the quality and training of labour and the volume and direction of consumers' expenditure, and hence on industrial investment and the general level of employment over good and bad times taken together—than it would do good in attracting capital. Indeed, it is hard to see how a general refund of income-tax would attract capital at all. It would certainly make it more profitable for people in Northern Ireland to own capital (by increasing the effective tax-free yield); but unless the refund on unearned income could be confined to income arising in Northern Ireland itself, it would not encourage the investment of domestic savings at home rather than in Great Britain or abroad. Even if it were practicable to devise a system for differentiating in this way, the tax remission would have to be very large in order to stem the outflow of investment funds, since it would be necessary to offset marginal cost disadvantages and other existing inducements for people to invest externally. Besides, by the terms of the Government of Ireland Act no concession could be given to non-residents, and so no inducement could be given to them in this way to invest their savings in Northern Ireland. It thus appears that the effective limit to the provincial government's power to reduce taxation is set not by the Constitution but by the adverse economic effects which would be likely to result from using the constitutional powers already possessed. The only qualification which must be made to this statement is that if, notwithstanding the foregoing considerations, it were thought desirable to try to influence the pattern of industrial development by means of tax manipulation rather than by other means, then Northern Ireland would probably need to control the rates of taxation over a wider section of the tax system than at present.

Flexibility in respect of an increase in taxation above the level in Great Britain is not nearly so great. Though Northern Ireland can vary the rates on the transferred taxes at its discretion, these cover only a narrow range of taxes and account for only a small part of total revenue. If for any purpose Northern Ireland decided to bring about, by means of its own taxing powers, a given proportionate increase in its disposable revenue—i.e. the amount remaining after deducting the Imperial charges —it would have to increase the rates on the transferred taxes in a very much greater proportion; for these nowadays yield only about one-tenth of the total revenue from all sources. Owing to the very limited variety of the taxes concerned, there would therefore be great difficulty in preserving equity among the different classes of taxpayers in respect of their total taxation. Even more important than the resulting inequity, however, would be the effects in repelling funds for investment. The main transferred taxes are death duties, motor-vehicle duties, stamp duties, and other taxes which fall principally on the owners of property. The increase in total taxation, above the combined rates applicable in Great Britain, would tend to swell the outflow of capital and dry up the inflow. Even if the extra revenue were all spent on projects designed to foster industrial growth, the effects on the supply of capital might nevertheless be significantly adverse on balance; and, even at the best, any net benefit would almost certainly be small.

Here once more the fundamental objection to the proposed increase in Northern Ireland's economic powers—in this case an increase in its powers of taxation—is that, even if the additional powers were granted, they could not be effectively used owing to the close economic integration with Great Britain. Any large divergence in economic policy, financed by an increase in provincial taxation, would tend to be self-defeating because of the reactions which it would cause on the inter-regional movement of labour and capital. Besides, so long as the Imperial Contribution is positive, there is in fact no need for Northern Ireland to tax more severely than Great Britain for this purpose, since it can get the money with which to encourage suitable industrial development without doing so. The principle is accepted that there should be parity of services with Great Britain provided there is equality of taxation; and expenditure on industrial development in the Development Areas is accepted as a subordinate part of the policy of full employment. Hence reasonable expenditure designed to stimulate industrial growth, on a scale sufficient to get rid of abnormally heavy unemployment, would presumably be accepted by the Joint Exchequer Board in computing the Imperial Contribution. Northern Ireland might conceivably, of course, wish to have greater powers of taxation in order to provide services on a more lavish scale, or over a wider range of functions than Great Britain. But this is merely a theoretical possibility. On a realistic view of the situation a change in the Constitution would not be justified on its account. There is, however, the possibility of a difference of opinion about what constitutes sound methods of stimulating industrial development, and Northern Ireland might, conceivably, wish to have greater powers of taxation in order to be free to adopt its own favoured policies. The real obstacle to action of this kind, however, is not the lack of constitutional powers of taxation but the basic facts of economic integration.

The kind of difference in opinion which might arise, and the difficulties which would be involved in independent action by Northern Ireland, can be seen by taking a concrete example. According to press reports, a suggestion was made to the British Government a short time ago that cross-channel transport should be subsidised. From Northern Ireland's point of view the case for such a policy is very strong. The natural obstacles to industrial development, translated into manufacturers' costs of production and distribution, largely take the form of extra costs of transport above those paid by competing firms in Great Britain. A subsidy on cross-channel transport would directly and obviously reduce this differential cost. It would therefore tend to be more effective in attracting new firms, than an equivalent (lump-sum) reduction in overhead costs, which is the form taken by most of the financial inducements offered under the New Industries Development Act and accepted by the Joint Exchequer Board as a reasonable charge in computing the Imperial Contribution. From the point of view of the British Government, however, there is a very strong case against the proposal; for even if a transport subsidy were admitted to be economically sound in this particular case, it would nevertheless, if granted, become a very awkward precedent. If in these circumstances the provincial government persisted in the plan to grant a subsidy, it would presumably have to impose higher comprehensive rates of taxation in order to finance it. In this event, the beneficial effect of the subsidy in attracting new industry would be partially offset, and perhaps more than offset, by the repellent effect of the differential taxation on both capital and labour. Not all of the extra taxation would be paid by business men. But neither would they receive the whole of the amount paid in subsidy. Part of it would go to consumers of imported consumption goods and would thus do something to offset the adverse effect on labour. The net effect on industrial development would depend on the incidence of the extra taxation and the incidence of the subsidy, and on how business men (and workers) would respond to the opposing stimuli. It is not clear, therefore, whether the net effect would be to stimulate industrial development or to retard it. It is clear, however, that Northern Ireland, as an integral part of the economy of the United Kingdom, has very little economic power, acting independently and without the support of the central government, to stimulate its own industrial development relatively to that of the whole country, and that an increase in its legislative powers over taxation would not make much difference.

As a self-governing dominion, Northern Ireland would possess all the extra powers over taxation and the expenditure of revenue that we have been discussing. In addition, it would have the right to institute a separate tariff of its own and a separate fiscal system and monetary system, with control over foreign exchange, including sterling. It would thus have all the legislative powers necessary for operating a fully independent economic policy. The final question left for discussion, therefore, is whether Northern Ireland would gain more from having tariff, fiscal and monetary independence—notwithstanding its lower taxable capacity—than it would lose through giving up the benefits which it now enjoys from having equality of services and equality of taxation with Great Britain.

The answer to this question depends on how Northern Ireland would be affected by economic independence in two different ways: firstly, on how real income would be affected by any resulting change in the level of governmental expenditure, and hence taxation; and, secondly, on how employment and income would be affected by erecting a customs barrier against Great Britain and by operating a separate fiscal and monetary policy, with separate rates of exchange. The basis for answering both parts of the question is provided by the foregoing study of Northern Ireland's economic structure and integration with Great Britain, and its relatively low income and employment. From that study it seems clear that under fiscal and tariff independence it would stand to lose in both ways.

So far as taxation is concerned, Northern Ireland would have to raise its rates of taxation above the British rates, or else reduce its expenditure on social or other services below the British standards, whenever employment and income, and hence tax yields, fell below the corresponding levels in Great Britain. As things are, it is partly shielded against this danger by its equal privileges in sharing the benefits of the Imperial services and by the arrangements for giving it the same standard of social services as in Great Britain on condition of equal severity of taxation. Thus, in relatively bad times, when its tax yields are low, Northern

Ireland is cushioned against rising expenditure on transferred services by the social reinsurance agreements. At the same time it is cushioned against the effects of a relative fall in revenue by the formula for calculating the Imperial Contribution; since it is only called upon to contribute what it can reasonably afford each year having regard to its necessary expenditure (including approved expenditure on industrial development) and its varying taxable capacity. Because of the disparity between Northern Ireland and Great Britain in employment and income, and because of the greater fluctuations in employment and income, these advantages in years of heavy expenditure and low tax yields are very substantial, and the loss of them would therefore be serious.[1] Besides, there would also be a considerable loss through having to duplicate the Imperial and reserved services, some of which (e.g. consular services) would be far more costly to run separately.

As against these adverse effects, however, Northern Ireland would be placed in a position in which it could, if it chose, cut out expenditure on defence without much sacrifice of security, since its defence would presumably continue to be a strategic necessity for Great Britain. Though it can be taken for granted that Northern Ireland would spurn to take advantage of this position, the fact remains that dominion status would give it the opportunity to reduce governmental expenditure by the equivalent of that part of the Imperial Contribution which is attributable to defence services. This amount would be much less, however, than the whole of the Imperial Contribution. Northern Ireland would have to provide the other Imperial services for itself, or go without them altogether, and it would presumably become responsible for a proportion of the national debt. The saving, therefore, would be limited to the

[1] In the last four pre-war years Northern Ireland received on account of unemployment reinsurance more than the whole of what it paid as Imperial Contribution and over one-tenth of its revenue from all sources, including the special payments from the Imperial exchequer. The actual figures for those years, as given in the *Ulster Year Books* for 1938 and 1947, are set out below. In all other years the net Imperial Contribution has been positive.

	Total Revenue £	Revenue from Unemployment Reinsurance £	Imperial Contribution £
1935–36 ..	10,958,000	752,000	365,000
1936–37 ..	11,597,000	1,039,000	900,000
1937–38 ..	12,693,000	1,615,873	1,200,000
1938–39 ..	12,822,000	1,786,752	1,300,000

amount of the Imperial Contribution attributable to defence when defence is regarded as the residuary element of it. Moreover, the case for claiming favourable treatment in the allocation of British defence orders would be forfeited. It is therefore safe to conclude that, apart from any reactions which it might cause on employment and income, and hence on tax yields, fiscal independence would make it necessary for Northern Ireland either to tax more severely than Great Britain or to stint governmental services as a whole.

As regards the effects of full dominion status on employment and income, a separate tariff would make it technically possible to shut out imports of any or all classes of manufactures—to any desired extent—not only from abroad but also from Great Britain. It would thus be technically possible to reserve the domestic market for any protected goods entirely for domestic manufacturers of them. But the mere exclusion of particular goods from entry would not be enough, by itself, to make sure that it would pay anyone to produce them in Northern Ireland. Unless the expected rates of profit in those particular industries were as high as those which could be earned on alternative investments in Great Britain, capital for establishing factories in them would not be attracted from Great Britain or other external sources, and (at any rate in the absence of rigid control of foreign exchange) domestic firms would not be able, because of the relatively poor returns, to obtain the necessary capital from internal sources. Hence, if costs of production in these industries were higher than in the same industries in Great Britain (and otherwise there would be no point in giving them protection), the prices obtainable for their goods in the domestic market would have to be correspondingly higher. It would consequently be necessary to supplement the tariff with some other measure, such as a policy of expansive credit or of deficit financing, for bolstering up the total monetary demand of consumers sufficiently to ensure a good market at these higher prices. The rising cost of living, however, would promote a rise also in wages and other money costs of production. It would therefore tend to defeat the intention of making investment in the protected industries more profitable. It would also tend to cause a contraction in the industries producing for export. For even if, as a result of the increase in total expenditure, these industries were able to charge higher prices than before in the home market, they would not be able fully to compensate for the increase in their costs of production, since they would be unable to charge higher prices also for their exports. In order to avoid these results it would be necessary to prevent wage rates and other money costs from rising along with prices.

It follows that, apart from the possibility of fostering infant industries which would be capable of doing without protection when established, the tariff and its supplementary measures could increase total employment only by forcing down the real earnings of wage-earners, salaried workers, rentiers, and others with relatively fixed money incomes. So long as the costs of production in the protected industries were not much above those of the corresponding British or foreign industries, this policy might nevertheless be sound. For though average real income per person employed would be less, the total number of persons in employment might, in those circumstances, rise enough to cause a net increase in the total real income of the community, and possibly even a net increase in the total real income of wage-earners as a group.[1] But if the average disparity in costs were large, as it almost certainly is in Northern Ireland, the lowering of average real income per occupied person would more than offset the effects of any resulting increase in the number of people earning incomes, and the total real income of the whole community would fall.

Even if the policy of protection were nevertheless judged to be desirable, there is a danger that it would be self-defeating. On the one hand there would be a very strong upward pressure on wages and other money costs, which, if it succeeded, would tend to cause a cumulative rise in internal prices and rates of exchange. On the other hand, in so far as the upward pressure was withstood, the heavy fall in real wages would adversely affect the economy by causing employed as well as unemployed workers, particularly the more skilled and adventurous workers, to emigrate to Great Britain or abroad, so causing the demand for goods in the home market to fall and costs to rise. Thus, if the differences between domestic and foreign costs in the protected industries were large, the policy would be unlikely to succeed even if all manufacturing could be protected against outside competition. In practice, however, unless money costs were pegged down rigidly notwithstanding the rising costs of living, the increase in employment in producing goods for the home market would be partially offset, and possibly more than offset, by a reduction in employment in producing goods for export. Hence, in that case, not only would there be a fall in total real income owing to the reduction in average real wages, but there would also be a serious danger of a net reduction in total employment. Moreover, this danger could not

---

[1] It has been persuasively argued that protection has had these effects in Australia. *Cf. The Australian Tariff: An Economic Inquiry* (Melbourne University Press), and L. F. Giblin, *Some Economic Effects of the Australian Tariff* (Joseph Fisher Lecture, University of Adelaide).

be avoided by allowing the external value of the currency to fall as money costs increased; for while that would have the effect of lowering the prices of exports in terms of sterling, thereby offsetting the rise in money wages, it would also have the effect of raising the prices of imported raw materials, fuel and capital goods in terms of the domestic currency.

Whatever may be true of protection elsewhere, conditions would be very much against it in Northern Ireland. In the kind of industrial environment in which a separate provincial tariff would have to operate, there would be very little scope for using it effectively to promote either the establishment of new industries or the expansion of the old. We can see why this is so by reminding ourselves of the kind of industries, actual and potential, to which development in Northern Ireland is limited by natural conditions, and by looking more closely at the effects of protection on the particular industries to which it is given.

As in other countries, there are some industries which are automatically sheltered from outside competition, without the help of a tariff, because they must of necessity be located near the consumers whom they supply. The industries in this category—e.g. building and construction and the various service industries—would not benefit from an import duty on their products because such products would not be imported in any event; and for a like reason they could not expand in size beyond the limit set by the domestic market. But apart from these naturally sheltered industries, most of the well-established industries produce far more than the provincial market could absorb at profitable prices, and they consequently have to sell a large proportion of their goods externally, chiefly in Great Britain. Even industries raised under the shelter of the tariff would generally have to engage in some exporting. For in order to be large enough to minimise their costs, most of them would have to be established on a larger scale than would be warranted by the home demand alone.

Now, in any industry in which part of the output has to be exported, it is unlikely that production would be stimulated by a duty on competing imports. The duty would not give producers an incentive to increase output unless it enabled them, by keeping out competing imports, to raise the domestic price. But the exclusion of imports would not enable them to do that if they were in competition with each other to sell in the home market. For in that case the domestic price would tend to be forced down, just as effectively as if there were no duty, to the point at which producers would gain no more by selling at home than by selling abroad. Thus the manufacture of any commodity produced partly for export would not benefit from an import duty unless the domestic producers were organised into a monopoly and so were able, with the aid of the duty, to exact a substantially higher price from domestic consumers than they could get for their exports. Moreover, if the imposition of a tariff enabled industries to develop such power, there would probably be adverse effects on total real income, and there would certainly be adverse effects on its distribution.

There remains for consideration the possibility of using a tariff to foster the establishment of industries which do not at present exist in Northern Ireland. Those who favour a separate customs system for Northern Ireland presumably have this possibility chiefly in mind. The idea would be to put up a customs barrier against some or all of the great variety of goods at present imported (from Great Britain or abroad) and so to encourage the production of these goods at home. The difficulty with this proposal is that if such goods were produced in Northern Ireland there would be a general tendency for them to cost the domestic consumers a great deal more than if they were imported. There are two main reasons. The first is that such an increase in self-sufficiency would generally involve the establishment of industries in which Northern Ireland's comparative disadvantages are substantial. The second reason is that for most individual commodities the unit of production would be uneconomically small if sales were confined to the provincial market. In order to be able to take full advantage of the economies of large-scale production, it would therefore be necessary to expand output beyond domestic requirements and to sell the excess, for what it would fetch, in Great Britain or abroad. But on most of the types of goods concerned this would mean heavy additional costs of transport to the outside markets, and also additional costs of transport in bringing in the raw materials from which to make the exports. On the average of the industries concerned, these additional transport costs would probably represent a considerable addition to the price—a much greater addition than that involved by the extra transport costs in the staple industries which have grown up without assistance. In these conditions the producers could only make a profit if they could organise themselves into a monopoly for charging a higher price for their goods in the protected home market than they could get in external markets. The cost of living would consequently rise. Hence either money wages would rise correspondingly (to the detriment of employment and earnings in the unprotected industries) or real wages would fall, to the detriment of the standard of living of the workers in protected industries as well.

Thus the possibilities of using tariff policy as a means of increasing the general level of industry in Northern Ireland are very slight. Northern

Ireland is so dependent on its external trade that anything which reduced the flow of trade would be likely, on balance, to have adverse effects on the economy. It is especially dependent on its trade with Great Britain, which is by far the most important single market. Quite apart from the other losses incidental to such a large degree of independence, the erection of a tariff barrier between Northern Ireland and Great Britain would be almost certain to do harm by itself.

These considerations contain an important inference regarding the question of the tariff barrier between Northern Ireland and the Irish Republic. Eire forms a natural market for some of Northern Ireland's manufactured goods; it is also a natural source of supply of some agricultural commodities, for use both in consumption and as raw materials. If the border were removed the flow of trade would consequently increase. As things are, however, economic union with Eire would mean economic disunion with Great Britain; the removal of the border with Eire would involve its erection between Northern Ireland and Great Britain. But owing to Northern Ireland's much closer economic integration with Great Britain than with Eire, an integration which is firmly based on the complementary relationship between them, the gain from such a change would be outweighed by the loss. This would be so even without taking into account the loss of the benefits derived from equality of services and taxation. The only way in which Northern Ireland could benefit from the removal of the border would be by getting rid of it altogether, not from shifting it from where it is to the coast. If located there, the harm done by it would be far greater.

Fiscal and monetary autonomy for Northern Ireland would tend to reduce even the existing flow of funds from Great Britain for the development of new undertakings. In deciding where to locate new factories investors are influenced by their judgment of the political risks to which their profits and the capital values of their business assets would be exposed. Under Section 21 of the Government of Ireland Act, the power to impose taxes on either profits or capital is explicitly withheld; and Northern Ireland has no power to interfere with the transfer of profits to Great Britain or with the repatriation of capital. Thus if Northern Ireland were given fiscal autonomy there would automatically be created a risk of additional taxation, both of the capital from Great Britain invested in new factories and of the profits which it yields. Likewise, if it were given monetary autonomy, there would be a risk that exchange control would be established and that, in consequence, restraints might at any time be placed on the withdrawal of profits and capital to Great Britain. In both of these ways the investment of British capital in industry in Northern Ireland would be discouraged. There is evidence that it is already discouraged to some extent by fears among British investors that, notwithstanding the British Government's assurance to the contrary, Eire's persistent agitation to be permitted to annex Northern Ireland may some day succeed.

As a self-governing dominion Northern Ireland could, of course, follow a policy of economic development out of keeping with the development which it would experience as an integral part of the British economy. But it could alter the current of its development in this way only through a large sacrifice in standards of living caused by severing the economic interconnections. For the truth is that, whatever its formal powers may be, or may become, Northern Ireland is a dependent part of the British economy in the sense that its economic prosperity, as indicated by the level of employment and income, is very largely governed by economic conditions and policy in Great Britain. Government action to offset the effects of Northern Ireland's natural handicaps, and so to keep the growth in industrial employment abreast of that in Great Britain, can most effectively, and with least hardship, be taken by the central government itself, or with its financial backing. Northern Ireland is too small and too dependent (in this sense) to be able to take effective action by itself. Thus full self-government would be against its economic interests. It would be against the whole trend of world development. For, with growing acceptance of the doctrine that governments have a duty to exercise deliberate control over the economic climate of their respective countries, and to co-operate in ensuring that they do not undermine each others' efforts in this respect, the whole drift is towards closer economic union, both within and between the different countries, coupled with devolution of administration.

CONCLUSION

DEVOLUTION AND PARTITION

By THOMAS WILSON

I

ON the face of it, it must seem somewhat ironical that Ulster should be
the only part of the United Kingdom to be governed under a Home Rule
Act. Admittedly Ulster's prolonged opposition to any such measure was
not in vain, for it is Home Rule with a difference: the local Parliament
sits in Belfast, not Dublin, and the loyalists have a majority that is both
substantial and assured. A separate Parliament for the North was not
open to the same objections from a Unionist point of view as a separate
Parliament for Ireland as a whole, but the fact remains that although
Home Rule on this basis was accepted by the North, it was never particularly desired. The Unionists would have been quite content with
direct government from Westminster, and the Nationalists, for their
part, had their eyes fixed on a much larger measure of self-government
to be enjoyed in company with the Nationalists in the South. Thus it
cannot be said that the new Parliament came into being in response to
local demands; it was created rather because the need for partition had
been so reluctantly accepted by Westminster and was still regarded as
perhaps only a temporary expedient which might be greatly modified,
under the provisions of the Act of 1920, should the two new Irish Parliaments so decide at a later date. Had the London government reconciled
itself at this stage both to the prolonged division of the island and to the
departure of the South from the United Kingdom, it seems unlikely that
any special measure would have been passed to provide Ulster alone
with a subordinate Parliament that she did not greatly want. Home
Rule in Ulster can therefore be regarded as something of an accident,
the unforeseen outcome of an unsuccessful attempt to solve the Irish
question as a whole.

To say this is not to imply that the only reason for advocating devolution is the desirability of satisfying nationalistic demands. On the contrary, there were two separate ideas running through the debates on
Home Rule in the latter part of the nineteenth century and the first part
of this: first, of course, the need to solve the Irish question, and secondly
the desirability of some reform in the machinery of government. Joseph
Chamberlain seems to have had both ideas in mind when he proposed

Home Rule all round, and in the anxious years before 1914 a number of other reformers—including F. S. Oliver and L. S. Amery—were advocating federalism for the United Kingdom.[1] By 1919 the proposal had attracted sufficient interest to be the subject of a debate in the House of Commons, and it seems to-day a curious fact that the following resolution was passed, if only with a small number of votes:

> "That, with a view to enabling the Imperial Parliament to devote more attention to the general interests of the United Kingdom and, in collaboration with the other governments of the Empire, to matters of common Imperial concern, the House is of the opinion that the time has come for the creation of subordinate legislatures within the United Kingdom. . . ."

A Speaker's Conference was formed to consider how devolution could best be put into operation in England, Wales and Scotland, without prejudice to any measure that might be contemplated for Ireland, and its report appeared in 1920. In the event, of course, no further action was taken with regard to Great Britain, and public interest in the project, never widespread or passionate, seems thereafter to have waned outside certain nationalistic groups in Scotland and Wales. Yet, if there was anything to be said for devolution thirty or forty years ago, there is far more to-day. It is a frequent complaint that the activities of the State have now increased so much that Parliament cannot hope to exercise effective control over the whole field. Many topics are inadequately debated, when debated at all, and a vast amount of authority is simply delegated to civil servants. Local needs cannot be properly voiced in sessions so crowded with business, and the private member has been reduced to almost chronic impotence. Thus, while the extension of the franchise has tended to make Parliament more representative in modern times, the inability of Parliament to cope with the ever-increasing flood of public business has tended to make government increasingly unrepresentative. It may be that the only really effective remedy would be to reduce substantially the amount of work undertaken by the State, although it need scarcely be said that any attempt to do so on a big enough scale to matter would raise a host of other difficulties and at every point a nice balancing of gain and loss would be involved. Here we are touching on one of the grand topics of contemporary political controversy, and to pursue it further would carry us well beyond the scope of this book. Nor is it appropriate to do more than record that these

[1] *My Political Life*, by L. S. Amery, vol. I, chapter XV; *cf.* also Mansergh, *The Government of Northern Ireland*, part I.

difficulties at the centre have been accompanied by a weakening of the independence and virility of local government, a development which has also been viewed with grave concern for the long-term effect on British democracy.[1]

What does concern us in this book is the possibility that some form of devolution, although incapable of affording anything like a full answer, might at least help a little to make government more representative. This is the constitutional argument for some kind of regional self-government, and whether convincing or not it stands on its own feet independently of any nationalistic sympathy for Home Rule.

"The question", writes Mr Amery, "is how far the principle of devolution can be extended and how far it can in that case lighten the excessive burden on Parliament itself. The successful working of provincial devolution in Northern Ireland suggests that there might be scope in the rest of the United Kingdom for what Mr. Churchill once described as the restoration of the Heptarchy, viz, devolution to Scotland and Wales, and to large provincial units in England. The powers assigned, to the English provinces at any rate, might not be as wide as those enjoyed in Northern Ireland. There would be obvious difficulties in transferring Commerce and Labour, for instance. But in agriculture, health, housing, education, poor relief and local government generally, provincial interest and inter-provincial emulation might well be more important than uniformity."[2]

The most serious objection to devolution is obviously the danger of conflict and confusion in public policy. If there were a number of regional assemblies their policies might be significantly different in some crucial respects, and all might diverge in varying degrees from the course of action which the central government, for its part, was trying to follow. Thus a reasonably workable degree of consistency in public affairs might not be achieved. We are accustomed to say that there should be more international co-operation and greater uniformity in the objectives that various countries are seeking to pursue. Would it not, then, be somewhat rash to contemplate any change that might divide a nation internally? If we are not yet part of one world, let us at least remain one nation! This is the argument against devolution, and it is a powerful one. At the

---

[1] Cf., e.g., H. Warren in British Government since 1918, ed. D. N. Chester: "the spirit of local initiative and responsibility, the sense of local community, and the process of mutual education that springs from the co-operation of groups, classes and individuals in the provision of communal needs, should not be allowed to perish because they lack suitable organs, adapted to the needs of the time, endowed with adequate power and providing a wide freedom with real initiative".

[2] Thoughts on the Constitution, Oxford University Press, p. 58.

same time it must be conceded that arguments couched in such general terms can scarcely be conclusive. There is, for example, no inescapable inconsistency between advocating greater international co-operation on the one hand and more independence for the English borough councils on the other! The real question is whether the line between different political authorities has been drawn at the right place, and it will scarcely do to oppose unity to disunity in a quite general way without distinguishing between the jobs to be done. With this somewhat obvious reflection, the abstract analysis can be set aside, and we can turn to some questions of fact. How have the opposing forces worked themselves out in those countries where the unifying activities of the central government encounter the authority of regional assemblies? In so far as the central power has grown, do the causes appear to be deep-seated and permanent, or do they seem to reflect special conditions that may not last? What were the effects, first of depression, and then of war? How far has a needlessly maladroit handling of public finance contributed to the growing power of the centre? And so on. If the answers must be sought in the main in the recent histories of the great federations, it is to Northern Ireland that one must turn in order to study the operation of the various forces within the United Kingdom itself. Has the granting of devolution been followed by a harmful conflict of policies between Stormont and Westminster? Or, if conflict has been avoided, is this because Stormont has imitated Westminster so closely as to make regional self-government seem a useless duplication of electoral and parliamentary effort? It is with issues such as these that this volume of essays has been in part concerned, and, as might be expected, some difference of opinion among the contributors can be discerned. Thus, whereas Sayers is inclined to come down in favour of devolution in a far from uncritical survey of Stormont's achievements, Newark, Isles and Cuthbert seem to doubt whether the net advantages have been really substantial. The evidence is too detailed and the argument too complex to make advisable any attempt at comprehensive summary in this concluding chapter, but it may be helpful to bring together some of the relevant considerations and also, perhaps, to add a little to what has been said about some of the services for which Stormont is responsible.

It will be convenient to analyse the evidence by considering in turn each of the three main reasons that may be advanced in favour of devolution in Ulster: first, the need for special measures to cope with those conditions in the province that may be regarded as a heritage from Dublin Castle; second, the need for such measures in order to cope with peculiar conditions of a more permanent nature; third the desirability of making government more representative by giving regions such as this the utmost possible say in determining their own destiny. I shall try to illustrate my remarks by references to some of the policies adopted by Stormont, in particular those relating to education, health and the nationalisation of industry. The chapter will conclude with a reference to some features of political life in the province that must be borne in mind in trying to draw any general conclusions from this experiment about the results of devolution: this will involve a brief glance at the wearisome struggle about the partition of the island.

II

1. The first consideration to be taken into account is that public policy in Ireland had differed materially from that applied to England even in the period before the North received devolution and the South dominion status. Although the Act of Union of 1800 had swept away the old Irish Parliament, Westminster did not thereafter legislate indiscriminately for the whole of the British Isles. Moreover Ireland was administered by a separate executive from its headquarters at Dublin Castle with important effects on the way in which various policies were implemented even when basically similar to those adopted across the Irish Sea. Indeed the public services in Ulster in 1920 were sufficiently different to make inappropriate any simple extension to the province of future policies designed to meet English needs. Special arrangements were clearly needed, but devolution was not necessarily called for. The previous system could have been retained but applied to Ulster alone: there would then have been from time to time special legislation applying to Northern Ireland and perhaps a separate executive in Belfast to run the specifically Ulster services after the fashion of Dublin Castle. The appropriateness of one method rather than another should depend at least in part upon whether or not these differences between the public services in Great Britain and Ulster are regarded as merely transient, the outcome of previous policies that did not really reflect basic differences in the needs of the two countries.

In the event the establishment of a new Parliament, even if it were made for quite different reasons, has given the Ulster people the chance of deciding for themselves the extent to which they want to come into line with England. It is against this background that we must consider the repeated declaration of the Unionist party that it has two objectives, the elimination of "leeway" and "step-by-step".[1] The first term "leeway", is

---

[1] *Cf.* Sayers, pp. 62 *et seq.* above.

the now conventional manner of referring to any inferiority in Ulster's services, while "step-by-step" means that British policy is imitated at Stormont. Now, it may well be the case that these objectives have been pursued more effectively because there is a local Parliament, but it will be appreciated that this affords only a temporary justification for Stormont's existence. Much of the "leeway" of 1920 has now presumably been made good—if not the Ulster electorate has genuine ground for complaint. Admittedly Stormont may not have succeeded in keeping pace at the same time with all new developments in Great Britain and new "leeway" may have resulted, but it should only be a question of time before any differences in the public services in Ulster as compared with those in England have disappeared—on the assumption that this is the official objective. That is to say, if the policy of overtaking "leeway" and of "step-by-step" were strictly and successfully followed, Stormont would ultimately deprive itself of its own *raison d'être*.

2. Notwithstanding the Unionist pronouncements, Stormont has not kept strictly "step-by-step", and it would have been inappropriate to do so because Ulster's needs are different in some important respects from those of the rest of the United Kingdom for reasons of a more permanent nature than the legislative and executive heritage we have just been discussing. There is no other area where about a third of the population wants to sever its connection with Britain and join what is now a foreign republic, and this is bound to raise complications, especially when a few members of the minority resort to terrorist activities. Thus, by establishing a local Parliament, Westminster has passed on to Stormont the unpleasant task of trying to keep the peace in conditions where the ordinary machinery for the preservation of law and order could not always work satisfactorily. That is to say, if there had been no Stormont, Westminster would have been faced with the need for some measure similar to the Special Powers Act.[1] Apart from terrorism, the mere existence of a large discontented minority is bound to cause complications, especially when the minority also happens to be Roman Catholic in religion. For the Catholic attitude to education, health services and the like gives rise to a number of issues which, if by no means peculiar to Ulster, are encountered there in such a form that special action is called for. We may conclude, therefore, that if devolution had not been granted, separate Acts of Parliament relating to Ulster would have been necessary at Westminster, and the existence of a separate legislature can thus be said to have done something to ease the pressure of business in London, as Professor Newark himself has conceded.[2]

[1] For a description of the Act, see Newark, pp. 46 *et seq.* above.   [2] p. 51 above.

On general grounds, it seems plausible to suggest that the policies actually adopted and the manner in which they have been carried out have been somewhat more satisfactory than would have been the case in the absence of a local Parliament. It is some advantage, for example, that civil servants dealing with provincial matters are in immediate contact with local cabinet ministers instead of being obliged to make constant trips to London in order to see busy men in whose eyes the complex needs of a remote area must seem a tiresome distraction from more important matters. In particular the existence of a local Ministry of Finance, provided it is not too closely tied to the Treasury, should be helpful in the conduct of business: whereas officials in the Scottish Office must seek advice and permission from a distant Treasury, their opposite numbers in Belfast need only walk along a corridor in order to consult the financial pundits, who are, moreover, full-time experts on local matters.

Such considerations are relevant in considering another of Ulster's special problems, its liability to severe unemployment. Here the popular verdict on Stormont's record would probably be unfavourable, but this is not necessarily conclusive. The Irish seem to be peculiarly prone to the fallacy that there is always a constitutional remedy for every ill: at one time it was Home Rule, but if devolution has "failed" in that it has not, for example, brought permanent full employment, then the remedy must be a return to Westminster, or the abolition of the border, or an extension of Stormont's powers.[1] Yet it is obvious enough that no mere provincial government could reasonably have been expected to provide work for all in the conditions of the thirties when there was heavy unemployment throughout the country as a whole, and Stormont was blamed for its failure to achieve what clearly lay beyond its powers. A more serious

---

[1] Of these the removal of partition is, of course, much the more fashionable, and it is not uncommon to hear Protestants as well as Catholics say that "all would be well if Ulster were not separated from its natural hinterland", and so on. In fact there is no convincing evidence in support of the view that union with Eire, which would mean separation from Great Britain, would help; on the contrary, conditions would probably be worse. *Cf.* the remarks of Isles and Cuthbert, p. 181 above

It must not be supposed that Ireland is an "economic unit" with an industrial North and an agricultural South. Both parts of the country export agricultural produce—to Great Britain. Nor would it be reasonable to expect that the great industries of the North—linen, shipbuilding, aircraft—would find much of a market in the South. Ulster's light industries, such as tobacco manufacture, might export more to the South in a united Ireland, but these are precisely the sort of industries that have developed in Eire behind the tariff wall.

The unwelcome truth is that Ulster and Eire are in the main competitive rather than complementary areas. It is with Great Britain, rather than with each other, that they tend to be complementary.

criticism is to point out that unemployment has been so much worse in Ulster than in the rest of the country since the end of the war, and to ask whether this can be attributed to the existence of devolution or to the alleged ineptitude of the particular government in power at Stormont. In reply it must first be observed that full employment in the Keynesian sense does not mean that no region will ever be allowed to decline; on the contrary, there must be mobility if there is to be progress and the price may be a little transitional unemployment. Lord Beveridge himself recognised as much when he took 3 per cent as his target for the nation as a whole, for this implied a higher percentage in some areas.[1] Thus the situation in Ulster in 1954, when there was 6 per cent unemployed, was not so gravely unsatisfactory as is sometimes suggested, especially when allowance is made for the fact that some of those registered as unemployed were not genuinely seeking work. The real cause for concern was that such a good figure might not be maintained: unemployment had been much higher shortly before—over 10 per cent in 1952—and might well rise once more because linen and shipbuilding, the two industries on which the province so much depends, are highly unstable. The real task has been to diversify the industrial structure, and for this purpose devolution is not essential. If Ulster were ruled directly from Westminster, the province would be a development area and as such would receive selective treatment. As Isles and Cuthbert have shown in their detailed and penetrating survey, it is by no means obvious where the balance of advantage lies, and the arguments summarised at the end of their second chapter need not be repeated here.

Let us rather turn for a moment to a different aspect of public policy which has been less fully discussed in the preceding chapters.

Education affords a clear example of some of the points made in a general way above. The new government inherited from Dublin Castle an educational system which was backward by English standards in organisation, in buildings and in scholarship. All the schools, apart from some technical colleges, were voluntary bodies run for the most part by the churches, and public policy was administered by three departments in Dublin which dealt direct with the numerous committees of management. One of the first major steps of the new Parliament was to pass the Education Act of 1923 which was designed to produce a modern system by constituting each county and county borough council the responsible education authority for its area. Provision was made for the transfer of voluntary schools to these new authorities, and secular education under the control of the State was thus inaugurated in Ireland. It is true that in

[1] *Full Employment in a Free Society*, pp. 124 *et seq.* above.

adopting this policy Stormont was not so much following a course of its own as trying to bring the provincial arrangements more into line with those already adopted in England; or, to resort to the jargon, "leeway" was being made good. But the transition was by no means a simple task, and it encountered so much opposition that modified arrangements were made reflecting more permanent differences between Ulster and England than mere "leeway". None of the churches were inclined to view with favour the diminution in their authority which the new policy implied, but whereas the Protestant sects capitulated fairly easily and surrendered nearly all their elementary schools, the Roman Catholic church decided that, here as elsewhere, it would not submit to secular education for its children. The compromise achieved by the Act of 1923 was that any voluntary body—in practice any church—could retain its schools if it wished provided it was prepared to face some financial consequences, and this the Catholics determined to do. As might be expected, the scale on which these remaining voluntary schools should receive assistance from the State became one of the principal issues in local politics, and it has provoked periodic explosions over the past thirty years. The Catholics claim that as taxpayers they are entitled to as much support for their schools as that given to the State schools. The authorities can reply that the Catholics can send their children to the State schools like members of other denominations and thus receive their due as taxpayers; if, however, the Catholics will have none of this, the government can refuse to accept *full* financial responsibility for their private schools because to make such support available to any and every sect, as it would have to be, would make nonsense of the modern scheme and foster a wasteful duplication of facilities. The issue is a familiar one in the politics of many countries, but from a Catholic point of view the compromise reached in Ulster stands up well in comparison with what has been done elsewhere. For the State pays virtually all the running costs in the voluntary schools, and it is only when capital expenditure is made that any significant burden falls upon their managers. Even then, the State pays 65 per cent of all the cost involved in putting up new buildings or in extending and improving old ones—an arrangement more generous than that adopted in England and vastly more generous than what is done anywhere in the U.S.A., where the Ulster government is nevertheless repeatedly denounced on the ground that it oppresses the Catholic population.

When a new Act of the Butler type was passed by Stormont in 1947, the voluntary principle again became a controversial issue, this time with regard to the future of the voluntary grammar schools.[1] The points

[1] Sayers, pp. 74-5 above.

at issue were the proportion of places reserved for the holders of public scholarships and the use for capital purposes of any part of the tuition fees that was paid by such scholarships. Ultimately the schools were divided into two groups: the "A" schools which must keep 80 per cent of their places for the holders of public authority scholarships but receive from the State 65 per cent of their capital expenditure, and the "B" schools which are under no such obligation and receive no such assistance. The details need not detain us, but it is worth observing that, since there is no question of taking over these schools completely or of interfering with their governors except with regard to the number of scholars, the controversy has not followed sectarian lines in quite the usual way. There are Catholic grammar schools of both the "A" and the "B" variety, and the non-Catholic schools are also divided.

The public examinations are, of course, the same for all schools, but Catholics normally choose Irish language and literature, which is an officially recognised option and is taught by teachers whose pay can be derived from public funds in the same way as that of the teachers of any other subject. It seems worth while to mention this point because attempts by the majority to impose its language on the minority have been such a regular feature of political oppression that something comparable might be expected in Ulster. In fact a very different course has been followed since Stormont came into being in 1920. Irish had already been killed by the joint efforts of the old Anglo-Irish executive and the Catholic Church, a somewhat surprising combination perhaps, but official Catholic support for the old national language is a comparatively recent development. Thus the Unionist Government, far from trying to destroy a living minority language, has given full practical support to the attempts to revive one already dead. There can be no doubt that this tolerant, not to say generous, attitude is a wise one, and if, in the event, Gaelic remains a very dead language, the fault does not rest with the authorities. In Eire, too, the persistent efforts to revive the language have failed.

The division between Protestants and Catholics fortunately becomes much less marked at the University level, for the Queen's University draws its students from all religious groups, although it is a secular institution like the ordinary modern English university. This implies a marked change of attitude on the part of the Catholics from that adopted in 1845, when the four Queen's colleges were first established at Belfast, Dublin, Galway and Cork. The Catholic bishops, supported by O'Connell, were apprehensive of this early experiment in secular education, and the growth of the new colleges in Dublin, Galway and Cork was greatly retarded by their hostility. These three now form the Catholic National University of Ireland and are under strict clerical control. The Belfast college, which had the support of the northern Protestants, continued to prosper and had become an independent university some years before Ireland was divided and the Stormont Parliament established. One of the developments that has helped to remove the Catholic suspicion of secularism has been the establishment at Queen's of a department of scholastic philosophy in addition to the ordinary philosophy department of the usual "secular" kind which looks after the non-Catholics.

The handling of the sectarian problem has of course been the aspect of educational policy that has provoked most controversy inside Ulster, and it is no doubt the one which deserves most attention from outside observers in view of the light it throws on the Unionist Government's treatment of its Catholic minority. But the other aspects of Stormont's policy should not be ignored if its record is to be fairly assessed. The new Ministry, as we have observed, has had an immense task in bringing up to date the backward system it inherited, and in trying to catch up with such new developments as meals in schools, the provision of proper medical attention and the like. Some "leeway" still remains to be made good: for example, the Act of 1947 makes provision for the further part-time education of young people between 15 and 18 years of age who have left school, but this is not compulsory, a departure from the English model which reflects not so much a disagreement about principle as a decision to give first priority to improving the facilities for full-time education; at the other end of the scale the provision of nursery schools is still felt to be inadequate. Such defects will be gradually remedied, and where the pace has at times seemed slow the fault has often lain with the local authorities rather than with Stormont.[1]

3. Education has been discussed at some length because it affords such a clear example of the way in which public policy has been adopted, under devolution, to meet local needs. But this, as we have seen, is not the only function of regional self-government. Some of the needs of any two areas may be basically very similar, but if the people in each area are free to choose, they will decide to meet these needs in different ways. Devolution may thus increase the effectiveness of self-government by allowing for local differences in majority opinion

A service which seems eminently suitable for such regional treatment is *town and country planning*, and Stormont has in fact enjoyed the right to independent action. But there can be no guarantee that a trans-

---

[1] *Cf.* p. 214 below.

ferred service, however appropriate its transference may appear to be, will in the event be successfully handled, and it cannot be said that Stormont has a particularly impressive planning record. Admittedly the province was spared any measure similar to Westminster's Town and Country Planning Act of 1947, for Stormont decided not to follow "step-by-step" when to do so would have involved the extravagances of "compensation and betterment"; Great Britain herself has subsequently abandoned the experiment. But it may be regretted that much more active measures have not been taken to protect the Ulster countryside, in particular the coast. In order to make such a policy more effective, it might have been appropriate to transfer to Stormont some of the functions that are rightly left to local authorities in England, where the alternative would be control by a distant and overburdened Whitehall. But little imagination or even interest has been shown. An admirable report, published in 1946 by the Planning Advisory Board, which recommended *inter alia* the creation of some national parks, has been ignored, and although Ulster's record may not be much worse than that of some parts of Great Britain, it is not so noticeably better as to count as one of the achievements of devolution.

When we turn to the *social services*, devolution seems to have been disappointing in another respect, for Stormont does not appear, at first glance, to have made any use of the self-government accorded to it, but has been content to follow "step-by-step". National insurance benefits and contributions are the same as in Great Britain, and the Health Act at Westminster was followed by a similar act at Stormont. This must seem surprising, for some of these measures have been much debated at Westminster, and the Ulster Unionists might have been expected to follow a different course from that which commended itself to the Socialist Government. Indeed, as Sayers has pointed out,[1] while the Unionist M.P.s at Westminster were opposing some socialist measures, their Unionist colleagues at Stormont were preparing to introduce similar measures for Ulster.

There may be two explanations of Stormont's attitude. First of all, it may be doubted whether the more moderate groups in the Socialist and Conservative parties at Westminster were really far apart in their attitudes to the social services, whatever may have been said in debate; secondly there are very good reasons, as Isles and Cuthbert have indicated,[2] for believing that a single province of the United Kingdom would find it extremely difficult to adopt a radically different policy in such matters as the social services from that adopted by the rest of the country.

[1] p. 69 above.   [2] pp. 173 *et seq.* above.

But it would be rash to suppose that devolution in this respect is therefore irrelevant and pointless. As we shall now see, Stormont has in fact been able to make some administrative modifications in adopting the new type of health service, and the policy of "step-by-step" has not been so strictly adopted as to imply slavish imitation.

As in Great Britain, the basic principle of the *Health Service* is the provision of comprehensive care and treatment to all members of the community with no direct payment—or very little—by the patients. At first no charge at all was made, but the rising cost of the service and the abuse by some patients of the privileges it conferred led to the introduction in 1951 and 1952 of charges for prescriptions, spectacles, dentures and dental services, a modification of the original policy which followed the English pattern exactly. General issues of policy of this kind are the concern of the Ministry of Health and Local Government at Stormont as at Westminster, but in other respects the Ulster Minister's responsibility is less direct, as we shall now see. The Act of 1948 established two new statutory bodies to which the main services were delegated: the General Health Services Board and the Hospitals Authority. Of these the first has broadly similar duties to those of a regional executive council in England, and is responsible for general medical services, dental services and pharmaceutical services. Its members are appointed by the Minister after consultation with the local authorities and the professional bodies, and Stormont has not, therefore, departed so far from English procedure as to experiment with boards consisting of elected representatives. The same applies to the Hospitals Authority whose members are also appointed by the Minister. Thus far the procedure follows the English pattern, but the Hospitals Authority, although constituted in much the same way as an English regional board, enjoys greater independence. The difference is indicated in a formal way by the fact that the hospitals taken over under the Act have been vested in the Hospitals Authority, not in the Minister. The latter, for his part, must promote the provision of all Health Services and must seek to co-ordinate the activities of the various bodies concerned, but it is not his duty to provide such services, as it is in England.

This procedure, it should be noted, did not originate in Ulster with the new Health Act, for the Northern Ireland Tuberculosis Authority, established two years earlier, had taken over the powers and duties of the county councils in regard to the treatment of a disease which was particularly prevalent in Ulster. The hospitals and other buildings formerly used by the councils for the treatment of tuberculosis were vested in the new body, not in the Minister, and the precedent was thus set for the treatment of the other hospitals when the general Act was passed.[1]

It has been suggested that it was the Unionist Government's dislike of outright nationalisation that made it favour a less centralised administrative arrangement. It has also been suggested that some of the administrators and doctors concerned hoped that by placing the administrative responsibility on special boards the new health service might be insulated to some extent from the day-to-day pressure of party politics. Whatever the reasons behind this departure from English policy, the new boards have clearly been successful and have demonstrated that a decentralised health service can work efficiently. In England, on the other hand, the satisfaction with which the establishment of regional hospital boards was originally greeted has tended to wane and some doubt has been expressed as to whether they fully justify their existence. In Northern Ireland, the Hospitals Authority is an active and vigorous body which performs much of the work of reorganisation and co-ordination left to the Ministry in England, and is very properly the originator of many of the proposals for modifying the service. The Minister, for his part, is close at hand and can be consulted at once when his sanction is needed, and local initiative and enterprise are less likely to be frustrated and discouraged when the chain of authority is short. Thus in assessing the relevance of Ulster's experience to the solution of regional problems in Great Britain, it must be recalled that delegation has been carried *two* stages farther in Northern Ireland: first by the establishment of a regional government with its Ministry of Health, and secondly by the subsequent transfer of administrative responsibility to three statutory bodies within the province.

The two special difficulties already mentioned in dealing with education are also encountered in dealing with health: "leeway" and sectarianism. Although some of the hospitals taken over by the new Hospital Authority were admirably equipped and staffed, others—especially some outside the Belfast area—were sometimes out-of-date and too small to cope with the needs of the districts dependent on their services. A heavy programme of extension and modernisation has had to be faced and the Ministry has provided the Authority with funds for capital expenditure on a more generous scale per head of population than has

[1] This body continues side by side with the boards established by the Health Act. There is, of course, some overlapping of duties: the Hospitals Authority has a large number of T.B. beds in its hospitals in addition to those provided by the Tuberculosis Authority. Fortunately there appears to be sufficiently close co-operation to prevent waste or conflict. The Tuberculosis Authority, it may be noted, deals with all aspects of prevention and cure, not only with hospital treatment.

been provided for any area in Great Britain. (Running costs remain sufficiently low to keep total expenditure below the general average across the Irish Sea.) As well as buildings and equipment more staff has been required, and the increase has been particularly marked at the consultant level, where the numbers have been roughly doubled to the benefit, in particular, of districts outside the Belfast area where there were very few consultants before the Act.

The elimination of "leeway" is a matter of time, not perhaps much time, but sectarianism is likely to be more permanent. Fortunately its effect on the Health Service has been much less important than its effect on education. The Roman Catholic Church refused to surrender its large Belfast Hospital, Mater Infirmorum, to the Authority, and was not compelled to yield. The Ministry, however, has made no offer of assistance comparable to that given to the Catholic schools, and the hospital continues to be supported by voluntary contributions. Admittedly these contributions, largely derived indirectly by means of a special football pool, are on a substantial scale, and the hospital appears to be able to carry on with this support. It need scarcely be said that Catholics are not obliged to go to their own hospital rather than to the State hospitals and many, of course, choose the latter. Nevertheless, some *ex gratia* payment to the Mater Hospital would be an act of goodwill, and it is only fair to add that, but for this hospital, the pressure on the accommodation provided by the Hospitals Authority would be that much the greater.[1]

The sober pages of the Sixth Annual Report of the Hospitals Authority, in which the first five years of the new services are reviewed, illuminates an aspect of political and social achievement in the province which normally receives too little attention. Over the period, hospital staffs increased by 50 per cent in total, while the medical staffs rose by no less than 70 per cent. Annual admissions to hospitals went up by two-fifths and out-patient attendances by three-quarters; the number of regular out-patient clinics increased to two and a half times its previous figure, and a substantial amount of hospital building had taken place. When we turn from the Report to the general statistics for public health, a marked improvement can be discerned since the 'thirties, and indeed since the mid-'forties when greater prosperity was already having its effect. This is not the place to detail the figures, but the conquest of tuberculosis is worth at least a passing reference: the death rate per thousand fell from

---

[1] If the big Catholic hospital stands apart in this way there is no distinction among the others between teaching hospitals and non-teaching hospitals corresponding to that in England; all are administered in the same way by the Authority.

1·67 in 1925 to 1·05 in 1935, 0·80 in 1945 and only 0·30 in 1952. The Ulster figure is no longer much above that for England and Wales, and is so very much below that for Eire that the benefits of a vastly superior health service can reasonably be described as one of the compensating advantages of partition.[1]

The recent improvement in health has not been confined to Ulster and is not the simple consequence of the Health Act. Although, among the possible causes, the conquest of unemployment has been less complete in Ulster than in Great Britain, the effects have not been insignificant, and higher real incomes, with better nutrition and better housing, have clearly contributed. There is no way of estimating separately the beneficial effect of the new health service, still less of assessing the importance of Ulster's modification of the English pattern. Nor is it, indeed, possible to describe in general terms the way in which the administration works in Ulster as compared with England, for the differences show themselves not as dramatic contrasts but rather as many variations of detail in the day-to-day working of the schemes. What can be said is that those who are familiar with both services and who are competent to judge seem to regard the sum of these differences as something significant, and those who feel that the direct responsibility for the health service in Great Britain should be transferred to statutory bodies with something of the independence of a public corporation can find some support for their views in Ulster's experience.

The last example we shall take is Stormont's *power to nationalise private industry*. It can scarcely be said of this transferred power, as it can of education, that the needs of the province are so peculiar as to call for special treatment; on the contrary, there are no very obvious reasons of a general nature for supposing that private enterprise will work better or worse in Ulster than in the rest of the country. What can be said is that devolution allows each case to be scrutinised on its merits from a regional point of view, and allows provincial party opinion to be clearly expressed. Presumably government is more effectively representative if such controversial issues are settled by the majority in a provincial parliament, rather than by the majority in a single central legislature for the whole country.[2] At all events, it cannot be held that devolution transfers no

[1] For both Northern Ireland and Eire, deaths per thousand were 1·47 in 1926. By 1948 the figure for Eire was still as high as 1·04 and even by 1952 it stood at 0·60.

[2] It is not suggested that it was for any such reason that Stormont was accorded the power to nationalise. The fact is that the power was transferred simply because it was not explicitly reserved (*cf.* p. 27 above). Presumably no one thought much about it in 1920.

powers of any significance when these powers include the right to deal with one of the most explosive topics in contemporary politics.

It would be only natural to suppose that the Unionist Government, whose party is affiliated to the Conservatives, had adopted a very different attitude to private enterprise from that adopted by the Socialists at Westminster after the war. These Unionists, indeed, are usually assumed to be well to the Right, and they, themselves, are wont to profess a respect for sturdy individualism and personal initiative that could not easily be reconciled with an affection for large State-owned public monopolies. With such considerations in mind Stormont's record, which we shall now review, must seem a little surprising.

At the start it must be recorded that the coal and iron-and-steel industries are not represented on a significant scale in the Ulster economy, and to this extent the scope for following an independent policy was narrowed. Nor is there, of course, any central bank in Northern Ireland, and the province was affected—or unaffected—by the taking over of the Bank of England in the same way as any other area in Great Britain. There is a point of departure in the treatment of public utilities owned by municipalities which have not been taken over by Stormont, a not unimportant case although the choice lay between local and central ownership rather than between private enterprise and socialism. But it is when we turn to transport that we find the most important case of independent action, and what is so remarkable is that Stormont has been more socialistic than Westminster. As long ago as 1935 the Unionist Government decided that road transport should be nationalised in order to ensure the proper co-ordination between road and rail. An Act of that year established the Northern Ireland Road Transport Board which was to acquire compulsorily firms carrying goods or passengers for hire and to operate the services so obtained; thus Northern Ireland had had ten years' experience of nationalised road transport before the Labour Government took office at Westminster. Although this experience had not been wholly reassuring it was decided to go further after the war and to take over the railways as well. The properties and duties of the Road Transport Board were transferred in 1948 to the Ulster Transport Authority which also acquired one of the railway companies, a second railway being added in the following year. (The province's third railway is also in public ownership, but since it operates in Eire too, it was acquired by a special board representing the governments of both countries. This is an interesting example of co-operation in dealing with a common problem.)

The Conservatives, who were helped to power in 1951 by Ulster

Unionist votes, implemented their pledge to restore the road services in Great Britain to private enterprise, but Stormont remained unimpressed and showed no signs of following suit. Thus Unionist Ulster became the only part of the United Kingdom where virtually all transport for hire was owned by a public corporation. There are, it is true such exceptions as the city transport in Belfast, but this is municipally owned and scarcely counts. The other exceptions are modest—local goods carriage within the city boundaries of Belfast and Londonderry, funeral transport, furniture removal and the like, together with some small concessions to the farmers. By contrast, the application to Ulster of the Socialist Act of 1947 would have left a far larger proportion of transport in private hands, for that Act provided only for the nationalisation of long-distance transport and allowed the private carrier to operate within forty miles of his base. In a small region like Northern Ireland, within which, moreover, much of the population is concentrated in one area, only a small part of road transport would have qualified as long-distance and therefore suitable for nationalisation under the Socialist Act. But, from the outset, Stormont was resolved to take over short-distance haulage as well, although in this case the arguments in favour of public ownership are generally admitted to be weaker. This policy the Unionists have unswervingly maintained.

Now there may be good reason to doubt whether the Unionist Governments have acted wisely in this, and it would be difficult to maintain that either the old Road Transport Board or the Ulster Transport Authority has been a resounding success. But our object here is not to pass judgment but to record the fact that the province has been free to take its own line and has in fact done so. To this we may perhaps be allowed to add that the Unionists, notwithstanding their "reactionary" reputation, which is not wholly unearned,[1] have been at least as socialistic in their attitude to transport as the British Labour Party.

III

In attempting to draw any conclusions about devolution as a form of government from the experience of Northern Ireland, it is necessary to bear in mind, first, that the present arrangements are not immutable and could perhaps be improved, and secondly, that the political environment in which the experiment has been made has some special features that might not be found elsewhere.

On the first of these points, I shall say little here. In several of the pre-

[1] *Cf.* Sayers, pp. 64 *et seq.* above.

ceding chapters the desirability of increasing Stormont's powers has been discussed, and it is of interest to record that no sharp differences of opinion between the various contributors appear to have emerged. There are, of course, a number of minor disagreements on specific points, and the emphasis is by no means always the same; but all seem to be in broad agreement that a wide extension of Stormont's powers would be useless or even dangerous. There may, it is true, be a case for some minor adjustments: for example, Stormont might have slightly more power to levy taxes, but I appear to be alone among our contributors in favouring this and would not, in any case, wish to describe the proposal as one of major importance. It is true that, apart from any formal changes in the Constitution, there may be a case for modifying somewhat the way in which existing powers are interpreted and used. Under this heading comes the argument advanced by Isles and Cuthbert that the principle of parity in expenditure and taxation should be consistently applied even if, at times, the Imperial Contribution is thus reduced to a negative figure. Perhaps most important of all is the need to ensure that the province does not fall between two administrative stools because certain issues which are held to be none of Whitehall's business lie beyond the practical competence of the provincial administration. Just after the war I was strongly inclined to suspect that Ulster's needs, especially with regard to the location of new industries, were very largely neglected in Whitehall and that the link with Stormont through the Home Office was too weak and indirect. No doubt the arrangements have been improved since then, but little information has been released. What may be needed is a Stormont representative permanently attached to each key committee and provided with offices and small staffs inside Whitehall itself—not with the object of engaging in special pleading but in order to ensure that the economic advantages the province has to offer are not simply overlooked.

Suggestions of this kind will of course be pointless if entirely adequate permanent arrangements for liaison between London and Belfast have now been made. One does not know. At Westminster, there are occasional perfunctory replies to questions on Ulster's affairs; at Stormont much is left obscure and uncertain on this and most other aspects of the arrangements with London because the Government cannot really be forced to lay its cards on the table. The same party has been in power since 1920 and is likely to remain so indefinitely; it would be surprising if such parliamentary security did not breed in both Ministers and civil servants some complacency and self-sufficiency and a reluctance to explain in detail just what they are about. Here we come to our second

point, the special political conditions that prevail in Ulster as a direct
and more or less permanent consequence of the debate about partition.

IV

It would have been pleasant to have been able to neglect altogether
this noisy and prolonged controversy and to have concentrated attention
in this book exclusively on other matters, such as economic development
and the Welfare State, which ought, perhaps, to be of more immediate
concern to all classes in the province. For, however much one may deplore
partition, it cannot, I think, be seriously denied that it has afforded the
only feasible compromise between the conflicting sentiments of loyalists
and republicans. This was undeniably so in 1920, but in the late 'thirties
a number of people in the North ventured to hope that Ireland could
ultimately be united within the Commonwealth as a Dominion. I must
confess that I myself shared this belief.[1] At the time it seemed to us that
the main obstacle was the obduracy of the Unionists, but in this Eire was
soon to prove us wrong, first by her policy of neutrality and then by her
repudiation of any link with the Crown and the adoption of republican
status. It must now be admitted, with satisfaction or dismay according
to one's point of view, that there is no prospect at all of both parties
reaching sufficient agreement for a United Ireland to be feasible in the
near future. These facts appear to be decisive, whatever the other
arguments for or against the division of the country, and it is therefore
tempting to try to escape entanglement in so bitter a debate by pleading
its irrelevance at the present time. This book has, in fact, concerned
itself in the main with other matters, but it has not been possible to
ignore altogether an issue that, however insoluble, continues to dominate
the politics of the area and to affect by its indirect ramifications nearly
every aspect of social and cultural life. In these concluding paragraphs,
the essential points will be passed very briefly in review.

Enough has been said in previous chapters by Mogey, Newark and
Sayers to allow us to dismiss with little delay the more extreme proposition that Partition is perpetuated only because a small group of Orange
bigots are maintained in power by a British garrison. It is true, of course,
that there are British troops in Ulster, including men at the depots of
those of the great Irish regiments that have survived the departure of
the South from the United Kingdom; but troops must be stationed
somewhere and their presence in Down or Tyrone does not by itself
prove that these areas are "occupied" any more than Yorkshire or Kent.

[1] *Cf.* my article "Ulster and Eire," *Political Quarterly*, 1939.

It is also true that, in view of the uncertainty of Eire's attitude in any subsequent war,[1] the Partition of Ireland is immensely in the interest of Britain and indeed of the U.S.A. and all the other N.A.T.O. Powers; as Falls has shown in chapter 4, the naval and air bases in Northern Ireland were a major factor in the struggle with Hitler and would be a major factor in any future submarine war. But it would be poor logic to infer from this that Britain has had to resort to undemocratic methods in order to keep Ulster under her control. However uncharitable some comments on Conservative policy may be, few people can really believe that Mr Attlee's Government kept a grip on the province by supporting a small reactionary "fascist" caucus in the teeth of popular sentiment.[2] As for the U.S.A., the Ulster loyalists have not received from that source even the private support that the republicans have enjoyed over a long period of years.

If Northern Ireland remains part of the United Kingdom, this is because the majority of her people want her to do so. Although their views have been expressed with great clarity on repeated occasions— once, indeed, with violent clarity—there is a strange reluctance in both Britain and America to accept what is after all a very obvious fact. This is not to say that partition is generally popular even among the Protestants, but if the choice is between partitioning the United Kingdom and partitioning Ireland the majority are unequivocal in opting for the latter. Reinforcing their allegiance to the British connection is their fear of Irish Catholicism. Many, of course, are inspired by an old-fashioned Protestant bigotry, and somewhat fanciful fears are often entertained about the fate of Protestants in the South; but it is fair to add that many others who are far from bigoted, and may indeed be fairly indifferent about religious matters, would be reluctant to become part of a professedly Catholic republic—as would many of Eire's left-wing supporters in England if they themselves were faced with such a choice. Those who have watched with approval as a modern Welfare State has come quietly

[1] As Falls has recorded, Mr De Valera was asked in the course of the last war whether he would abandon neutrality if partition were abolished, but he refused to commit his government. In a future war against the U.S.S.R., the sympathies of Catholic Ireland would presumably be on the side of the Western Powers, but there could be no certainty that, even if partition had gone, Eire would not remain neutral, perhaps from a sense of grievance, real or imaginary, about some other minor issue. Or, grievances apart, she might simply find the attractions of neutrality as irresistible as did Norway, Holland and Belgium in 1939. At all events there is a risk here. While partition remains, on the other hand, there is a certainty that at least some of the Irish bases will be available.

[2] It is worth recalling that it was the Labour Government which was responsible for the Act of 1949 by which Ulster's status can be changed only with the consent of her own Parliament.

into being in the North would be inclined to hesitate before exchanging Unionist rule, with all its faults, for the clericalism of the South.

To some, such views may appear wrong-headed and foolish; it requires little effort of the imagination to understand the impatient disagreement of those who advocate a united Irish Republic. The Unionists, for their part, whatever the merits of their case, are exceedingly bad at presenting it and tend to be either inarticulate or boisterous, to remain dourly silent or to shout. But it is enough for our immediate purposes to record that the majority hold such Unionist views and do not want to be forced out of the United Kingdom into the Republic of Ireland. Our task is to record what opinions are held, not to pass judgment upon them.

If the Irish nationalists had some sort of moral right to withdraw from the United Kingdom, and if the Northern loyalists can claim a similar right to stay, what is one to say about the large minority within the borders of Northern Ireland itself? Roughly a third of the population consists of Catholics, and of their number a large, although perhaps declining, proportion demands union with the South. How can one apply the principle of self-determination in such circumstances? The answer would appear to be that beyond a certain point the principle cannot be applied at all, and some *modus vivendi* must be accepted by both sides. The Catholic population is more heavily concentrated in some areas than in others; in parts the Catholics—and Republicans— are clearly in the majority. It may be that the border could be better drawn, but unfortunately it would be over-optimistic to suppose that any readjustment would produce an acceptable solution, for Eire continues to demand the *whole* of Northern Ireland. Moreover, the Catholics are widely scattered—in Belfast itself they make up a quarter of the population; an attempt to choose areas even smaller than the six counties for the application of the principle of self-determination would lead to a preposterous segmentation of the country. At some point a halt must be called even if the consequence is a minority problem of the kind so familiar in many other countries. The really interesting questions, then, are whether the minority receives fair treatment and whether it, in turn, is prepared to co-operate with the majority in making the State work as well as may be.

The main reason for suspecting that the minority may be repressed is the extent to which people in Northern Ireland can be deprived of the traditional British liberties under the *Civil Authorities* (*Special Powers*) *Act*.[1] It is not surprising that this measure should have aroused grave

[1] *Cf*. Newark, pp. 46 *et seq*. above.

concern in England, for the powers given to the executive are far-reaching and could undeniably be used to establish a Unionist dictatorship. But there are two questions that ought to be considered before judgment can be passed. First, could law and order have been preserved without some special powers? Secondly, has the Act really been used for sinister party ends?

A confident answer to the first of these questions can be given only by those who are thoroughly familiar with all the circumstances. But it is sobering to reflect that had events taken a slightly different course in the early 'twenties, Westminster might have remained responsible for law and order in Ulster. Would it really have been possible to do without special measures?[1] It is fair to say that the British Fascists detained during the war were a less serious threat to security in England than the I.R.A. has been for many years to security in Ulster. Mr De Valera himself used special powers against these terrorists, and the Eire legislation of 1939 remains in force although Mr Costello has not been inclined to use it. The Government of India has special powers of detention (the Preventive Detention Act), and Mr Nehru's difficulties have always been treated with sympathy and understanding in this country. Clearly we must be careful in criticising the Ulster Government lest we imply that it ought to be able to get along without powers that other governments in similar circumstances have held to be indispensable.

There can be little doubt that the Act was needed in 1922 when disorder was widespread, but it may be asked whether it has really been necessary to keep it in force ever since. As Newark has emphasised, a distinction must be made between the Act itself and the Orders made under it. A long and alarming list of Orders did, it is true, remain in force for many years—not entirely without reason, for there were periodic outbreaks of terrorism. In 1949 and 1951, however, the majority of these Orders were withdrawn, including the Detention Order which had attracted so much adverse comment.[2] The Government's attitude appears to have been that the Act itself should be retained for the time

---

[1] The Special Powers Act had been preceded by a comparable Westminster measure, the Restoration of Order in Ireland Act, which lapsed when the Government of Ireland Act of 1920 came into effective operation and Stormont assumed responsibility for law and order.

[2] The only regulations then left in force that call for comment are: the right to examine bank accounts in certain circumstances, a measure that can be better understood when one recalls the extent to which terrorism in Ireland has been financed from the U.S.A.; the ruling that membership of the I.R.A. and certain related organisations was illegal. The power to ban meetings and processions when the peace is likely to be threatened is now provided by the Public Order Act of 1951, which may be compared with the Westminster Act of 1936. Cf. my article in the *Manchester Guardian* April 5, 1955.

being because it allowed new Orders to be brought in quickly in an emergency, but it can be said that for a time the Act was almost inoperative.

In 1954 the I.R.A. embarked upon a new campaign which differed from the last in that it was directed only against the authorities in England and Ulster but not against the Government of Eire as well. There can be no doubt that this policy paid dividends. Although Mr Costello, the Prime Minister, expressed disapproval he took no steps to control I.R.A. activities. It should be borne in mind that there is no working extradition arrangement with Eire. (The High Court in Dublin decided in 1929 that Northern Ireland warrants could not be executed.) Thus terrorists have only to slip across the long land frontier in order to be safe. Even the informal wartime co-operation between the police forces in Ulster and Eire was stopped in Dublin, and Eire thus became a safe base for terrorist activities against Ulster. It is rather as though a band of gunmen who had raided Chester barracks, shot some soldiers and stolen some arms could find ready sanctuary by slipping across the frontier into Wales.

In June 1954 the I.R.A. attacked an army depot and made off with some arms. The Minister of Home Affairs then made an Order by which the police were given the right to search without warrant any person suspected of "carrying any firearms, ammunition, explosive substances or any article or document for any purpose or in any way prejudical to the preservation of peace or the maintenance of order". In the following October another barracks was raided. No arms were captured, but there was a fierce gun battle in which several soldiers were wounded. No immediate action was taken by the Government, but a couple of months later two I.R.A. publications were banned. The special power of detention was not restored, and anyone charged under the Act was to be tried in a court of summary jurisdiction or indicted.[1]

After the bomb outrages of 1950 the Minister of Home Affairs observed that: "The Government hopes it will not be necessary to revive the powers of internment which were previously in force". Stormont is faced, here, with something of a dilemma. The case against restoring special powers is obviously strong. Although such powers might be directed only against terrorists, they would no doubt be regarded as a grievance by the minority, and this would conflict with the official policy of conciliation followed in a number of fields, notably education. Moreover Stormont's reputation in Great Britain and America has been

---

[1] When the Detention Order was in force, those detained could always appeal to a special tribunal with a judge or senior barrister as chairman, in the knowledge that any recommendation for their release would be accepted by the Government.

greatly damaged by the Special Powers Act, and it may be feared that a revival of emergency measure would do fresh harm. Yet without such powers—and without co-operation from Eire—it may be impossible to prevent further outrages.

Let us now turn to the second question? Has the Act been used to suppress legitimate and peaceful opposition to the Government? To this an unequivocal and reassuring answer can be given. Although Parliamentary Government does not work as well as might be wished in Ulster, the reason is not that the Special Powers Act has been used improperly for party ends. It is true that two I.R.A. publications have been banned, as we have observed above, but these were seditious by any standard. "No one pretends", writes Mill, "that actions should be as free as opinions. On the contrary, even opinions lose their immunity when the circumstances in which they are expressed are such as to constitute their expression a positive instigation to some mischievous act." The ordinary republican newspapers, published in both Belfast and Dublin, circulate as freely in Ulster as any other newspapers, and freedom of speech extends even to the most vehement visiting politicians from the South. These are not matters on which any difference of opinion is possible. A tourist who arrives in Belfast can buy from a newsagent papers and pamphlets that urge not merely a change of Government but the abolition of the State in its present form; he can listen to republican speeches in the Parliament at Stormont; he can attend public meetings where union with Eire is fiercely demanded; he may perhaps be amused to hear —from people who are obviously safe, secure and uninhibited—that he has come to a totalitarian country where all liberty has been cruelly destroyed and where any criticism will be savagely punished. The very fact that such angry complaints about Unionist tyranny can be made in public with complete impunity is in itself an indication that rhetoric has taken charge and truth has been left behind.

To say this is not to imply that there is no discrimination against the minority. We have been concerned with the possible use of security measures for improper party ends and have reached a reassuring conclusion. But it may still be true that in other and milder ways the minority is put at a disadvantage. It is indeed the case that, just as it is better to be a Catholic in Eire, so it is better to be a Protestant in Ulster; but the margin of advantage is usually small. Entrance to the Civil Service is by competitive examination,[1] and there is no question of excluding Catho-

---

[1] Recruitment to Grade I is by means of the ordinary Home Civil Service examination administered by the Civil Service Commissioners. A large number of the officials in the administrative grade come from other parts of the United Kingdom. So do

lics from the public departments—or even from the police; nor is there any obstacle to their entering business or the professions. What discrimination there is tends to be private rather than official, and what it amounts to is that, as between two candidates, a Protestant employer will tend to engage a Protestant if he has the choice and both are more or less equally competent. In the same way, Catholics favour Catholics, but there are not so many Catholic employers. There may be similar discrimination in the appointments made by some local authorities. Lack of evidence makes it difficult to reach definite conclusions. Moreover, even if figures were available for the proportion of Catholics in each occupation, they would prove little: there is no reason *a priori* why Catholics, who are one-third of the population, should have one-third of the chairs at the university, one-third of the administrative posts and so on, for ability and inclination, together with the competition of people from outside Ulster altogether, may dictate differently. As for business life, Presbyterians and Jews are probably endowed with more business acumen than Irish Catholics.

From any objective point of view it cannot be said that the grievances of the Catholics are always very real.[1] They have less to complain about than the U.S. negroes, and their lot is a very pleasant one as compared with that of the nationalists in, say, the Ukraine. But political dissatisfaction is not always based on concrete grievances, and it is perfectly natural that so many Catholics should resent their inclusion in the United Kingdom and long to see the North brought into the Catholic Republic. Ulster is the scene of many of the great Celtic legends and the home of some of the national heroes; Ulster was for long the centre of Celtic resistance to English aggression; it seems monstrous to nationalist sentiment that this historic area should lie outside the national State. Moreover, just as it is necessary to understand the "planter" psychology, so it is necessary to understand the psychology of those who were supplanted. For generations they were the underdogs, the despised "croppies", the adherents of a persecuted religion, who were kept out of public affairs by the Protestant conquerors. They were made to feel inferior, and to make matters worse they often *were* inferior, if *only* in

---

many of the staffs in the University and in the schools. Whereas Eire is run by Irishmen, a large part of the public business of Northern Ireland is conducted by first-generation immigrants who have never been involved, either personally or through their families, in the feuds of their new environment.

[1] The most substantial is that their local government representation is unfairly small in some towns because, in part, of the way in which the area boundaries are drawn. *Cf.* Sayers, p. 61 above.

those personal qualities that make for success in competitive economic life. Their material grievances may now often be more imaginary than real,[1] but spiritual discontent remains, and could only be met in full by a reversal of status such as would follow from incorporation in the Republic. While the Protestants would no doubt be well treated, their status would then clearly be inferior in the same subtle way as that of the Catholics still is in Ulster, and the latter for their part would regain self-confidence and self-respect.

I have tried here to make explicit the feelings that may really lie behind more extravagant complaints about persecution, and may have suggested a deeper sensitivity than is general. But, although the intensity with which they are held may vary, these are, I believe, the sentiments of a large part of the Catholic minority, certainly of those who are politically vocal. It is clear that, whether we are trying to understand the Unionists or the Republicans, we must allow for such complex habits of mind which can be understood only by the study of Ulster's unhappy history.

Admittedly there are Catholics who do not seem to share this discontent with their position, and some will admit—in private—that they would not really like to see the North leave the United Kingdom. I suspect that a good many would in fact be dismayed by the blow to the Welfare State and to the Ulster economy in general that such a change would imply. Some, indeed, are believed to have voted Unionist in recent elections. The Government, for its part, has pursued a policy of conciliation since the war, and its spokesmen have clearly been at pains to avoid the provocative utterances that used to be too frequent, although still considerably embarrassed at times by the outbursts of the more intransigent back-benchers. Perhaps, in time, this statesmanlike policy will yield more impressive fruit, but the fact remains that a large proportion of Ulster's population refuses to accept the present constitutional status and in such circumstances Parliament cannot function effectively.[2]

"The Westminster system", writes Professor Newark, "is based on the healthy alternation of parties in power. . . . But at Stormont the

[1] It is surprising how unreal these grievances can be. I know from experience that when a Catholic child fails a public examination, his parents are liable to say that this is an example of Orange persecution.

[2] The Southern Protestant is no better off than the Northern Catholic. The basic difference is that the former has resigned himself to the position, whereas the latter still believes that a constitutional change is possible. The minority in the South is, of course, very small and has declined since 1922. By contrast the number of Catholics in the North has grown, partly by immigration from Eire.

Unionist party has never gone out of office since 1921, and there is no likelihood of this happening in the foreseeable future." So long as the constitutional issue dominates politics, the Unionists will consist of a sort of informal coalition of loyalists of various sentiments, and both the official socialists and the anti-partitionists will remain futile groups with no real prospect of defeating the government. If Eire politicians could be persuaded to abandon their agitation about the Border, and if the nationalists in the North could be induced to accept the fact that there is no immediate prospect whatsoever of ending partition, a new alignment of forces would gradually appear at Stormont. There can be no doubt that from the nationalists' own point of view this would be the best way of ensuring that their domestic grievances—including "gerrymandering"—were fully investigated and, where substantiated, reformed.

Here then is the main reason why it is unfortunate that the first experiment in devolution should have been carried out in Ulster. In other areas, where a normal rotation of parties might have taken place, some greater achievements might have been possible.

When account is taken of all the difficulties with which the Ulster Parliament has been confronted from the early days of civil disturbance and administrative confusion to recent times, with the hostility of the large minority still strong and outbreaks of violence still recurrent, one is left, I think, with a feeling of surprise that it has worked so well. For this full credit must go to the Unionist Ministers and the civil servants who have toiled away at the practical problems while all the shouting has been going on. But we must also allow for another special feature in the situation which, unlike the one we have just discussed, operates in favour of efficient government. This is the determination of the Unionists, with their strong pro-British sentiments and their chronic feeling of insecurity, not to allow public policy in Ulster to diverge too much from Westminster. As we have seen, a number of important differences have been made on a scale which, in my view, justifies the existence of a separate Parliament, but the general path of development has been the same at Westminster and Stormont. Had this not been so, devolution might not have worked as well as it has done; it would not, I suspect, have proved so successful in the South if the Act of 1920 had ever come into effective operation, because nationalist sentiment would have led the Dublin Parliament to seek wherever possible a separate course of action if only as a means of asserting independence. By contrast, there was no nationalistic pressure behind the granting of devolution to Northern Ireland, and the successive Unionist governments have never felt impelled to differ from Westminster unless there appeared to them to be good reason for doing so on the merits of the case. Devolution backed by nationalism might have produced some more lively actions and perhaps some more individual achievements; but the risk of harm from too much independence, with all the confusion and administrative conflict that would follow, might be much greater than the likelihood of gain.

Perhaps, then, our final conclusion should be this: that Home Rule can be tried with most confidence in those regions where the majority of the people do not particularly want it! It is precisely when national sentiment demands Home Rule that Home Rule may do serious harm. When there is no such sentiment, a regional Parliament may prove to be a valuable addition to the machinery of government by easing the burden on Westminster and by allowing local policies to be adapted to local needs. When such sentiment is strong, the Parliament may always be straining to the utmost its powers of independent action, and the Administration will be engaged in a perpetual and mutually-frustrating conflict with Whitehall. Admittedly our experience of devolution is too restricted to allow us to advance these propositions with great assurance, but on the face of it they do not appear to be lacking in plausibility. On this speculative and slightly cautionary note our observations on the Ulster experiment may be suitably brought to an end.

STANDARDS OF PUBLIC EXPENDITURE IN NORTHERN IRELAND

By PETER ROBSON

THE financial relations between the Exchequers of Northern Ireland and the United Kingdom have been described elsewhere in this book. It has been explained that the principle underlying existing arrangements is that of parity of taxation, parity of services. More precisely, there is to be absolute parity in the cash social services and relative parity in the other services according to Northern Ireland's special needs. In addition it has been agreed that Ulster is to be permitted to incur additional expenditure for the purpose of making up "leeway" in the social services.

The purpose of this section is to present briefly some estimates which show how these principles and their earlier variants have affected, and are affecting, the level and distribution of transferred expenditure. It must be said at this point that the notion of parity is not precise and little is known of the way in which it has been interpreted, except in a few fields. The simplest way to interpret parity is to define it in terms of equality of expenditure per head of population. This is inadequate, however, for it is in some sense parity of standards which underlies existing arrangements, and parity of expenditure will only produce parity of standards if the cost of providing a service and the need for it are the same in the two regions. It seems reasonable therefore, to interpret parity to mean that level of expenditure which will produce equivalent standards of benefit or service. This is, in fact, the way in which parity has been interpreted so far as the cash benefit in social security services is concerned. Here, conditions of eligibility and rates of benefit are identical in the two regions, and parity emerges automatically. Regional levels of expenditure are automatic reflections of differences in need.

In the field of the social services given in kind, such as the Health Service, and in relation to other public services, what is meant by parity of standards is by no means as clear. Here, qualitative comparisons and judgments of need are necessary, and the scope for administrative discretion is considerable. Actual rates of expenditure on these services reflect that discretion, and they must be evaluated in the light of what is known about the special conditions of the province.

It can probably be assumed that, taking into account the special conditions of Northern Ireland (greater sparsity and dispersal of population, geographical position, etc.), the costs of providing particular real services of an equivalent standard to those in Great Britain will be, in general, at least as high as the cost in Great Britain. It may be possible to provide some services of equivalent standard at lower cost, on account of different and more efficient methods of administration, but these cases are likely to be of limited importance.[1] In

[1] Cases in question are, possibly, the child care service and the dental services.

general, if parity is to be attained, expenditure per head in Northern Ireland must be at least as high as that in Great Britain. In many cases local needs and cost conditions will demand a higher outlay if equivalent benefits are to be provided. How far these needs will be taken into account will depend partly on the way in which similar local needs in Great Britain receive attention, and partly on political negotiation.

The problem of leeway is very relevant to a consideration of expenditure in Northern Ireland since the war. Where leeway exists one would expect expenditure in Ulster to be higher than whatever standard current equivalent seems appropriate. The excess would depend not only on the magnitude of the leeway, but also on the rate at which it is made up. The existence of leeway, however, in the sense of a relatively low standard of capital equipment in a particular field, may set sharp physical limits on the rate of current expenditure.

In Table 1 figures are given showing rates of social and economic expenditure from votes of supply in the two areas for the period 1923–4 to 1951–2. The figures exclude expenditure on the cash benefit social services, for which conditions of eligibility and rates of benefit have always been the same in the two areas. It can be seen that, during this period, taking economic and social expenditure together, standards of expenditure per head of population have been consistently higher in Northern Ireland than in Great Britain, except for a few years in the thirties and for one post-war year. The marked relative reduction in Ulster's standards of expenditure in the 'thirties reflects the disuse of the Colwyn Special Formula, which was probably given a good deal of weight in determining permissible levels of expenditure in Northern Ireland when finances were buoyant.

For post-war years, standards of expenditure in Northern Ireland are not adequately indicated by expenditure from votes, on account of factors discussed below.[1] When adjustments are made on this account, overall rates of expenditure in Northern Ireland are somewhat reduced. It is difficult to make accurate estimates for all years owing to the complexity of the accounting procedures, but it seems clear that for the earlier post-war years up to 1949–50, total *economic and social* expenditure per head in Northern Ireland was if anything lower than that in Great Britain. Since then standards of expenditure in Ulster have been higher than in Great Britain and the excess has shown a tendency to increase. There has, however, been a marked difference between relative levels of economic and social expenditure in the two regions in the post-war years.

Since the war, rates of *economic* expenditure per head have generally been much higher in Northern Ireland mainly because of the higher rate of expenditure on industrial development services in Northern Ireland. In 1951–2, for example, expenditure per head on industrial development services was six times as high as corresponding expenditure on development area services in Great Britain.

In the field of *social* expenditure the situation has been different. Whereas before the war social expenditure in Northern Ireland was generally substantially higher than in Great Britain in the post-war years, up to 1951–2 it appears to have been lower—in earlier post-war years, considerably lower. This is in part a consequence of the fact that the authorities in Great Britain

[1] *Cf.* p. 222 below.

have, in the post-war period, taken over responsibility for services which were more highly developed than the corresponding services in Northern Ireland. The distribution of specific expenditure by central government on the social services in the two regions is set out in Table 2, where for comparative purposes expenditure on the social security cash benefits is included. It can be seen from line 3 of the total that in this year less per head was being spent in Northern Ireland than in Great Britain on the non-cash social services. If the whole of non-specific grants to local authorities is included as expenditure on social services, then Northern Ireland's relative level of expenditure is increased, but it still falls short of the rate of expenditure in Great Britain.

Table 2 includes both *current* and *capital* expenditure. If these two elements are distinguished, it becomes clear that in 1951–2 Northern Ireland was spending at a much higher rate on *capital* account than was Great Britain on education, hospital services, and water and sewerage. This reflects the efforts to make up leeway by increasing the supply of social capital—schools, hospitals and environmental services. This higher rate of *capital* expenditure was however more than offset by lower rates of *current* expenditure in a number of fields, particularly health and housing. In the earlier post-war years, Ulster appears to have been spending less per head on social services on both capital and current account than was Great Britain. Since 1951–2 the higher rates of capital expenditure in Northern Ireland have been maintained. The situation currently appears to be that the overall rate of expenditure on the social services given in kind per head of the population is now rather higher in Northern Ireland. The much higher rates of capital expenditure are to a considerable extent still accompanied by lower rates of current expenditure on the services mentioned.

It is of considerable interest to compare aggregate public expenditure on social services in the two regions. This is done in Tables 3 and 4, which are consolidated accounts of social service expenditure of *all public authorities* in the two regions. The figures relate to 1949–50, the latest year for which the local financial statistics are available for Northern Ireland. The tables show that, in this year, Ulster was spending less per head of the population on all social services, on both current and capital account, than was Great Britain. Perhaps the most significant feature which emerges from consolidation is the effect which the inclusion of local authority expenditure has upon relative levels of expenditure on education in the two areas. The inclusion of local authority expenditure reduces Northern Ireland's relative standard of expenditure per head on this service greatly. A more interesting comparison is between expenditure as a rate per head of population of school age. On this basis in 1949–50 public current expenditure on education in Great Britain amounted to £40·5 per head. In Northern Ireland the corresponding rate of expenditure on the age group 5–14 was only £28·6. (No doubt the independent schools—mainly Catholic—at the elementary level form a larger part of the total in Ulster than in Great Britain, but a great part of the expenditure of these schools is provided by public funds in any case. This point accounts only for a small part of the difference in these rates of expenditure.) The question which suggests itself is whether the local authorities are bearing their share of the burden. The average level of rates in Northern Ireland is lower than in Great Britain, but this is not conclusive. It is none the less alarming that local expenditure should reduce the standard by so much notwithstanding the much higher rate at which the General Exchequer Contribution is running in Northern Ireland. This perhaps points to the need for reconsidering the principles on which these grants are made in Northern Ireland. At present they take local poverty into account only to a small extent.

In conclusion, it can be said that standards of current expenditure from central sources on education and health will necessarily increase in Northern Ireland as the school and hospital building programmes are completed. A closer approximation to parity is then to be expected in these services. Expansion of educational expenditure is, however, likely to raise acute problems in the field of local finance. The adequacy of current levels and the question of future levels of economic expenditure is a more problematic matter. These estimates of expenditure are intended only to provide a broad financial background to a discussion of Ulster's problems. The appropriateness of these levels of expenditure must be considered in the light of the special financial, economic, and social problems of the province, which are fully discussed elsewhere.

TABLE 1

NORTHERN IRELAND

	Social		Economic		Total Social and Economic	
	£000	£ per head	£000	£ per head	£000	£ per head
1923–4	2,551	2·03	252	0·20	2,803	2·23
1924–5	2,280	1·81	327	0·26	2,607	2·07
1925–6	2,393	1·90	425	0·34	2,818	2·24
1926–7	2,331	1·86	670	0·53	3,001	2·39
1927–8	2,318	1·85	721	0·58	3,039	2·43
1928–9	2,437	1·95	676	0·54	3,113	2·49
1929–30	2,897	2·34	719	0·58	3,616	2·92
1930–1	3,502	2·83	674	0·55	4,176	3·38
1931–2	3,388	2·73	753	0·61	4,141	3·34
1932–3	3,434	2·75	711	0·57	4,145	3·32
1933–4	3,446	2·74	832	0·66	4,278	3·40
1934–5	3,436	2·72	622	0·49	4,058	3·21
1935–6	3,609	2·84	629	0·49	4,238	3·33
1936–7	3,544	2·78	638	0·50	4,182	3·28
1937–8	3,526	2·75	731	0·57	4,257	3·32
1938–9	3,698	2·88	916	0·71	4,614	3·59
1939–40	3,724	2·87	1,111	0·86	4,835	3·73
1940–1	3,826	2·95	698	0·54	4,524	3·49
1941–2	3,914	2·99	838	0·64	4,752	3·63
1942–3	4,215	3·17	1,331	1·00	5,546	4·17
1943–4	4,421	3·30	1,476	1·10	5,897	4·40
1944–5	4,684	3·45	1,379	1·02	6,064	4·47
1945–6	5,817	4·28	1,328	0·98	7,145	5·26
1946–7	8,535	6·32	1,690	1·25	10,225	7·57
1947–8	9,071	6·71	1,948	1·44	11,019	8·15
1948–9	15,963	11·72	2,971	2·18	18,934	13·90
1949–50	19,878	14·50	4,026	2·94	23,904	17·44
1950–1	21,437	15·57	3,795	2·76	25,232	18·33
1951–2	23,926	17·43	3,840	2·80	27,766	20·23

Source: Appropriation Accounts, United Kingdom and Northern Ireland.
Notes: Figures exclude expenditure on departmental administration, and expenditure on civil government—i.e. justice, defence and police. Expenditure on cash benefit social services, for which conditions of eligibility and

OF SUPPLY 1923-4 TO 1951-2

GREAT BRITAIN

	Social		Economic		Total Social and Economic	
	£000	£ per head	£000	£ per head	£000	£ per head
1923-4	62,809	1·45	17,518	0·40	80,327	1·85
1924-5	64,231	1·47	17,272	0·40	81,503	1·87
1925-6	65,188	1·49	18,665	0·42	83,853	1·91
1926-7	72,503	1·65	19,794	0·45	92,297	2·10
1927-8	70,252	1·59	22,192	0·50	92,444	2·09
1928-9	68,006	1·53	20,344	0·46	88,350	1·99
1929-30	84,226	1·90	24,062	0·54	108,288	2·44
1930-1	115,729	2·59	31,205	0·70	146,934	3·29
1931-2	117,464	2·62	32·772	0·73	150,237	3·35
1932-3	115,047	2·55	27,159	0·60	142,205	3·15
1933-4	115,221	2·55	23,964	0·53	139,185	3·08
1934-5	114,821	2·53	23,693	0·52	138,514	3·05
1935-6	127,446	2·80	24,256	0·53	151,702	3·33
1936-7	129,148	2·82	29,600	0·65	158,748	3·47
1937-8	134,697	2·93	27,711	0·60	162,408	3·53
1938-9	137,418	2·97	33,847	0·73	171,264	3·70
1939-40	140,337	3·01	25,642	0·55	165,979	3·56
1940-1	138,728	2·96	18,256	0·39	156,984	3·35
1941-2	139,953	2·98	18,223	0·39	158,176	3·37
1942-3	142,974	3·04	24,221	0·51	167,195	3·55
1943-4	146,936	3·10	21,573	0·45	168,509	3·55
1944-5	153,322	3·22	20,902	0·44	174,224	3·66
1945-6	192,460	4·02	21,057	0·44	213,516	4·46
1946-7	229,251	4·79	46,616	0·97	275,867	5·76
1947-8	327,992	6·80	74,050	1·54	402,042	8·34
1948-9	547,293	11·24	68,750	1·41	616,044	12·65
1949-50	701,378	14·32	59,500	1·21	760,878	15·53
1950-1	733,821	15·05	83,266	1·71	817,087	16·76
1951-2	767,289	15·69	66,791	1·37	834,081	17·06

rates of benefit are the same, has also been excluded. Food and other general subsidies have been excluded. Social expenditure includes broadly, education, housing, health and non-specific grants to local authorities. Economic expenditure includes road expenditure, agriculture, and industrial and commercial services.

TABLE 2

SOCIAL EXPENDITURE BY CENTRAL GOVERNMENT 1951–2
(Capital and Current)

Service	Great Britain £mn.	Great Britain £ per head	Northern Ireland £mn.	Northern Ireland £ per head
National Insurance				
Grants to National Insurance Fund	104·5	2·14	2·332	1·70
Grants to N.I. (Industrial Injuries) Fund	6·0	0·12	0·128	0·09
Extended Unemployment Benefit ..	3·4	0·07	0·158	0·12
Family allowances	63·1	1·29	2·760	2·00
Non-Contributory Old-Age Pensions	23·5	0·48	1·654	1·20
National Assistance	71·2	1·46	3·578	2·61
Industrial Rehabilitation	3·8	0·08	0·038	0·03
Nutrition Services				
Grants to Local Authorities (School Meals)	29·5	0·60	0·311	0·23
Milk in Schools	9·4	0·19	0·451	0·33
Other Milk and Welfare Foods	29·5	0·60	0·907	0·69
Education	B		A	
General	197·4	3·83	6·534	4·76
University	23·0	0·47	0·365	0·27
Child Care	7·9	0·18	0·170	0·11
National Health Service				
Hospital Services	265·0	5·42	6·003	4·37
General Medical	144·0A	2·94	3·648	2·66
Grants for Local Authorities Services	18·6	0·38	0·480B	0·35
Other	4·9	0·10	0·347	0·25
Housing				
Grants to Local Authorities ..	38·4	0·79⎤	C	
Annuities under Housing (Temporary Accommodation) Act, 1944	21·8	0·45⎦	4·653	3·39
Water and Sewerage	4·0	0·08	0·642	0·47
(1) TOTAL	1068·9	21·85	35·159	25·61
(2) Total with N.I. Housing on Annuity Basis	1068·9	21·85	31·394	22·86
(3) Total as (2) but excluding Cash Benefit Services	797·2	16·30	20·784	15·14

Table 2 (*contd.*)

Sources: The figures for Great Britain are derived from the Appropriation Accounts. The figures for Northern Ireland are made up from the Appropriation Accounts and the Consolidated Fund Services Account.

Notes: A Excludes School Medical Services.

B Includes School Medical Services. Estimated Amounts:
N. Ireland— £125,000
G. Britain—£4,000,000

C On a comparable (Annuity) basis to the figures for Great Britain this item is estimated to be:

	£mn.	£ per head
Grants to Local Authorities	.. 0·633	0·46
Temporary Accommodation	.. 0·255	0·18
	0·888	0·64

Non-specific Grants

	£mn.	£ per head
Exchequer Equalisation Grant (G.B.) 1951–2	55·46	1·15
General Exchequer Contribution (N.I.) 1951–2	2·94	2·14

Expenditure per head on non-cash social services including non-specific grants (i.e. (3)+Grants):
N.I. .. .. £17·28
G.B. .. .. £17·45

Administrative Expenditure excluded throughout.

R

TABLE 3

CONSOLIDATED CURRENT EXPENDITURE ON SOCIAL SERVICES[1]
BY ALL PUBLIC AUTHORITIES 1949–50

Service	Great Britain		England and Wales		Scotland		N. Ireland	
	£mn.	£ per head	£mn.	£ per head	£mn.	£ per head	£mn.	£ per head
Contributory Insurance Scheme	398·2	8·1	356·3	8·1	41·9	8·0	10·31	7·5
Extended Unemployment Benefit	5·5	0·1	4·3	0·1	1·2	0·2	0·23	0·2
Family Allowances	62·6	1·3	54·6	1·2	8·0	1·5	2·72	2·0
Non-Contributory Old Age Pensions	27·0	0·5	24·3	0·5	2·7	0·5	1·87	1·4
National Assistance	62·9	1·3	55·6	1·3	7·3	1·4	2·85	2·1
Industrial rehabilitation ..	1·7	(0·04)	1·6	(0·04)	0·1	—	0·10	—
Nutrition Services	60·6	1·2	54·3	1·2	6·3	1·2	1·32	1·0
Education ..	267·5	5·4	235·5	5·4	32·0	6·1	6·27	4·6
Child Care ..	14·0	0·3	12·9	0·3	1·1	0·2	0·14	—
National Health Service ..	411·1	8·4	365·4	8·3	45·7	8·8	9·00	6·6
Housing ..	67·0	1·4	56·0	1·3	11·0	2·1	0·90A	0·7
TOTAL ..	1378·1	28·1	1220·8	27·9	157·3	30·2	35·62	26·0

Sources: Annual Abstract of Statistics 1952. Appropriation Accounts for U.K. and N. Ireland Local Government Financial Statistics (G.B.) and Local Government Taxation Returns (N.I.).

Notes: A. Estimate on equivalent basis to figures for Great Britain.
B. Estimated.

[1] Excluding environmental Services.

TABLE 4

CAPITAL EXPENDITURE ON SOCIAL SERVICES BY ALL PUBLIC AUTHORITIES FOR 1949-50

Service	Great Britain		N. Ireland	
	£mn.	£ per head	£mn.	£ per head
Education ..	37·3	0·8	0·600	0·5
Health	22·4	0·5	0·200	0·2
Housing	254·5	5·2	6·225[1]	4·5
Other	13·5	0·3	0·050	(0·04)
Total	327·7	6·7	7·075	5·2

Source: Great Britain: Annual Abstract of Statistics 1952. N. Ireland: Estimates based on Appropriation Accounts and Local Taxation Returns.

[1] Includes lump-sum subsidy to private subsidised building.

R*

Statistical Notes

For the post-war years expenditure out of vote of supply is an inadequate basis for comparing standards of expenditure in Great Britain and Northern Ireland. Since the war the Northern Ireland government has adopted a policy of issuing money from the Consolidated Fund and setting it aside in special funds to meet future capital expenditure. This policy began in 1946–7 with the creation of the Housing Commutation Fund and the Tuberculosis (Capital Purposes) Fund. In the following two years a number of other funds were created, but in August 1949 they were all, with the exception of the Housing Fund, amalgamated into a new Capital Purposes Fund. The money issued to these funds has come from revenue surpluses and capital receipts into the Exchequer, from the Reserve Fund, and from voted moneys. In general the Ministry of Finance has authority to meet expenditure on the different services for which the funds were established, from the Capital Purposes Fund, the Consolidated Fund, or from vote, as they think fit.[1] For comparative purposes adjustments must be made to take account of these transactions.

Table 2 sets out specific expenditure by central government on the social services in 1951–2. For Great Britain the figures are derived from vote of supply. For Northern Ireland the figures are derived from vote adjusted to take account of expenditure through the channels just mentioned. From the table it appears that expenditure per head in Northern Ireland on these social services was appreciably higher than that in Great Britain. For comparative purposes, however, the housing figures for Northern Ireland require adjustment, because whereas in Great Britain housing subsidies are paid to local authorities in the form of annuities, in the case of Northern Ireland the greater part of these annuities is commuted after six months for a lump sum payment. Northern Ireland's expenditure on housing has therefore been adjusted to show the level at which subsidies would be running if they had not been commuted. For this purpose annuities have been estimated, taking sixty years as the basis for the permanent housing programme (except for the pre-war residue) and ten years for the temporary housing programme. On this basis, housing expenditure in Northern Ireland in 1951–2 would have amounted to approximately £888,000, giving a rate of expenditure per head of 0·64 as against 1·19 for Great Britain. The second line of the total in Table 2 reflects this adjustment. A further distinction requires to be drawn between the social security services and the rest, since expenditure on the former indicates precisely the levels of expenditure required to produce parity of standards. The third line of the total excludes expenditure on these services. It can then be seen that whilst expenditure per head on the social security services is higher in Northern Ireland, expenditure on the remaining services is lower.

The table displays clearly the marked differences in the pattern of expenditure in the two regions. Looking first at the social security services, it can be seen that payments to the Insurance Funds in Ulster were lower, reflecting the smaller proportion of insured workers in Northern Ireland. The higher rate of non-contributory pensions is to some extent the other side of the medal. The greater expenditure on family allowances reflects differences in the family

[1] See Report of the Comptroller and Auditor-General on the 1950–51 Appropriation Accounts (N.I.), p. xi.

structure in Northern Ireland as compared with Great Britain. Payments in respect of National Assistance in Ulster are almost double the average for Great Britain. For this there are two main reasons; first, there is a larger number of cases per head of population; second, the size of family relieved is in general larger in Ulster, which results in the average payment per case being higher. These differences in rates of expenditure on the cash benefit services reflect differences in the industrial and social structure, in level of employment, and in income per head as between Great Britain and Northern Ireland.

In relation to the other social services, expenditure is significantly lower in a number of cases. In the nutrition services there is a much lower rate of expenditure on school meals. The percentage of pupils participating in the school meals service in fact falls far short of the corresponding figure for Great Britain. On the other hand, almost all children in attendance at grant-aided schools in Northern Ireland benefit from the free milk service, and the rate of expenditure per head on this service is higher in Northern Ireland than in Great Britain.

Expenditure on University education is very much lower in Northern Ireland than in Great Britain, but recently increased rates of grant will do much to remove Northern Ireland's backwardness in this field. General educational expenditure per head of population from central sources is much higher in Northern Ireland than in Great Britain. To a considerable extent this difference is accounted for by the much greater rate of expenditure on capital development in Northern Ireland, which in this year amounted to £740,000 as against £600,000 in Great Britain. If this capital expenditure is subtracted, current expenditure per head of the population is still higher in Northern Ireland. A more interesting comparison is between relative expenditures per head of population of school age. A comparison of expenditure on this basis shows a different picture. Current educational expenditure per head of the age group 5–15 amounts to £28·8 in Great Britain. In Northern Ireland expenditure per head of the age group 5–14 is £26·5. Thus not only is educational expenditure in Northern Ireland lower on account of the lower school-leaving age, but less is being spent on the existing school population.

A substantial difference in the relative rate of expenditure in the two regions shows itself in connection with the health services. In aggregate, expenditure per head on the health services in Great Britain amounted to £8·8 per head. The corresponding figure for Northern Ireland is £7·7. The addition of the local authority contribution to the Northern Ireland Tuberculosis Authority which should be made for comparative purposes makes no significant difference to the figures for Northern Ireland. This relatively low rate of expenditure in Northern Ireland is a feature of all years since the establishment of the health service. The difference is least marked in the case of the General Medical Services. Here the final small difference is the result of a number of small offsetting differences in the pattern of expenditure in the two regions. The rate of expenditure on the Pharmaceutical Services is higher in Northern Ireland, partly because of the higher cost of prescription, partly because of the higher rate of morbidity. On the other hand, the cost of dental services appears to be lower. This may be attributed partly to the lower level of demand for these services, partly to the lower cost of the treatment which is provided. The really marked difference in rates of expenditure arises in connection with the hospital services. In 1951–2 expenditure per head on these services in Great Britain amounted to £5·42 per head, as compared with only £4·37 in Northern Ireland. In this year, however, Northern Ireland was spending at a much greater rate on capital account on these services. In absolute terms, capital expenditure on the hospital services in Great Britain amounted to £14·6 million. The corresponding figure for Northern Ireland appears to have amounted to approximately £1 million. Current expenditure per head on the hospital services in Northern Ireland was therefore very much lower than in Great Britain.

In the field of housing expenditure, the lower effective rate seems remarkable when considered in conjunction with the facts that Northern Ireland has since the war built 50 per cent more houses per head than Great Britain, and that the Northern Ireland subsidy is the same as the Scottish subsidy, which itself is higher than the standard general amount payable under the Housing Act 1946 (and subsequent amendments) for houses built in England and Wales. The explanation of the much lower rate of expenditure per head in Northern Ireland, notwithstanding these facts, may be attributed to a number of factors. In the first place, one-third of the houses built with public assistance in the post-war period in Northern Ireland have been for the account of owner occupiers. These houses carry a capital subsidy from the government,[1] but this is equivalent to a very low annual rate of subsidy. In the second place, although the maximum general subsidy on local authority houses is higher than in England, the actual rate in Northern Ireland depends on the size of the house, and diminishes with size. In England and Wales, on the other hand, the rate of subsidy is not related to the size of the dwelling. Since the average local authority house in Northern Ireland is smaller than that in Great Britain, the effective advantage is correspondingly reduced. On the other hand, the Northern Ireland Housing Trust receives, in addition to the ordinary subsidy, a grant equal to the ordinary local authority contribution from rates. Further factors which contribute to an explanation of the difference include the greater importance of the temporary housing programme in Great Britain, the effective cost of which is higher, and the greater volume of subsidised building which took place before the war in Great Britain. Finally the 1946 Act gave the authorities in Great Britain powers to pay higher rates of subsidy in certain special cases. Part of the difference may be associated with the exercise of these powers. Housing is obviously a case in which, owing to the different methods of administration in the two regions, judgments about parity based on comparative rates of expenditure are likely to be misleading. However, from the budgetary point of view the lower rate of expenditure in Northern Ireland is of great importance.

In the field of environmental services standards in Northern Ireland are recognised to be much below those in Great Britain and there is much leeway to be made up. This situation is reflected in the levels of expenditure on water and sewerage in the two regions. In 1951–2 Northern Ireland was spending six times as much per head as Great Britain. The following figures show the different rates of expenditure in this field in the four main regions of the United Kingdom:

[1] At present a maximum of £360.

			England	Wales	Scotland	N. Ireland
£000 ..	..	..	2,167	768	1,052	642
£ per head	..	..	·05	·3	·2	·47

Table 2 does not give a complete picture of central expenditure on the social services in 1951–2, because it does not include the non-specific Exchequer Equalisation Grant for Great Britain, or the General Exchequer Contribution for Northern Ireland. The greater part of these items is to be regarded as expenditure on the social services. In 1951–2 the amount paid in this respect for Great Britain was £5,545,700. For Northern Ireland the corresponding amount was £2,944,000. In terms of expenditure per head of population the respective amounts were £1·15 and £2·14. The aggregate amount paid under this head in Northern Ireland is much more than Northern Ireland's population proportion—as it should be, for local authorities there are poorer, in terms of rateable value per head, than the average local authority in Great Britain. The grant is also running at a much higher rate than would be payable if the amount were computed according to the principles of the British Exchequer Equalisation Grant, using as the standard of reference Northern Ireland's average rateable value per head of weighted population. This basis of computation, however, would not take into account at all Northern Ireland's relative poverty. If instead the standard employed was the average rateable value per head of population in England and Wales, then the amount payable would be more than is at present being paid by between 10 and 20 per cent. The size of this grant, however, should not be considered in isolation from the rates of expenditure incurred through specific grants for social services.

INDEX

Abercorn, Duke of, 34 n.
Agrarian agitation, xvi, xx, 8, 57
Agriculture:
Acts of 1924–33, 139
— and food-processing industries, 148–9
government assistance to, 138 et seq.
Livestock Breeding Act, 1922, 139
Marketing Act (N.I.), 1933, 139
mechanisation, 99–100
numbers employed, 97–9
organisation of, 12, 98–100
total income from, 100
volume of production and exports, 142–3
Amery, L. S., 184 n., 185
Andrews, J. M., xxiii
Anglo-Scottish Union of 1603, xiii
Anti-Partition:
— League, 70–1
— Parties, 60
Antrim, ix, xiv, 2, 7, 9, 45
Armagh, ix, xiv, 2, 6, 7, 45
Armed forces in Ulster, 83 et seq., 202–3
Attlee, C. R., 66, 203

Banking Policy, 160
Baldwin, Stanley, 26
Bases in Northern Ireland:
future needs for, 88–90
war of 1914–18, 81–2
war of 1939–45, 82 et seq.
Beckett, J. C., 6
Belfast, xviii, xix, 20, 45, 57, 65, 70
Beveridge, Lord, 190
Border, ix, xx, xxii
and Boundary Commission of 1925, 25–6
and minority, 204
See also Partition
Boyne, Battle of the, xviii, 7, 10, 81
Brookeborough, Lord, xxiii, 64
Browne, Dr. Noel, 58 n.

Campbell, T. J., K.C., 70
Canadian forces in Northern Ireland, 84
Capital:
and financial institutions, 168–9
shortage of in industry, 150 et seq.
Ulster as exporter of, 151–7, 168

Capital Grants to Industry Act, 65
Carson, Sir Edward, 21, 22, 59
Cavan, ix, xiv, 1, 6
Celts, 4–5
Celtic law, 42–3
Census of Production, 1935, 110
Chamberlain, Joseph, 19, 20, 183
Chester, D. N., 185 n.
Church of Ireland, 9, 12
disestablishment of, xx, 8
revenues of, 18
Churchill, Sir Winston, 83, 185
Civil disabilities of Catholics and Dissenters, xvi–xvii, 8
Colwyn Committee and formula, 40, 63, 127, 134, 213
Commonwealth Labour Party, xxii, 72
Communism, 73
Companies:
predominance of family businesses, 12, 67
public and private, 130, 154–6
Constitutional history, 15–22
Cost of living, 109
Costello, J. A., 205
Cotton Spinning (Re-Equipment Subsidy) Act, 1948, 157
Craigavon, Lord, xxiii, 36, 59, 60, 62
Crewe, Lord, 21

De Valera, Eamonn, 203 n., 205
Development Areas, 62, 92, 162–3
Development of new industries, 144 et seq.
Devlin, Joseph, 70
Devolution, xxii
assessment of, 51–4, 76–8, 95 et seq., 158 et seq., 183 et seq., 210–11
"functional", 167
and federalism, 164–5, 167–8
Speaker's Conference on, 184
Donegal, ix, 1, 6
Down, ix, xiv, 2, 7, 9
Duggan, Dr G. C. 66 n.
Dublin Castle, 37, 186–7, 190
Dublin Rebellion of 1916, 22

Economic classes, 12–13
Education, 74–5, 190–3, 214, 223